Introducing Neuroed[ucational] Research

Among educators, scientists and policymakers there is a growing belief that the field of education can benefit from an understanding of the brain. However, attempts to bring neuroscience and education together have often been hampered by crucial differences in concepts, language and philosophy. In this book, Paul Howard-Jones explores these differences, drawing on the voices of educators and scientists to argue for a new field of enquiry: neuroeducational research.

Introducing Neuroeducational Research provides a meaningful bridge between two diverse perspectives on learning. It proposes that any such bridge must serve two goals that are critically related to each other: it must enrich both scientific and educational understanding. This challenge gives rise to unique conceptual, methodological and ethical issues that will inevitably characterize this new field, and these are examined and illustrated here through empirical research. Throughout the book, Paul Howard-Jones:

- explores 'neuromyths' and their impact on educational thinking;
- highlights the opportunities to combine biological, social and experiential evidence in understanding how we learn;
- argues against a 'brain-based' natural science of education;
- introduces clearly the concept of an interdisciplinary neuroeducational approach;
- builds a methodology for conducting neuroeducational research;
- draws on case studies and empirical findings to illustrate how a neuroeducational approach can provide a fuller picture of how we learn.

Presenting a blueprint for including our knowledge of the brain in education, this book is essential reading for all those concerned with human learning in authentic contexts: educators, scientists and policymakers alike.

Paul Howard-Jones is Senior Lecturer at the Graduate School of Education, University of Bristol.

Introducing Neuroeducational Research

Neuroscience, education and the brain from contexts to practice

Paul Howard-Jones

Routledge
Taylor & Francis Group

LONDON AND NEW YORK

First published 2010
by Routledge
2 Park Square, Milton Park, Abingdon, Oxon OX14 4RN

Simultaneously published in the USA and Canada
by Routledge
711 Third Avenue, New York, NY 10017

*Routledge is an imprint of the Taylor & Francis Group,
an informa business*

© 2010 Paul Howard-Jones

Typeset in Galliard by Keyword Group

British Library Cataloguing in Publication Data
A catalogue record for this book is available from
the British Library

Library of Congress Cataloging-in-Publication Data
Howard-Jones, Paul.
    Introducing neuroeducational research: neuroscience,
education and the brain from contexts to
practice / Paul Howard-Jones.
        p. cm.
    Includes bibliographical references.
    1. Learning. 2. Education—Research. 3. Neurosciences.
I. Title.
    QP408.H695 2010
    612.8072—dc22   2009016870

ISBN 13: 978-0-415-47201-2 (pbk)
ISBN 13: 978-0-415-47200-5 (hbk)
ISBN 13: 978-0-203-86730-3 (ebk)

ISBN 10: 0-415-47201-6 (pbk)
ISBN 10: 0-415-47200-8 (hbk)
ISBN 10: 0-203-86730-0 (ebk)

For the children: Dylan, Harvey, Miranda, Theo and Finn

Contents

Acknowledgements   ix
Introduction   x

PART I
Contexts   I

1   What has neuroscience got to do with education?   3

2   Neuromyths   20

3   Educators on the brain, neuroscientists on education   37

4   Neuroscience and education in dialogue   59

PART II
Neuroeducational research   **77**

5   A multi-perspective understanding of learning   79

6   Methodology in neuroeducational research   98

7   Neuroeducational ethics   122

8   Neuroeducational research case study A:
    Creativity   138

9   Neuroeducational research case study B:
    Learning games   164

PART III
The future   **183**

10   Neuroscience, education and the future   185

Appendix 1: Some neuroanatomy   197
Appendix 2: Glossary   200
Notes   203
References   206
Index   229

Acknowledgements

I am grateful to the many people whose voices and opinions have contributed to the writing of this book. I would like especially to thank Ros Sutherland and the many other members of the Graduate School of Education (University of Bristol) whose continuing efforts and support are helping to establish this new field of enquiry, and also Andrew Pollard, Sarah-Jayne Blakemore, Rafal Bogacz, Ute Leonards, Liane Kaufmann, Ian Summers, Malek Benattayallah, Anne Cook, Guy Claxton, Mary O'Connell, John Geake, Claire O'Malley, Christine Howe, Uta Frith, Usha Goswami, Dénes Szücs, Sue Pickering, Aaron Williamon, Jonathan Sharples, Anne Diack, Futurelab, Chris Brookes, Sally Barnes, Tony Brown and the late Rosemary Stevenson. I would also like to thank the various institutions that have funded NEnet research and seminar initiatives reported upon in this book: ESRC, TLRP, The Life Long Learning Foundation, The Innovation Unit and ESCalate. The views, opinions (and any errors) expressed are, of course, those of the author.

Many thanks also to my partner Katie for love and support, and the café staff of Coffee #1 and the Rainbow Café (Chepstow), and Grounded (Bristol) where most of the book was written.

Introduction

The 'big idea' of including the brain in educational thinking and practice has been around a long time. Early enthusiasts included the first educational psychologists, who claimed a physiological basis for learning. As long ago as 1926, Edward Lee Thorndike wrote 'Intellect, character and skill have their physiological basis in the structure and activities of the neurons and accessory organs which compose the nervous system' (Thorndike, 1926). More recently, educational interest in the biology of learning has increased, and with it some voices of objection. Some educators have expressed concern that neuroscience might have little to say about behaviour in complex culturally dependent contexts such as school classrooms, with some suggesting the contribution of brain science to understanding learning is limited in principle (Davis, 2004). Scientists have voiced their own anxieties: the risk of raising false hopes and expectations of prescriptive solutions (Willingham, 2009), of ignoring the educational value of research from other areas (Stern, 2005) and, in particular, of the dangers of making links between neuroscience and education without involving the mind (Bruer, 1997).

The debate, however, also reflects a step change in efforts to bring together neuroscience and education, and is a natural outcome of dialogue between two diverse fields. Collaboration presents both opportunities and potential pitfalls, but enthusiasts are now heard in both fields, with an academic journal[1] founded on interdisciplinary dialogue and research, and some funding for national and international projects.

Already, ideas about the brain have become involved with educational thinking and practice although, as we shall see, this involvement often needs a better scientific and/or educational basis. This book is in response to this need, and to the rapidly growing interest to develop educational understanding that involves consideration of brain processes. This text moves beyond simply exploring the potential relevance of neuroscience to education. It focuses less on whether neuroscience can, or should, involve itself with education. It concerns itself more with how we can develop a research-based process of knowledge construction across these two very different areas, a process that maintains both scientific and educational sense.

Debates around neuroscience and education, of course, will continue and so they should. Rather than holding back progress, the concerns voiced in these debates are essential to developing this new field, in tempering the attitudes and ideas of its proponents and in the generation of its concepts. Indeed, the dialogue and debate have influenced the very aims of the interdisciplinary venture. Early discussions were about 'cognitive neuroscience informing education' and 'education learning from neuroscience' but many educators now insist that the venture must be two-way (Christodoulou and Gaab, 2009). Consensus appears to have emerged that neuroscientists in isolation cannot provide classroom-ready information any more than educators can independently retrieve it from scientific journals. Essentially, no such classroom-ready knowledge from neuroscience is ever likely to exist. With the abandonment of the transmission model, a new idea has surfaced: that neuroscience and education can somehow work together in research activities that construct the required knowledge. This book asks *how* such neuroeducational[2] research might be achieved in practical and theoretical terms. What sorts of methods and techniques are available and how they can be applied? What are the key challenges? Which areas of education might benefit?

To begin answering these questions requires understanding of the present state of neuroscientific and educational knowledge, of the different ideas about learning and the brain that already exist within neuroscience and within education, and the concerns and hopes that have been expressed in recent dialogue. Part I of this book is focused on exploring these contexts. This provides the basis for Part II, which considers the practical and theoretical implications of these contexts for researchers whose work spans two, quite different, worlds of understanding. Part III consists of a single chapter considering the likely implications of neuroscience, and a developing field of neuroeducational research, for the future of education.

The first chapter in this book considers what has seeded interest in neuroscience and education collaborating together, i.e. advances in brain science that appear potentially relevant to education. Chapter 1 seeks out the sorts of shiny nuggets of neuroscientific knowledge presently attracting attention. But, shiny though they are, these nuggets are only possible starting points and their educational effectiveness is usually untested. They do, however, also provide a helpful illustration of what, in scientific terms, counts as authentic scientific understanding, which is a useful counterpoint to the next chapter.

Having visited scientific concepts about the brain, Chapter 2 introduces the 'parallel world' of neuroscience already established in education. This world comes complete with books, learning resources, in-service training and usually a fee to a private company marketing unscientific ideas about the brain. We will find that other entrepreneurial interests, including water companies and makers of food supplements, have also stepped into the knowledge vacuum created by educational enthusiasm and an absence of accessible science. Chapter 2 takes the reader on a brief journey through this neuromythological world, attempting to unpick the fact from the fiction.

In Chapter 3, the constructions that educators have about the mind and the brain are investigated in more depth, together with neuroscientists' ideas about education. Just as teachers currently receive no training in brain function, neuroscientists are usually not trained as educators and their scientific backgrounds can impact on their views about education. Thus, into the collaborative arena, neuroscientists and educators bring with them expectations and beliefs about each others' fields that have influence on collaboration. It appears our neuroscience and education 'bridge' must span worlds not just full of different ideas, but which also attach different meanings to the same terms.

So what happens on first contact? Chapter 4 draws on instances when experts came face-to-face and discussed what might be gained from their professions collaborating. The discussants identified the types of aims that could be pursued, the types of evidence sought, and their general concerns and hopes regarding such a venture. By the time you reach the end of Chapter 4, you should have a clear impression of the gulf dividing neuroscience and education, but also a sense of willingness and even some agreement about the work required to bridge it. When neuroscientists, psychologists and educators sit down and discuss the idea, consensus forms around many issues, such as the desirability of interdisciplinary dialogue and research as a means to tackle neuromyths, the importance of scrutiny and communication in developing concepts, and the need to manage expectations and test concepts in both the lab and the classroom. Also, there appears clear agreement about the importance of cognitive psychology and our understanding of the mind when interrelating what we know about the brain with behaviour, including learning behaviour. However, some seemingly fundamental issues also arise in these discussions, such as differences in the use of language, about how learning is conceptualized and the value placed on different types of evidence.

Part II is about pulling apart the issues that surfaced in Part I to understand how to construct knowledge that is both educationally relevant and scientifically valid. Chapter 5 tackles potential philosophical challenges, beginning with the meaning of the term 'learning'. Even within the two camps, differences exist, but it is fair to say that neuroscience considers learning chiefly in terms of changes in an individual's biological system. Education, on the other hand, prefers a view of learning as a distributed process of social construction, within and across individuals, groups, institutions and cultures. The distance between definitions and the challenge of interrelating them is sobering and it deserves serious appreciation. However, perhaps a more insidious and dangerous type of misunderstanding involves conceptualization of the brain–mind relationship. Neither is this misunderstanding restricted to education, with researchers within neuroscience standing accused of occasional bouts of confusion. The brain–mind-behaviour model of cognitive neuroscience is helpful in avoiding these difficulties. To support consideration of social learning processes within education, an extension of this model is proposed for neuroeducational research that includes emphasis on meaning-based communication between individuals. Such a model is also useful for reflecting upon the potential role of different traditions of enquiry, such as those found in the social and natural sciences, in informing a multiperspective understanding of learning.

Chapter 6 argues that a two-way approach to neuroscience and education implies twin interrelated goals that produce both scientific and educational insight. These goals, in turn, suggest three types of neuroeducational study: scientific, bridging and practice-based. Building on the model developed in Chapter 5, Chapter 6 then deconstructs existing approaches to research methodology by first identifying three fundamental types of evidence that can be helpful in understanding learning: biological, social and experiential. It then builds upwards from these types of evidence to consider a representative range of different techniques used to produce them, and some of the methods that employ these techniques to answer specific research questions. However, when employing these methods in neuroeducational research, with its goals that demand the interrelation of different types of study, it is argued that these methods and techniques should be adapted to serve such interrelation. Thus, the twin goals of neuroeducational research can give rise to methodology that departs from what is conventional in either neuroscience or educational investigations.

Despite the controversy surrounding some aspects of neuroscientific research and the highly political nature of education, discussion about research involving neuroscience and education often omits ethical issues. Perhaps this is because both traditions boast well-established forums, guidelines and procedures. Chapter 7 compares current ethical perspectives within neuroscience and education as separate areas of research, but demonstrates how neuroeducational researchers cannot simply follow two sets of ethical guidelines. Fresh reconsideration of many of the issues may be required. In addition, it argues that the communication and scrutiny of concepts has special ethical significance for this emerging field, and also reviews imminent developments where decisions by educational policymakers will soon involve new ethical dimensions.

Chapters 8 and 9 provide case studies of investigations involving the author to show what neuroeducational research can look like in practice. These chapters re-emphasize the need to be able to interrelate different types of studies and the evidence they produce, in order to provide concepts of learning that are educationally relevant and scientifically valid. Their narratives revisit and illustrate much of what has been discussed in the earlier sections of the book, providing a meaningful context to reflect on the theoretical and practical challenges that may come to characterize neuroeducational investigation.

In the final part of the book, Chapter 10 indulges in some horizon scanning. It assumes that the less scientific ideas about neuroscience and education will fade away as the field of neuroeducational research advances, developing forums that can scrutinize educational ideas about the brain more carefully. As the sciences of brain and mind continue to flourish, and neuroeducational research becomes an established and potentially innovative force in educational thinking, this final chapter identifies where new understanding is likely to make the greatest impact on educational theory and practice.

Part I

Contexts

Chapter 1

What has neuroscience got to do with education?

Many teachers, policymakers and scientists now believe neuroscience is providing insights about the brain that are relevant to education and, as the number of these grow, so do the calls for education to take note of them. This belief is driving the new field of intellectual enterprise to be explored critically in Part II. First, however, it is important to understand the scientific evidence underlying this enthusiasm. What insights appear, at least on the face of it, to have something to do with our efforts to improve teaching and learning?

In this chapter you will encounter some of the 'low-hanging fruit' that may be most accessible to interdisciplinary researchers, i.e. where understanding in neuroscience is most closely approaching topics of educational interest. But this review is by no means exhaustive and, with the number of new findings in neuroscience each year increasing, it will soon be out of date. Nevertheless, it provides some idea of why the idea of 'neuroscience and education' is generating excitement, and an impression of the breadth and diversity of its potential impact in our educational institutions and beyond.

Note: in this chapter, and all others, you will encounter some jargon, such as technical names for brain regions and processes. Readers who are not specialists in the brain may wish to read Appendix 1, which provides a brief tutorial that explains these terms, and also see Appendix 2 which provides a glossary.

Brain development

Our brains are plastic, which means their structure and connectivity can change with experience; but the most drastic changes occur during childhood and into adolescence. There has been considerable interest in understanding these aspects of brain development, not least because they may suggest changes in readiness to respond to environmental stimulus,[1] including the type provided by formal education. So, this chapter begins with a brief review of how our brains develop with time.

Early years

The vast majority of the neurons we possess as adults arrive within three months of our conception. There are two regions, the hippocampus and cerebellum, where neurons continue to be produced after birth. In the hippocampus, there is evidence that *neurogenesis*, the birth of neurons, continues even in adult life, although the full significance of this in terms of learning is still unclear. Learning is chiefly associated less with the birth of neurons and more with *synaptic plasticity* – changes in the connectivity between neurons. These changes appear to occur in waves. After birth there is a massive increase in synaptogenesis, i.e. there is a huge blossoming of connections, such that an infant's brain is more connected than an adult's. Then follows a wave of synaptic pruning, in which connections are cut back. These changes occur at different rates in different parts of the brain. For example, in the visual cortex the number of connections peaks at about 8–10 months, whereas in the frontal and parietal cortices the decline begins around the beginning of puberty, reaching adult levels at around 18 years or later (Huttenlocher and Dabholkar, 1997).

Described in this simple way, these changes may sound genetically programmed but the situation is more complex than this. Views on the role of genetics in development vary across different fields of science. It has been said that the instructions encoded in DNA have acquired a unique causal status in developmental outcomes due to their unidirectional influence (Plomin *et al.*, 2007). It is true that some specialist genes, such as those linked to reading disability, have been identified (Paracchini *et al.*, 2007), as well as a set of so-called 'generalist genes' that appear largely responsible for genetic influence across domains of academic achievement and cognitive ability (Plomin *et al.*, 2007). Such valuable insights make it likely that genetic indicators can contribute to devising personalized learning approaches for children of all ability, in much the same way as personalized medicine is moving away from the 'one size fits all' treatment (Abrahams *et al.*, 2005). Such indicators will, however, only indicate probable rather than certain outcomes. In molecular biology, a unidirectional formula of DNA→RNA→protein is often assumed, in which the proteins that go on to form biological structures, including those found in the brain, are translated from the intermediary ribonucleic acid (RNA). However, modern neuroconstructivist theories, currently favoured within developmental cognitive neuroscience, reject this maturational unfolding of pre-existing information in the genes (Johnson, M.H. 2004). Instead, they assume this process of protein synthesis is *bidirectional*, since it is known that proteins can act on RNA and DNA and, in exceptional cases, RNA can even transform DNA in a process called reverse transcription (Gottlieb, 2004). Furthermore, these processes are affected by normally occurring environmental influences. So, even at the level of gene activity, interaction with experience and the environment is likely to play a crucial role in normal brain development. Our genes contribute to, but do not define, who we are.

Periods of both increased synaptogenesis and synaptic pruning can be considered as indicating increased sensitivity to learning, and may explain so-called sensitive periods when we are more able to learn particular things. In the future, it may be possible to determine sensitive periods for particular aspects of cognitive function relevant to different educational areas but, at present, our knowledge of sensitive periods for human development is quite limited and is restricted to basic perceptual functioning. A famous example includes our inability to distinguish new speech sounds if we are not exposed to them before the age of 6 months (Kuhl *et al.*, 1992). However, the idea that environments enriched with copious amounts of stimulus are needed by children in their earliest years to promote the development of their brains cannot be supported by neuroscientific evidence. This neuromyth is explored more fully in the next chapter.

Brain development in adolescence

The frontal lobes, more than other region, are associated with the types of higher-level processing fostered by education and these, together with parietal regions, are still undergoing radical structural changes until the late teens. Thus, the science suggests that all of childhood, including adolescence, can be considered as a special time for learning. Apart from synaptic pruning, a second type of change occurs in these brain regions during puberty called myelination. This is the process by which the axons, carrying messages from and to neurons, become insulated by a fatty substance called myelin, so improving the efficiency with which information is communicated in the brain. In the frontal and parietal lobes, myelination increases considerably throughout adolescence and, to a less dramatic extent, throughout adulthood, favouring an increase in the speed with which neural communication occurs in these regions (Sowell *et al.*, 2003). For these reasons, one might expect the teenage brain to be less ready than an adult brain to carry out a range of different processes. These include directing attention, planning future tasks, inhibiting inappropriate behaviour, multitasking, and a variety of socially orientated tasks. Indeed, psychological testing has even shown a 'pubertal dip' in some areas of performance, such as matching pictures of facial expressions to descriptors. In this task, 11–12-year-olds performed worse than younger children (McGivern *et al.*, 2002). Discontinuities have also been shown in abilities underlying social communication, such as taking on the viewpoint of another person, or so-called 'perspective-taking'(Blakemore and Choudhury, 2006; Choudhury *et al.*, 2006).

Just as linguistically sensitive periods have been linked to synaptic pruning in very young children, continuing synaptic pruning in adolescence suggests the possibility of sensitive periods here too. For example, research has shown that teenagers activate different regions of the brain from adults when learning algebraic equations, and this difference has been associated with a more robust process of long-term storage than that used by adults (Luna, 2004; Qin *et al.*, 2004).

However, an important point here is that, while young children's development in areas such as language is advantaged by biological start-up mechanisms specific to these language skills, no such start-up mechanisms for adolescents are likely to exist that are specific to the KS3 curriculum. Thus, formal education, as well as social experience, may have a particularly important role in moulding the teenage brain.

Teenagers often tend to perceive risks as smaller and more controllable than do adults, and they are generally more vulnerable than adults or children to a range of activities which are inappropriately risky, such as gambling and drug taking. Appropriate decision making appears to require a balanced engagement between harm-avoidance and reward orientating processes that is regulated by processes associated with the prefrontal cortex, where development is thought to lag during adolescence (Ernst *et al.*, 2005). An imaging study comparing adults and adolescents showed reduced activity in these prefrontal regions when making risky decisions, and that this reduced activity correlated with greater risk-taking (Eshel *et al.*, 2007). Such studies are providing new insights into adolescence that may influence educational perspectives on teenage behaviour and help understand a potentially problematic, and sometimes even dangerous, period of children's development (Baird *et al.*, 2005).

Brain development in later adulthood

Although the changes are less radical than during childhood, the brain continues to change and develop through adulthood. Reductions in grey matter volume are detectable in the thirties in some regions of the brain but not in others, and this reduction continues with age (Good *et al.*, 2001). Although some neural atrophy has been reported, such changes are unlikely to be explained in terms of losses of neurons (Morrison and Hof, 1997). There appears little evidence for developmental changes in connectivity beyond 60 (Scheff *et al.*, 2001) and, in at least one region of the brain, the hippocampus, new neurons are produced in adulthood that are associated with new memories (Shors *et al.*, 2001). It may be wrong, therefore, to expect an inevitable general decline in mental functioning with aging. Indeed, older adults are generally slower to process information and have reduced working memory capacity, but show improved general and verbal knowledge, and an accumulation of sophisticated social expertise (Leclerc and Hess, 2007).

The brain's continuing plasticity suggests it is well designed for lifelong learning and adaptation to new situations and experiences, and there is clear evidence that such adaptation can bring about significant changes even in its structure. In a recent study of juggling, the brain regions of adults activated at the beginning of a three-month training period increased in size by the end of it (see Fig. 1.1 in colour plate section). After three months of rest, these regions had shrunk back and were closer to their original size (Draganski *et al.*, 2004). This graphic example of 'if you don't use it, you lose it' demonstrates the potential importance of education in mediating brain development throughout our lives. Further evidence of the effects of education on brain structure comes from research into Alzheimer's disease, which is associated with the death of brain cells due to deposits (or plaques) and development of dense bundles (tangles of fibrils) within cells. Despite the biological basis of the disease, it is becoming increasingly clear that the risks of developing Alzheimer's in later life are reduced not only by previous educational attainment (Elkins *et al.*, 2006), but also by the level of challenge encountered in one's working life (Wilson, 2005). Even after the onset of Alzheimer's, there is evidence that the progress of some symptoms can be diminished by training (Acevedo and Loewenstein, 2007).

Brain imaging has increased understanding of how older brains process information, and also provided additional evidence for continuing plasticity. These studies have often contributed to notions of 'successful aging', rather than adding to a deficit model of growing old. For example, one study has shown that older adults produce more bilateral frontal activity than younger adults. This result was observed in tests of episodic memory at which they performed equally well, suggesting compensatory changes in brain functionality (Rossi *et al.*, 2004). The plasticity of the brain is also illustrated by the positive effect of exercise on the ageing brain's capacity to learn (Cotman and Berchtold, 2007; Hillman *et al.*, 2008; Colcombe *et al.*, 2004).

Strategies for teaching and learning

Commercial 'brain-based' educational programmes

This section will briefly review some of the key findings that may be relevant to enhancing mainstream teaching and learning. It excludes consideration of the many educational programmes that have been marketed in the last two decades that claim to have a 'brain basis'. The misconceptions and neuromyths promoted by many of these unscrutinized 'brain-based' programmes will be explored in Chapter 2. Leaving these aside, we find neuroscientific understanding is only just approaching the point where some limited educational implications and applications can be made that are of general significance to mainstream education. Here, we examine present progress in developing these scientific insights and their genuine potential significance for mainstream education.

Memory

It has been known for some time that presenting material in both visual and textual form can enhance memory (Paivio and Csapo, 1973). This type of finding has provided an important basis for the design of multimodal educational approaches. Such results are now joined by more recent evidence showing that multimodal stimulus produces additional brain activity over and above that produced by experiencing each mode separately (Beauchamp *et al.*, 2004).

The additional activity was observed in the posterior superior temporal sulcus and middle temporal gyrus. The location of this region suggests it has an important role in making links between visual and auditory features. Such automatic recruitment of additional processing may account for our improved memory for multimodal stimuli.

Neuroimaging has also helped provide insights into a study of individual learning strategies (Kirchhoff and Buckner, 2006). In this investigation, the brains of adult participants were scanned while they tried to memorize images of pairs of objects for a test. They were then asked to complete a questionnaire about the strategies they used. There are many reasons to be sceptical about such self-report approaches, but the brain images confirmed that self-reported use of visual and verbal encoding strategies predicted activity in distinct regions of the brain associated with visual and verbal processing. These strategies had an additive effect on memory, such that participants who used multiple strategies showed improved memory performance.

Research into the effects of stress on memory has produced apparently conflicting results. Most of us might feel we need a little stress to stay alert when learning, although too much stress can be unhelpful. It is also true that many people are unable to forget some very stressful experiences (Olff *et al.*, 2005), yet the details of such events can be unreliable (Christianson, 1992). Physical or psychological stress appears to facilitate learning and memory of an event when it occurs in the same context and at the same time as the event. Additionally, neuroscientific studies demonstrate that stress hormones and transmitters must also converge in time and space with the brain activity produced by the details of the event if they are to enhance their memory (Joels *et al.*, 2006). For example, stress hormones appear to facilitate memory when they are present at the time of learning, but have the opposite effects when they are present before, or for a considerable time after, the learning event (de Quervain *et al.*, 2000; Kirschbaum, 1996; Kuhlmann, 2005). Physical stressors, such as temperature and hunger, activate lower regions in the brain than the psychological stress of receiving a stressful emotional message, which is more likely to activate limbic regions such as the amygdala (Herman and Cullinan, 1997). Such a stressor is also likely to produce noradrenaline in these regions, and the coincidence in time and place promotes memory for the message, but not for any unrelated contextual information (McGaugh, 2004). Such models provide insights into, for example, the effects of examination stress on memory. If psychological (but not physical) stress occurs before the exam, and is associated with the learning, it may be beneficial. If it occurs during the exam, it can be detrimental.

Many of the studies mentioned have studied learning in the context of memorizing abstract material. Factual recall, such as a list of steps when carrying out a process, may not appear as important as being able to carry out a process with understanding and efficiency, and the repetition required to achieve well-rehearsed automatic and effortless processing may not appear as important as covering new material. However, neuroscience has provided striking images of the educational importance of such rehearsal as a means of liberating working memory (WM). Working memory refers to our capacity to temporarily hold a limited set of information in our attention when we are processing it, and is another area where neuroscience is helping to 'concretize' psychological concepts. Our WM limitation is the reason why we prefer to write down a telephone number a few digits at a time rather than be told the whole number and then start writing. The average upper limit of this type of memory is about seven chunks of information, but there are individual differences in this limit that are linked to differences in educational achievement (Pickering, 2006). Pupils' dependency upon working memory is graphically revealed when brain activities associated with, for example, mathematical training are visible. In a recent study involving functional magnetic resonance imaging (fMRI), adults learning long multiplication demonstrated a shift, with practice, in the regions of the brain they were using to complete their calculations (Delazer *et al.*, 2003). At first, considerable demand upon working memory was demonstrated by activity in the left inferior frontal gyrus, as students explicitly and formally followed the processes they were learning (see Fig. 1.2 in colour plate section). After practice, this activity reduced and was replaced by activity in the left angular gyrus, as processes became more automatic. The images generated by this study provide a helpful and very visual illustration of how the types of mental resource required for solving a problem change with practice. They resonate well with classroom observations of the difficulties faced by many learners when engaging with new problems. In such situations, it can be particularly helpful for pupils to show their working since, apart from many other advantages, external representations can help offload some of these heavy initial demands upon working memory. Cognitive Load Theory (CLT), which is based around reducing load on working memory, has formed an important basis for much instructional design (Merrienboer and Sweller, 2005) which may be developed further through the application of neuroimaging techniques that reveal activity shifts during learning.

Learning and emotion

There has been much interest in the possibility of neuroscience shedding light on the role of emotion in classroom learning but, beyond the stress effects described above, these hopes are still largely to be realized. To a large extent, this is due to the present distance between concepts about emotion that have been developed in neuroscience and the conceptual frameworks used to study emotion in psychology. Indeed, reflection on this distance has led at least one author to conclude that:

> Given the lack of overlap between these traditions in the case of emotions, it might be said that the available neuroscientific work on emotion is largely irrelevant to the field of education.
>
> (Byrnes, 2001, p. 12)

However, in the future, it appears likely that neuroscience will be helpful in integrating concepts of emotion in our understanding of learning, if only because, as understanding in this region grows, it seems increasingly unhelpful to consider emotion and cognition as separable in terms of neural processes. In a review article, Immordino-Yang and Damasio (2007) point out the neurobiological evidence that learning, attention, decision making and social functioning are all both profoundly affected by and subsumed within emotional processes. They suggest evidence from brain-damaged patients emphasizes the particular importance of emotion-related processes in transferring learning achieved within school to the outside world (Immordino-Yang and Damasio, 2007).

Understanding about the human reward system has also provided insight into the motivation provided by games of chance. Additional dopamine is generated in the reward system when the reward we receive is uncertain, and dopamine has been shown to peak at odds of about 50:50 success (see Chapter 9). When the additional motivation provided by elements of chance is combined with formal learning processes, as in learning games, Howard-Jones et al. demonstrated that the emotional experience of the learning was also influenced (Howard-Jones and Demetriou, in press – now published online). This has provided a basis for understanding how learning games can enhance motivation, attention and learning in the classroom. In a computer based knowledge quiz in which points available were subject to chance, modelling of reward signals can even predict when a player learns quiz knowledge from a mistake, based on the points that had been available (Howard-Jones et al., 2009).

Learning by imitation and visualization

There are many other psychological insights being explored by neuroimaging that have broad implications for teaching and learning strategies. For example, it has been known for some time that visualization is a useful strategy for learning. As well as being able to produce strong physiological responses, we now know that visualizing an object recruits most of the brain regions activated by actually seeing it (Kosslyn, 2005). This ability of mental imagery to engage so much of the brain circuitry involved with a real perceptual experience emphasizes its potential power and usefulness as a learning tool.

Brain imaging is also promising insight into vicarious learning. When we observe others carrying out actions, some of the same cortical regions are activated as if we were carrying out the actions ourselves (Rizzolatti and Craighero, 2004). The so-called mirror neuron system may support imitation-based learning, and is thought to have evolved as a type of 'mind reading'. The goal of the observed action influences mirror neuron activity, suggesting it may have developed as a means to anticipate others' actions (Gazzola et al., 2007).

Vicarious learning

This mirror neuron system also activates when we merely hear of human actions being performed, suggesting ways in which the potential effectiveness of visualization can be further realized (Tettamanti *et al.*, 2005). The restriction of mirror neuron activation to biological movement may help untangle apparent inconsistencies surrounding claims that animation can support learning (Tvesrky and Morrison, 2002). The existence of a mirror neuron system may explain why animation is most advantageous when the learning involves human movement (van Gog *et al.*, 2008).

Learning about the brain

Ideas about biologically defined limits to mental ability may influence self-perceptions and motivation, suggesting that learning about the brain may support learning in other areas. A recent study of adolescent pupils showed that pupils who conceived of intelligence as a malleable entity were more likely to receive grades with an upward trend for the subsequent two years, whereas concepts of intelligence as a fixed entity predicted a flat trajectory in school performance (Blackwell *et al.*, 2007). In the same report, the authors of this study also implemented an intervention with low-achieving teenagers. They informed pupils about the structure and function of their brain, how learning changes the brain by producing new neuronal connections, and provided the clear message that the pupils themselves were in charge of this process. This promoted a positive change in classroom motivation. Grades for the control group, who had not received the intervention, continued downward, while this trend was reversed for the intervention group.

Curriculum areas

Maths

Neuroimaging involving adults has shown that calculating answers exactly increased activity in regions of the brain involved with word association and language tasks, in the left frontal and angular gyri (Dehaene *et al.*, 1999). This suggests that the acquisition of formal mathematics relies on our ability to learn rules and procedures. However, when the same individuals attempted to estimate answers, the role of a more ancient and innate ability to approximate was linked to bilateral activity in the intraparietal sulci (see Fig. 1.3 in colour plate section).

Even at six months, it seems, most of us can approximately differentiate between large numbers of items for ratios of between 1:2 and 2:3 (Starkey and Cooper, 1980) and we share this approximate number sense with other animals (Boysen and Capaldi, 1993). Such innate mathematical ability may have a critical role in 'bootstrapping' our capacity to formally grasp exact differences and procedures (credited to Spelke and Carey in (Johnson, M.H. 2004); see also (Carey, 2004)).

There have been few imaging studies on the effects of teaching, but one fMRI study has revealed striking differences in the brain activities of learners who had been taught by rote or by strategy (Delazer *et al.*, 2005). In the rote condition, learners were taught to associate a particular result with two operands, and in the strategy condition they were taught to apply a sequence of arithmetical operations. Greater activation of the left angular gyrus was associated with drill learning, reflecting greater reliance on the retrieval of automatic mappings of arithmetic problems to their solutions. This shift towards left angular gyrus activity was mentioned in the discussion of working memory above, after adults had trained and improved their performance in a complex multiplication task (Delazer *et al.*, 2003). The role of this region in the learning of exact mappings prompted the suggestion that it might play a role in individual differences in mathematical ability. A recent study with adults confirmed that low scorers in a mathematical test, with otherwise normal intelligence, produced less activation of the angular gyrus during multiplication than their peers, even when accuracy and response time differences were controlled for (Grabner *et al.*, 2007). This lends weight to the notion that such differences in brain activity are related to functional differences, rather than arising from performance alone. However, increases in angular gyrus activation were not recorded when, in another study, participants became trained in subtraction (Ischebeck *et al.*, 2006). Here, compared with training in multiplication, brain activities suggested faster and more efficient strategies, rather than a shift towards automatic retrieval processes. In summary, it would seem that **teaching strategies, learner differences and the type of mathematical operations involved** all influence mathematical processing, and neuroscientific experimental approaches have a major role to play in studying these effects.

One example of the potential influence of neuroscience on mathematics education comes from research into the role of fingers in early mathematical development. **Finger gnosis** (being able to differentiate between different fingers in response to, say, one or more being touched) has been identified as a strong predictor of mathematical ability (Noel, 2005). Links between finger discrimination and mathematical ability have been studied in children and adults. An fMRI study has shown that, although behavioural outcomes can be the same, the activities produced when fingers are used to help approximate varies with age (Kaufmann *et al.*, 2008). Eight-year-old children produce an increase in activity in the intraprietal sulci when fingers are involved, but not adults. Kaufmann suggests fingers represent concrete embodied tokens involved in the estimation of number magnitude – an intimate involvement with our basic 'number sense'. On this basis, children should not be discouraged from using them and teachers may be able to exploit their natural role more fully (Kaufmann, 2008). Indeed, recent evidence for linking finger gnosis and mathematical ability is now producing interventions based on these concepts. New arrivals at three Belgian schools were identified as having poor finger gnosis and some of them received two-weekly 30 minute sessions of finger training for eight weeks (Gracia-Bafalluy and Noel, 2008). After training, these children were significantly better at quantification tasks than those who had not received the training. The disproportionate number of split-five errors made in later years, due to intermediate results represented by hands being forgotten, bears witness to the continuing influence of our fingers on our mathematical training. Neither does the relationship between our fingers and our mathematical abilities entirely disappear in adulthood. In an adult study, it has been shown that repetitive transcranial magnetic stimulation (TCMS) of the left angular gyrus, which can be expected to disrupt function in that region, interferes both with access to finger gnosis and numerical magnitude processing (Rusconi *et al.*, 2005). As already discussed, the angular gyrus is more associated with retrieval strategies than number sense, so these results suggest some level of explicit processing of estimated outcome, and that also some 'cortical trace' of finger processing remains in adulthood even when formal retrieval strategies are being used.

Dyscalculia may arise from a deficit in our 'premathematical' estimation abilities. A study of low birth-weight adolescents with numerical difficulties revealed less grey matter in the region linked to these abilities (i.e. the intra-parietal sulcus, Isaacs *et al.*, 2001). Further research is needed to confirm the direction of cause and effect in such studies, but insights from brain imaging research are contributing to models of mathematical development useful in developing interventions. In one such intervention, it was demonstrated that children with dyscalculia showed considerable improvements in a broad range of calculation abilities when teachers focused on basic numerical and conceptual knowledge in the early stages of mathematics education (Kaufmann *et al.*, 2003). The neuroscientific research of Stanislav Dehaene has emphasized the importance of our animal 'number sense' in our acquisition of mathematical ability. Building on this research, he has helped develop and evaluate educational software aimed at remediating dyscalculia. The software is based on the hypothesis that dyscalculia derives from a core deficit in number sense, or in relating number sense to numerical symbols (Wilson *et al.*, 2006).

Reading

Behavioural studies suggest the acquisition of early reading ability follows in stages. It begins with recognizing simple words based on their salient visual features, but without any letter-to-sound connections, as illustrated by recognizing an advertising logo even if one or more letters are removed. This logographic (Frith, 1985) or pre-alphabetic (Ehri, 1995) stage gives rise to a partial alphabetic stage when the more salient letters are used to attempt a pronunciation, such as the word 'on' being recognized as a short word beginning with a small circle. In the full alphabetic stage, letters become fully associated with particular sounds. Readers can now also make phoneme-grapheme mappings of sight words – whole words that have acquired a memory of their whole sound. Blending the pronunciation of letters, and some combination of letters such as 'ch', allows the sounding out of new complete words. Finally, in the orthographic stage, awareness and memory of recurring letter patterns is consolidated (so 'chest' might be identified as two sounds 'ch' and 'est' instead of 'ch,e,s,t', also allowing rapid identification of new words by analogy with old ones (e.g. 'feed' from 'need').

Reading in adults is known to involve a network of language regions in the left hemisphere including the posterior superior temporal cortex (Fiez, 1998). This part of the brain appears to be crucially involved in our ability to separate words into sound-based components. Such phonological skills are a good indicator of later reading ability, and a study of young readers has shown that the amount of activity in this brain region correlates with these early phonological skills (Turkeltaub et al., 2003). The same study showed how reading development was associated with increasing activity in the language region of the left inferior frontal gyrus and decreasing activity in some right hemispheric regions linked to visual processing. This suggests a decreasing reliance on recognizing words using non-lexical cues such as their shape, and thus supports the behavioural model just discussed. Interestingly, these decreases were predicted by the early reflections of Samuel Orton in 1925, who suggested children may need to disengage posterior right hemisphere visual representations that interfere with proper word identification. Children with developmental dyslexia display reduced activation in typical left hemisphere sites for reading, and also show atypical engagement of right hemisphere sites (Simos et al., 2002; Shaywitz et al., 2002; Shaywitz et al., 2003; Temple et al., 2001). Some educational interventions that improve language outcomes have also been shown to help remediate these differences in neural activity (Shaywitz et al., 2004; Simos et al., 2002; Temple et al., 2003). Such studies demonstrate the plastic nature of the brain regions involved and the potential for remediation, and our increasing knowledge of reading development has helped encourage interventions (e.g. synthetic phonics) that emphasize the importance of phonological processing.

As our understanding improves and techniques are further developed, it may be possible to identify children at risk from dyslexia well before they begin school, allowing the earliest possible intervention. One promising technique is electroencephalography (EEG), which involves placing a net of electrodes on the scalp to detect and record the minute patterns of electrical activity produced by the brain. These patterns of electricity sometimes change in predictable ways in response to particular events. Several types of these event-related changes, known as ERPs, or Event-Related Potentials, have been identified in relation to language processing. Because it is quite non-invasive and child-friendly, this technique has already proved immensely useful in revealing the earliest stirrings of linguistic processing ability. Some ERP waveforms of newborn infants have been identified that can differentiate between children who will later, at eight years old, be poor readers or be dyslexic (Molfese, 2000). ERPs have been shown as effective in predicting dyslexia in newborns with and without a family history of dyslexia (Guttorm *et al.*, 2005), and such techniques could form the basis of very early screening, so that 'at-risk' children are able to benefit as quickly as possible from suitable intervention.

Learning of scientific concepts

Neuroimaging has also prompted questions about the nature of knowledge construction in scientific concept learning. In an MRI scanner, non-physics and physics students were asked to watch Newtonian and non-Newtonian movies, i.e. when balls of unequal mass fall at the same rate (according to Newtonian physics) and at different rates respectively (Dunbar *et al.*, 2004; Dunbar and Fugelsang, 2005). Regions of the anterior cingulate and regions associated with motor activity increased their activity when physicists watched non-Newtonian movies, and when non-physics students watched Newtonian movies, apparently indicating that both groups were detecting inconsistencies with their current beliefs. This also confirmed, together with behavioural data, that the physicists had developed their concepts of motion beyond the common naive belief that heavier objects should fall faster. More interestingly, the physicists also demonstrated increased medial frontal activation when watching naive non-Newtonian movies, a type of activity linked to pre-existing representations. The authors suggest this challenges the view that students restructure their knowledge when learning. It may be, instead, that these physicists were inhibiting their naive knowledge while concurrently activating their Newtonian knowledge.

Induction of rules, by trial and error exploration, can be considered an important part of exploratory concept learning in science. In an fMRI study of adults, participants attempted to maximize their score in a number sequence task, by working out a system for predicting outcomes (Sailer *et al.*, 2007). As participants learnt the rule for predicting outcomes, their task became more one of merely applying that rule, and a number of brain sites associated with learning from feedback were seen to reduce their activity. One of these regions, the frontopolar region (the most forward part of the frontal lobes), has a well-established role in rule induction rather than rule application. Interestingly, however, this region's activity was greater for gains than losses and it was this gain-related activity that reduced with learning, rather than its response to losses. The researchers promote this as evidence for the power of positive, over negative, reinforcement in stabilizing strategies held in working memory, i.e. that positive feedback has a greater significance in deriving and consolidating such learning than negative feedback.

Music

Musical studies involving biological perspectives have provided a number of educational insights, particularly in our understanding of the role of experience over innate giftedness. For example, we appear born to appreciate a broad range of different music. A sensitive window of music appreciation is present for a few months following birth, during which we are eclectic in our appreciation of rhythms from diverse cultures. After this period, however, we are chiefly sensitive only to those we have already experienced (Hannon and Trehub, 2005a, 2005b). Such research has also shown that the intense emotion we can experience from music recruits the same brain region as that activated by a range of other powerful pursuits of pleasure, such as sex, eating and the consumption of illicit drugs such as cocaine.

When musicians were asked to search for bars of musical notation amidst musically meaningless ones, it was shown that a period of training on the target bars set in motion a series of neural events related to learned music responses for those bars. These automatic responses allude to the power of even brief periods of musical training to grant musical notes a significance that cannot be easily suppressed. Structural analysis of the brains of musicians has shown enlargement of the corpus callosum (Schlaug *et al.*, 1995), auditory (Schneider *et al.*, 2002) and motor regions (Amunts *et al.*, 1997) but, again, such changes speak of the critical influence of experience. Structural alterations appear dependent on the age at which training began (Elbert *et al.*, 1995; Hutchinson *et al.*, 2003) and the intensity of training received (Gaser and Schlaug, 2003; Hutchinson *et al.*, 2003; Schneider *et al.*, 2002). Although neuroscience cannot promise that 'practice makes perfect', it does offer clear and observable evidence of how the brain adapts to the demands of extensive training. In contrast to notions of biology as destiny, neuroscience places emphasis more upon practice and experience than on giftedness (Stewart and Williamon, 2008).

Music is also a curriculum area where the potential benefits of neurofeedback have been studied. Neurofeedback refers to the monitoring of one's own brain activity with a view to influencing it. Recent work investigating EEG neurofeedback concluded that it helped improve the performance ability of music students. Conservatoire students received training using neurofeedback and improvements in their musical performance were highly correlated with their ability to progressively influence neural signals associated with attention and relaxation (Gruzelier and Egner, 2004). Similar results have been found for dancers (Raymond *et al.*, 2005). This is an interesting and unusual example of a technique being borrowed from neuroscience to provide direct improvements for learners. Despite its apparent success, these interventions are not built around any particular cognitive model and the processes involved are not completely understood. However, the helpfulness of EEG feedback in raising levels of attention indicates its potential benefit in a broad variety of educational areas (Egner and Gruzelier, 2001).

Creativity

Creativity is considered a key thinking skill but the fostering of creative thinking in the classroom has been hampered by a lack of understanding of the thinking processes involved. Psychological research has suggested that creativity requires switching between two very different types of mental process: generative and analytical thinking, each benefiting from a different attentional state. Analytical thinking, in which we research the background to a problem or evaluate a potential solution, requires the type of focused attention most often encouraged by a school environment. The generative thinking needed to produce ideas and potential solutions, however, requires more diffuse attention – the type supported by relaxed environments, changes in context and the absence of critical evaluation by self or others. A recent EEG study demonstrated the relationship between unfocused, diffuse attention and generative thinking at an individual level (Kounios *et al.*, 2008). The EEG of individuals with high and low insight problem-solving ability was recorded when they were at rest. Such measurements, when brain function is more spontaneous and less controlled by the experimenter than when an individual is performing a set task, can be helpful in identifying individual differences in brain function. Results confirmed psychological models by revealing that the brain activities of high insight problem solvers reflect greater attentional diffusion, even at rest.

Other studies have shown how creative ability is not just about individual differences but can be influenced by the sorts of typical strategies used by teachers in the classroom. One such strategy requires the student to incorporate elements into their creative outcome which are not related to each other. A brain imaging study investigated the generation of stories from words that were unrelated and showed that such strategies can increase the brain activity associated with creative effort, supporting their likely effectiveness in fostering longer-term creative ability (Howard-Jones *et al.*, 2005). As will be discussed in Chapter 8, these and other insights have been used to co-construct with educators an educationally relevant and scientifically grounded understanding of creativity, as a basis fostering it in the classroom (Howard-Jones, 2008).

Brain care

Caffeine

Although caffeine is classed as a stimulant, its tendency to suppress the cognitive function of habitual users is less well publicized. Caffeine is found in many drinks (tea, coffee, cola) and some foods (e.g. chocolate). It influences our physiology and behaviour through blocking the action of adenosine, an inhibitory neurotransmitter. Adenosine is produced naturally by the body and its levels increase with each hour of wakefulness until we sleep, decreasing neural firing rates and inhibiting neurotransmitter release in a number of key brain regions. Caffeine interrupts this action but, with regular consumption of caffeine, counter-regulatory changes occur in the adenosine system, which result in adverse effects when caffeine is withdrawn. Thus, when faced with cognitive tests at breakfast time, coffee drinkers appear unable to perform as well as non-caffeine users until after they have had their usual dose. So, rather than being a helpful means to wake up, habitual caffeine use tends to suppress cognitive function, which only returns to baseline levels after ingestion of caffeine and then, of course, only temporarily (James and Rogers, 2005).

More worryingly, caffeine is the only psychoactive drug legally available to children, and their consumption of it has become very widespread. Even a small 500 ml bottle of cola, such as those dispensed by a vending machine, has the same amount of caffeine as a cup of coffee. It is hardly surprising, therefore, that children commonly experience caffeine withdrawal (James, 1997). In a study of children aged 9–10 years, those who habitually consumed the equivalent of two cans a day showed decreased alertness relative to low users (Heatherley *et al.*, 2006). As with the adult study, the alertness of these children only rose to baseline levels when they had received some caffeine. It would appear that, rather than making children fizzy for their lessons, the cola 'caffeine fix' provides only a momentary return to the state of alertness offered by a caffeine-free life-style. Recently, a clinical review of the evidence confirmed clear links between caffeine and daytime sleepiness, for both adults and children, and concluded that these effects are greatly underestimated by the general population and physicians (Roehrs and Roth, 2008). Part of this effect may be due to suppression of cognitive function, but part of it may also be due to caffeine's effect upon disrupting nighttime sleep. This is important because, as well as ensuring we are fully alert the next day, sleep can also contribute more directly to our learning.

Sleep

Neuroscience is beginning to reveal more clearly the processes by which sleep helps us 'lay down' our memories and consolidate them, ensuring they remain more robust when we wish to access them later. This nighttime consolidation process may explain why, during sleep, the brain has been shown (see Fig. 1.4 in colour plate section) to reproduce the neural activities characterizing whatever we experienced in our preceding hours of wakefulness (Maquet *et al.*, 2000).

The neurotransmitter ACh (acetylcholine) has been identified as a 'switch' that changes our state of wakefulness and plays a central role in how we process information. High levels of ACh help maintain a wakeful state that supports the encoding (or storing) of information, while low levels of ACh during sleep minimize the encoding of new memories and maximize consolidation of what has already been experienced (Rasch *et al.*, 2006). As well as helping us remember what we learnt yesterday, sleep also helps us prepare to learn more and use what we know to generate insights (Wagner *et al.*, 2004). Regular and sufficient sleep is thus essential for the brain to learn efficiently.

Exercise

Exercise is also linked to brain health and development throughout life. Many studies have linked levels of physical activity to school achievement (Sibley and

Etnier, 2003) and, in a study of over-65s, those who exercised at least three times a week were 38 per cent less likely to have developed dementia six years later than those exercising less than this (Larson *et al.*, 2006). At present, the mechanisms by which exercise influences mental ability are not well understood. However, a recent study showed improvements in short, medium and long-term memory after only three minutes intense aerobic exercise. This study linked these effects to the production of brain-derived neurotropic factor (BDNF) (Winter *et al.*, 2007). As we understand more about the mechanisms involved, this knowledge should help develop exercise programmes that most effectively deliver academic benefits. In Chapter 2, we shall look more closely at what is, and what is not, known about this link between exercise and learning.

Summary

There are a wide variety of areas where advances in neuroscience are of potential interest to educators. These include brain development, particularly during adolescence, and the brain's continuing plasticity throughout life. From neuroscience, we have come to understand more about the effect of strategies and stress on memory, and the vital role of working memory in learning new mental processes. Neuroscience is providing explanations and illuminating the processes involved with motivation and the effects of different types of feedback. It may help us understand more about learning through visualization, imitation and observation. Some research findings offer new insights in specific curriculum areas, including the development of reading ability and the early acquisition of number. Insights have also been provided in the teaching of science, in terms of the learning of concepts and the inference of rules, and also in music and the arts, in terms of the role of experience over innate giftedness and the effects of strategies intended to foster creativity. More broadly, neuroscience has helped reveal the processes by which our daily habits, such as those involving sleep, exercise and the ingestion of caffeine, influence the development and function of our brains.

This is all exciting news for those seeking fresh approaches in education, and so it is unsurprising that many educators are keen to apply scientific concepts about learning in their teaching as soon as possible. However, history suggests much caution is needed. As we shall see in the next chapter, rather than prompting more effective educational solutions, uncritical excitement and enthusiasm has spawned a number of unhelpful and/or unscientific educational approaches.

Chapter 2

Neuromyths

Neuromyths may abound more freely in education but the original use of the term comes from the medical sciences. It can probably be accredited to the neurosurgeon Alan Crockard, who became frustrated in the 1980s by how easily some unscientific ideas about the brain were embedding themselves in medical culture. He noticed, for example, that Lhermitte's sign[1] had become almost synonymous with a diagnosis of multiple sclerosis, despite also being generated in a number of other conditions. Crockard used the term 'neuromyth' in his lectures, and later in written articles, to describe a misleading type of 'received wisdom' within medical circles about clinical symptoms and causes (Crockard, personal communication; Crockard, 1996). In 2002, the OECD's Brain and Learning project drew attention to the many misconceptions around the mind and brain arising outside of the medical and scientific communities. They redefined the term 'neuromyth' as a 'misconception generated by a misunderstanding, a misreading or a misquoting of facts scientifically established (by brain research) to make a case for use of brain research, in education and other contexts' (OECD, 2002b, p.111).

As we shall see in later chapters, such neuromyths have had a major influence on shaping the perceptions and views of educators about neuroscience and its potential role in education. To unpick some of these ideas and understand more about the existing relationship between neuroscience and education (real and imagined), the most salient neuromythologies will be examined in this chapter. However, as will become clear, this task of examination is not just a process of deciding whether an idea is true or false. In the sense used in this chapter, the term 'neuromyth' will refer to a story about the brain formed and reformed by countless retellings, rather than some fundamentally misconceived notion. Indeed, neuromyths frequently originate from, and to a lesser extent retain, some genuine scientific understanding. This residual element of real science remains an important part of their enduring power. It affords them credibility long after they have divorced themselves from the scientific community and become effectively protected from its scrutiny. Since some original science remains in the myth, the task here becomes not a matter of determining if an idea is right or wrong, but what part of the story can be supported by valid evidence and what cannot.

Multiple Intelligences (MI) theory

Gardner's MI theory proposes that it is more useful to describe an individual as possessing a small number of relatively independent intelligences, rather than possessing a single all-purpose intelligence (Gardner, 1983). Possible candidates for these intelligences include linguistic, musical, logical-mathematical, spatial, bodily-kinaesthetic, intrapersonal sense of self, interpersonal; and Gardner has later proposed other possibilities such as naturalistic and existential intelligence (Gardner, 1999). MI theory is in direct opposition to the idea of a unitary general intelligence factor 'g', reflecting overall brain efficiency and the close interconnection of our mental skills. MI theory resonates with many educators, who see it as a robust argument against IQ-based education.

In a critical review of the evidence for MI theory, Waterhouse examined the empirical scientific evidence (Waterhouse, 2006). MI theory claims to be drawn from a wide range of disciplines including neuroscience. Indeed, Gardner has claimed 'accumulating neurological evidence is amazingly supportive of the general thrust of MI theory' (Gardner, 1999). In terms of an empirical basis, one might point to neuroscientific evidence showing that achievement in different types of task is correlated with activity in different regions of the brain such that the behavioural influence of one region's efficiency may vary according to task. Additionally it is also true that a single measure of intelligence is inadequate in explaining individual behavioural differences. Both types of evidence might help argue against the likely usefulness of a single IQ measure as a strong general predictor of educational achievement.[2] This is not the same, however, as suggesting that the limits of our mental and/or neural performance arise from a small distinct set of components, and that these limitations, in combination, account for the diversity of performance we observe across individuals tackling different tasks.

Gardner suggests that each intelligence operates from a separate area of the brain although, in response to Waterhouse, Gardner rephrased this claim more carefully. In this response, he refers to intelligences as being 'composites of fine-grained neurological subprocesses but not those subprocesses themselves' (Gardner and Moran, 2006) Gardner refers to the type of test he believes would invalidate his MI concept when he argues that if musical and spatial processing were identically represented in the cortex that fact would suggest the presence of one intelligence, and not two separate intelligences. Yet, many shared and overlapping brain processing pathways have been found between, for example, language and music skills (Koelsch et al., 2004), music perception and nonverbal reasoning (Norton et al., 2005) and distributed networks for emotion that are shared with reasoning, memory and action (Adolphs et al., 2003; Morgane et al., 2005; Phelps, 2006). Neither do two tasks recruiting the same shared region provide strong evidence for a single intelligence. The idea here is that if a single region is linked with two different tasks, then performance in these two tasks might be effected only by the processing efficiency in this single brain region. This could contribute to the notion that these two tasks require the same single type of intelligence. Such functional isolation in the brain would be unusual, with processes often employing different pathways between and within the same broad regions. In short, the general processing complexity of the brain makes it unlikely that a theory resembling MI theory will ever emerge from it. Cognitive neuroscience is exploring the brain in terms of processes (vision, hearing, smell, etc.) but not in terms of *seeing intelligence, auditory intelligence* or *smelling intelligence*. In the realm of neuroscience, it appears neither accurate nor useful to reduce the vast range of complex individual differences at neural and cognitive levels to any limited number of capabilities.

Despite the absence of MI theory in the neuroscience literature, teachers heavily associate MI theory with neuroscience. (To confirm this, the author returned to the data collected from the 150 UK teachers who were asked the question 'Please list any ideas that you have heard of in which the brain is linked to education' (Pickering and Howard-Jones, 2007). Of those teachers who responded to this question (121), most listed no more than two to three ideas. Of these, MI theory occurred 17 times (14 per cent)).

In Gardner's response to Waterhouse, provocatively titled 'The science of multiple intelligences theory', he summarizes two ways in which MI theory may come to be assessed in the future. The first is by intelligence testing, using systems of assessment he describes as 'intelligence fair'. Such tests may indeed raise awareness of how diverse our individual profiles of cognitive ability are, and provide evidence against the idea of a unitary measure of that ability. Less certain is the possibility that they will also indicate a limited set of clearly defined and relatively independent intelligences.

The second way that Gardner suggests his theory will be assessed is by whether it improves the lot, formally and informally, of students in schools where practices have been informed by MI theory. There are already a great number of studies claiming the successful application of MI theory in the classroom, but these studies assume the validity of the listed intelligences rather than test them. At this level of investigation, the principle under investigation is the pedagogical value of understanding pupils in terms of their many different strengths and weaknesses, something most teachers aspire to. Nothing in the above suggests there should be no practical advantage to educators in considering performance in these terms. The point here is just that, however useful the concept is in practice, it does not arise from neuroscience and is unlikely to be proven or disproven by neuroscience. So, although Gardner reviewed the scientific literature when developing MI and may have been inspired by it, it essentially remains an educational theory, with its power and validity being assessed (and sometimes debated) only within educational domains. The neuromythological part of MI theory is that it is a scientific theory, since it does not derive directly from empirical evidence and, in its present form, it is not testable. This is, not least, because Gardner is unwilling to define the components involved.

MI theory is very popular with educators and promotes the worth of children's individual and diverse talents rather than how generally 'bright' they are. Thus, in educational terms, MI theory appears like a liberator – providing teachers with the 'scientific' licence to celebrate diversity. In terms of the science, however, it seems an unhelpful simplification. No clearly defined set of capabilities arises from either the biological or psychological research. MI theory may, therefore, also be an example of an idea that has been inappropriately imbued with a sense of neuroscientific authority although, in fairness to Gardner, this is not wholly due to arguments put forward by its author. As he reported recently:

> I have come to realize that once one released an idea – 'meme' – into the world, one cannot completely control its behaviour – anymore than one can control those products of our genes we call children.
>
> (Gardner, 2003)

Learning styles

An individual's learning style can be considered as a set of learner characteristics that influences their reponse to different teaching approaches. A survey in 2004 identified seventy-one different models of learning styles and our own survey showed almost a third of UK teachers had heard of learning styles, with most of those who used this approach reporting it as effective (Pickering and Howard-Jones, 2007). As with MI theory, which is also often interpreted by educators as a means to identify preferred modes of learning, the promotion of learning styles has benefited from a strong association with neuroscience. Many learning style models have a distinctly biological justification, with one of their major proponents (Rita Dunn et al., 1990, p. 86), commenting that 'at least three fifths of style is biologically imposed'.

There are many instruments used to measure and explain learning styles and these consist almost entirely of self-report questionnaires. The validity of only a few of these instruments has been explored and even here, findings are not always conclusive. For example, the Learning Styles Inventory has been shown by some to record stable measurements (Heffler, 2001; Marshall and Merritt, 1986), while other researchers have been critical of its reliability (Lam, 1997; Loo, 1997).

Perhaps the best-known inventory within education is the one categorizing individuals in terms of their preferred sense modality for receiving, processing and communicating information: visual, auditory or kinaesthetic (VAK). However, the educational enthusiasm for learning styles does not stop at identifying a preferred sense modality. Instead, it usually goes one step further in assuming that there is some educational value in tailoring educational experience to suit the learning style reported by each individual. Perhaps the assumption that learning can be improved in this way is not wholly unreasonable. If a learner expresses a preference during the learning process, then a learner-centred response seems logical. However, if identification of this preference is via a very limited and closed questionnaire consisting essentially of three options, based wholly upon sensory modalities, the extent to which VAK can meaningfully personalize learning seems very questionable.

Very many educational projects have pursued improvement through tailoring programmes to meet individual learning styles but, as yet, there is no convincing evidence that any benefit arises. A review of such studies failed to find convincing evidence that matching instruction to meet an individual's sensory strengths was any more effective than designing content-appropriate forms of education and instruction (Coffield *et al.*, 2004). Furthermore, in a laboratory study of memory performance, participants' own self-assessment of their learning style (as is commonly used) was shown to be out of line with more objective measures, and memory scores in different modalities appeared unrelated to any measure of dominant learning style (Kratzig and Arbuthnott, 2006). There was, instead, evidence that participants' self-rating as kinaesthetic learners was related to visual performance, that they were self-rating their learning styles in ways possibly promoted by the inventory itself, and objective evidence from memory testing that suggested visual and kinaesthetic/tactile tasks were tapping the same underlying memory process. The authors concluded that educators' attempts to focus on learning styles were 'wasted effort'.

The implicit assumption of the VAK approach appears to be that, since different modalities are processed independently in different parts of the brain, differences in the efficiency of these parts results in a clear modality-based method of classifying how learners are able to process information most efficiently. However, as pointed out by Geake and already discussed in terms of MI theory, this flies in the face of what we know about the interconnectivity of the brain (Geake, 2008). Education seeks chiefly to develop higher order types of thinking processes, and brain areas associated with higher level thinking activate in a similar way when a problem is presented in different modalities, as might be expected from existing models of cognition (Qin *et al.*, 2003). As yet, no evidence arising from neuroscience, or any other science, supports the educational value of categorizing learners in terms of their sensory modality or any other type of learning style. In the meantime, the buzz words visual, auditory and kinaesthetic have developed a pedagogical meaning in all sectors of education, even enjoying promotion, for a period, on government web-sites (Sharp *et al.*, 2008).

Another popular way of categorizing learning style is in terms of 'left-brain right-brain' theory (Springer and Deutsch, 1989). According to this theory, learners' dispositions arise from the extent to which they are left or right brain dominant. This idea has become part of the theory used by many to underpin their learning style models, such as Hermann's Brain Dominance Instrument (Hermann, 1989) and the 4MAT system (McCarthy, 1997), or cited as an influence upon outcomes (Dunn *et al.*, 1990). The detail of such categorization varies with different educational programmes and learning style models but, for example, an 'intuitive learner' may be considered more right-brained and step-wise sequential learners are supposedly dominated more by their left hemisphere (McCarthy, 1987, 1997; Sloan *et al.*, 2002; Hoffman, 2002). Many educational texts encourage teachers to determine whether a child is left or right brained before they attempt to teach them (e.g. Hoffman, 2002). It is a well-established scientific fact that many processes are associated with extra brain activity predominantly occurring in one hemisphere or the other. For example, language is considered to be left lateralized. Imaging techniques can be used to identify areas of the brain that increase activity (usually in terms of blood flow) during tasks that require language function and, among the great majority of right-handed participants, these areas are in the left hemisphere (although they are in the right hemisphere for around a third of left-handed individuals). Here, as perhaps with MI theory and VAK, neuroimaging studies that present static pictures of well-defined islands of activity may have helped mislead non-specialists in suggesting a new phrenology of isolated well-defined functional units.

In reality, activity has only exceeded a statistical threshold defined by the experimenter. No part of the brain is ever normally inactive in the sense that no blood flow is occurring. Furthermore, performance in most everyday tasks, including learning tasks, requires both hemispheres to work together in a sophisticated parallel fashion. Even many language tasks produce additional activation in areas of the right hemisphere. For example, Carol Seger and her colleagues (Seger *et al.*, 2000) measured the extra brain activity produced when participants generated an unusual verb to follow a noun, rather than the first one that comes into our heads (e.g. 'the cat painted', rather than 'the cat purred'). The additional processing required was linked to a widely distributed set of 'hot spots' in the right hemisphere (see Fig. 2.1 in the colour section). However, these are in addition to the activities (excluded in this analysis) in other language networks usually found in the left hemisphere. A task that required the production of a complete sentence – perhaps the beginning of a story – would involve a host of further additional networks, including regions concerned with syntax, memory and the integration of concepts. Very quickly, as the task becomes closer to something resembling a simple classroom activity, you would find that most areas of the brain are more active than when our brains are completely at rest (if such a state can be said to exist). Thus, the types of hotspots seen in brain images such as Fig. 2.1 merely *appear* to support the neuromyth that we use just a small percentage of our brains.[3] In fact, brain activity at any moment is occurring, to a greater or lesser extent, throughout the brain. Also, these static brain images belie the rapidly changing nature of real brain activity. If the technology were better, scientists would be able to show the spreading and contracting of regions of increasing and decreasing activity all over the brain, on time scales of milliseconds. The idea that we use the left side of our brain for one task and the other side of our brain for another is very far from the mark.

The division of people into left-brained and right-brained takes the misunderstanding one stage further. The confusion in such an approach is reflected by the contrasting ways in which different learning style models attempt to allocate their dimensions to the two hemispheres. In the Learning Styles Inventory model, concrete experience is associated with right-brain thinking (Kolb, 1999). In the Cognitive Styles Index, the intuition-analysis dimension is allocated to the right brain (Allinson and Hayes, 1996), whereas in Cognitive Styles Analysis, the global-analytic dimension (whose definition is close to intuition-analysis) is characterized by its unrelatedness to hemispheric preference (Riding, 1998). At the end of their extensive review, Coffield *et al.* (2004) concluded that the dearth of rigorous research prevents any clear implications for pedagogy arising from existing models of learning styles.

Enriched environments

Contrary to much popular belief, there is not a convincing neuroscientific case for starting formal education as early as possible. Three such arguments for this approach have been used, but each involves the erroneous interpretation, or overinterpretation, of the evidence.[4] First, it is true that *synaptogenesis* (the making of synapses, or connections between neurons) occurs at a greater rate among children than in adults, as does *synaptic pruning* (in which infrequently used connections are eliminated). It is fair to consider that such overt changes in brain connectivity may help make childhood a good time to learn. Much of what we know about synaptogenesis and pruning is derived from research with other primates. In monkeys, these processes occur early, suggesting that the first three years of their life may be especially significant in terms of learning (Rakic, 1995). However, we now know that such structural changes continue in the human brain well beyond the first three years of life. In fact, the brain is still developing in adolescence, particularly in the frontal and parietal cortices where synaptic pruning does not begin until after puberty (Huttenlocher, 1979).

A second argument, often linked to the first, has been constructed from the concept of the critical period – a window in time when a child can learn a particular skill or ability. For example, it is known that adults have more difficulty in discriminating sounds that they did not hear in the first six months of life (Kuhl *et al.*, 1992). However, scientists now believe that critical periods should be referred to as sensitive periods. They are not fixed and rigid. They exist more as subtle differences in the brain's ability to be shaped by the environment. Furthermore, they chiefly involve visual, movement and memory functions that are learned naturally in a normal environment. Thus, research on sensitive periods may be potentially valuable for education but it cannot yet contribute to meaningful discussions regarding formal curriculum. The third argument points to research into the effects of enriched environments on learning and the development of synapses (e.g. Diamond *et al.*, 1987; Greenough *et al.*, 1987). However, this research involved rats living in environments that were no more enriched than their natural habitat. These rats were compared with caged rats existing with no stimulus in their cages at all. As researchers themselves suggested (Greenough *et al.*, 1987), the enriched condition was an incomplete attempt to mimic a wild environment and was enriched 'only in comparison to the humdrum life of the typical laboratory animal' (p. 546).[5] Thus, the results may say more about the effects of deprived environments than enriched ones, resonating with studies of neglected children showing delays and deficits in cognitive development. Overall, there is some evidence to suggest that impoverished environments inhibit neural development, but no evidence that enriched environments enhance it (for further discussion, see Blakemore and Frith, 2005, pp. 26–36).

Educational kinesiology (Brain Gym)

Educational kinesiology (or Edu-K, also often sold under the brand name of Brain Gym) was developed by Paul and Gail Dennison as a means to 'balance' the hemispheres of the brain so they work in an integrated fashion and thus improve learning (Dennison, 1981). According to the Dennisons, 'When one side of the brain is in control, the other side either cooperates and coordinates its movements with the controlling hemisphere, or it may "switch off" and block integration' (p. 8). The idea of cerebral dominance as a cause of learning difficulty can be traced back to Orton in the 1930s and 1940s who expressed the view that reading difficulty could be attributed to mixed cerebral dominance (Orton, 1937). Perhaps surprisingly, given the lack of imaging evidence when Orton made this claim, a recent fMRI study did produce findings confirming a shift from bilateral to left hemispheric activity with reading development, and evidence that this shift was delayed in poor readers (Turkeltaub *et al.*, 2003). However, Brain Gym also draws on theories of neurological repatterning and, more specifically, the Doman-Delacato theory of development (Dennison and Dennison, 1994). This proposes that efficient neurological functioning requires the acquisition of specific motor skills in the correct order (Doman, 1968), on the basis that ontogeny (individual development) recapitulates phylogeny (the development of the species). According to this view, if a particular developmental stage is skipped, such as when a child learns to walk before crawling, then this has a detrimental effect on later development of more complex processes such as language. Treatment in this case might be to encourage the child to rehearse crawling movements, in order to *repattern* their neural connections and improve their academic progress. Due to the methodological issues involved, it is difficult to test such a theory directly, but several careful reviews of scientific findings have concluded that the theory is unsupported and contradicted (Chapanis, 1982; Cohen *et al.*, 1970; Cummins, 1988; Robbins and Glass, 1968), and practical approaches based upon such ideas have been revealed as ineffective (AAP, 1998).

Brain Gym also draws on ideas about perceptual-motor training, i.e. that learning problems arise from inefficient integration of visual, auditory and motor skills. These ideas have generated training programmes that seek to ameliorate learning difficulties through exercises rehearsing integration of perceptual and motor skills. These approaches were shown to be ineffective by numerous studies in the 1970s and 1980s, and yet similar ideas have continued in circulation

(Arter and Jenkins, 1979; Bochner, 1978; Cohen, 1969; Hammill *et al.*, 1974; Kavale and Forness, 1987; Sullivan, 1972). Indeed, as recently as 2003, a paper was published in the respected journal *Dyslexia* promoting the value of such an approach, although its specific details were omitted on the basis that they were 'commercial sensitive' (Reynolds *et al.*, 2003). The article provoked a flurry of highly critical attention from well-established researchers in the field of dyslexia, who drew attention to fatal methodological flaws such as: the absence of standardized reading tests, inappropriate statistical analysis, lack of control for placebo effects, smaller student/teacher ratios in the experimental group, using unbalanced control and experimental groups, using an experimental group with few of the difficulties that the programme was intended to ameliorate, and inadequate reporting of essential details on the basis of 'commercial sensitivity' (Rack, 2003; Richards *et al.*, 2003; Singleton and Stuart, 2003; Snowling and Hulme, 2003; Stein, 2003). In a review of the assessment of perceptual-motor skills (Salvia and Ysseldyke, 2004), it was concluded that such tests were neither theoretically nor psychometrically adequate and that 'the real danger is that reliance on such tests may actually lead teachers to assign children to activities that do the children no known good' (p. 538). Texts on Brain Gym (e.g. Cohen and Goldsmith, 2000) now often include additional exercises for vision therapy – 'vision gym' (p. 66). Learning can easily be disrupted by vision defects and these should be corrected. However, given the lack of evidence for the effectiveness of carefully directed visual training by medically trained vision specialists, except in a very limited sense (Helveston, 2005), it seems extremely improbable that self-directed or teacher-directed exercises can help in this way. The broader literature reveals no convincing evidence to support the use of visual training as a means to tackle learning problems (Keogh and Pelland, 1985; Sieban, 1977; Silver, 1995).

Together with these flaws in its theoretical basis, there is a lack of published research in high quality journals to make claims about the practical effectiveness of programmes such as Brain Gym to raise achievement. Of the studies published elsewhere, the lack of information about the exercises undertaken and/or the insufficient or inappropriate analysis of the results undermine their credibility (Hyatt, 2007). However, many teachers and learners remain enthusiastic about Brain Gym and convinced that it supports learning, with reports of increased reaction times following Brain Gym exercises suggestive of some positive effect on cognition (Sifft and Khalsa, 1991).

Indeed, it may even be that programmes such as Brain Gym are contributing to learning, but for reasons entirely different from those used to promote them. There is an emerging body of multidisciplinary research supporting the beneficial effect of aerobic exercise on selective aspects of brain function that happen to be particularly important for education (Hillman *et al.*, 2008). A meta-analysis that drew together results from forty-four studies concluded that levels of physical activity are correlated to many categories of cognitive performance in school-age children, including IQ and achievement, and mathematical and verbal testing (Sibley and Etnier, 2003). The effect size was similar to that observed by another review of studies across the lifespan (Etnier *et al.*, 1997), suggesting that early intervention in terms of developing physical exercise habits might have significant implications for the rest of an individual's life. Correlations between physical activity and academic performance have sometimes produced variable results (from no effect to a positive effect) but this may reflect the diversity of research methods employed. However, one important and consistent finding has been that increasing the amount of time directed towards health-based activities, such as physical education, has never been shown to impinge upon academic performance (Ahamed *et al.*, 2007; Castelli *et al.*, 2007; Kim *et al.*, 2003). Physical fitness has been associated with blood flow in frontoparietal areas that are also strongly associated with cognitive functions of educational significance, such as higher-order processing and mathematical reasoning (Colcombe *et al.*, 2004). In animal research, exercise has been associated with increased prolifera- tion and cell survival in hippocampal areas together with an increased ability to learn (Olson *et al.*, 2006; van Praag *et al.*, 1999). The hippocampus is strongly linked to the consolidation of memory and, although our understanding of the role of postnatal neurogenesis remains incomplete, it seems likely the birth of new neurons in this area may also help facilitate human learning and memory. In human studies, even short periods of exercise have been shown to improve learn- ing in the short term and long term, if they are intense. A study of healthy adults revealed increased levels of brain-derived neurotrophic factor (BDNF) after two 3-minute sprints (Winter *et al.*, 2007). When compared to sedentary or moder- ate exercise conditions, participants showed a 20 per cent increase in the speed of recall for words they learnt immediately following their intense exercise. BDNF plays an important role in synaptic plasticity. It is an essential contributor to the process of Long Term Potentiation (LTP), thought essential to the changes in connectivity that underlie learning. Additionally, it supports the survival of new neurons and may also be implicated in the hippocampal neurogenesis (Cotman and Berchtold, 2007). In this human study by Winter *et al.*, data was based on peripheral measurements of these chemicals in blood samples, but this finding is consistent with non-human studies showing that BDNF in the brain mediates the positive effects of exercise on cognition (Vaynman *et al.*, 2004).

Given the beneficial effects of exercise for learning, the present anxieties around childhood obesity (Haslam and James, 2005) and the contribution made by exercise in school to general physical health, it seems unwise to dis- courage schools from pursuing an exercise programme they feel works for them, whatever the validity of the claims made by its promoters. However, the use of poorly evidenced theories to successfully promote some exercise programmes has inevitably detracted from the development and uptake of more appropriate and effective ones. Brain Gym is not designed to deliver aerobic exercise, but focuses on co-ordination. In the case of Brain Gym, factors thought to promote processes of so-called repatterning, which appears to be a neuromyth, take precedence over factors known to promote BDNF, such as the intensity of the exercise. The successful marketing to schools of exercise programmes that are quite sedentary in their nature emphasizes the importance of asking 'why' as well as 'whether' something works. When developing effective educational programmes and interventions that attempt to draw on our present knowledge of the brain and mind, scientific scrutiny of the theories involved and how they are applied is likely to be essential for success.

Water

In a popular book on Brain Gym (Cohen and Goldsmith, 2000), teachers are asked to encourage their children to sing (to the tune of 'Frere Jacques'):

> Let's drink water,
> I love water.
> It gives me
> En-er-gy

The drinking of water is often promoted as a way to improve learning, with some schools enthusiastic in their promotion of water as a means to raise attainment. In a BBC report headed 'Water improves test results', the headteacher of a school in Edinburgh explains 'the human brain uses water in its transmission of neural messages … if children are regularly hydrated their brains are better physically equipped to learn'. (BBC, 2000)

It is true that even small amounts of dehydration can reduce our cognitive ability. There are very few studies investigating the effects of dehydration on children, but these few, together with adult studies (Cian *et al.*, 2000), confirm the deleterious effect of even mild dehydration on our ability to think. However, drinking too much water can also be dangerous, resulting in water intoxication and even death (Vreeman and Carroll, 2007). Moreover, a recent adult study has shown that drinking water when not thirsty can also diminish cognitive ability (Rogers *et al.*, 2001).

As we shall see in the next chapter, many believe their brain may dangerously shrink if they fail to regulate their own water intake. In fact, very serious dehydration can increase the concentration of sodium in the blood and can produce a reversible shrinkage of the brain. In recent years, this fact was graphically illustrated when a man in Japan tried to commit suicide by overdosing on soy sauce (Machino and Yoshizawa, 2006). As with more common cases of serious dehydration, unusual pressure gradients can develop between the brain and the rest of the body. That means sodium levels needed to be restored slowly and carefully to avoid water entering the brain itself. The medical team thus had plenty of time to image the patient's brain and note the striking extent of brain shrinkage. Three weeks later, after appropriate treatment, the man's brain was shown to have returned (mostly) to its original dimensions. However, this was a rare case and one caused by vast amounts of soy sauce, not by forgetting to drink water.

In fact, forgetting to drink water is not usually a problem, because our brains have evolved a sophisticated system that makes us thirsty when our bodies (and brains) need more fluid. So, encouraging and enabling children to drink water when they are thirsty may be a more sensible approach than constantly monitoring the amount of water they consume. Exercise and unusually hot weather are the exception to this rule, when there is evidence that the body's own monitoring system becomes less reliable and then children should be encouraged to drink in order to avoid dehydration (Bar-David *et al.*, 2005; Bar-Or *et al.*, 1980). Apart from these special circumstances, there is no evidence to suggest that normally functioning children are generally prone to voluntary dehydration. Indeed, the only study showing voluntary dehydration among children comes from schools in the Dead Sea area – the lowest point on the planet and notoriously hot (Bar-David *et al.*, 2005).

So, where does the concern about learners having to drink enough water come from? It may be associated with the older myth of having to drink 6–8 cups of water a day. This is not an easy goal for many adults, and more challenging for a child. A possible original source for the 8 glasses-a-day myth is the nutritionist Fredrick J. Stare, whose obituary stated he was 'an early champion of drinking at least 6 glasses of water a day'. In a text co-authored by Dr Stare (p. 175), the issue is explicitly dealt with (although without consideration to the dehydrating effects of alcohol!):

> How much water each day? This is usually well regulated by various physiological mechanisms, but for the average adult, somewhere around 6 to 8 glasses per 24 hours and this can be in the form of coffee, tea, milk, soft drinks, beer, etc ...
>
> (Stare and McWilliams, 1974)

However, a review of the literature has concluded that 'such large amounts are not needed' in the case of healthy individuals in a temperate climate leading a generally sedentary existence (Valtin, 2002).

Omega-3

Omega-3 and Omega-6 fatty acids are termed essential fatty acids (EFA) because they must be provided through diet, rather than be provided by the body itself. The longer-chained versions of these are called the highly unsaturated fatty acids (HUFA) and are vital for brain development. These HUFAs can be produced by the body from their corresponding EFAs. They are produced from these precursors rather inefficiently by the body, especially the male body, and intake of EFAs are low compared with our historical past. The key Omega-3 HUFAs are found in significant quantities only in fish and seafood, with an Omega-3 EFA in green vegetables and some nuts and seeds. In contrast, the key Omega-6 HUFA is provided directly by meat, eggs and dairy products, which also contain its precursor EFAs that can be converted to Omega-6 HUFA by the body. The ratio of Omega 6 to Omega-3 HUFAs in the human population is estimated to have risen from 1:1 in our hunter-gatherer past to a present ratio worse than 16:1. High ratios of Omega-6 to Omega-3 are associated with a range of disease, psychiatric illnesses and developmental disorders, many of which appear to have arisen alongside our modern Western lifestyle and diet (Mazza et al., 2007; Simopoulos, 2002).

Many potential mechanisms have been identified for the deleterious effects of low Omega-3 HUFA levels in the brain including, at a cellular level, the survival and proliferation of neurons and their ability to communicate with each other (Salem et al., 2001). The formula-feeding of infants has been linked to low Omega-3 HUFA levels in the brain (Makrides et al., 1994), and breast feeding is associated with better cognitive development when results are adjusted for potential confounding factors, such as socio-economic status (Mortensen et al., 2002). Additionally, the improvement in cognitive outcome when Omega-3 HUFA is added to the formula of milk for preterm infants adds strongly to the case for it being a significant factor influencing cognitive developmental outcomes (Judge et al., 2007).

The long-standing interest in the potential positive effects of Omega-3 supplements has extended to trials involving children with developmental disorders such as ADHD. Findings here have been contradictory and no clear consensus has emerged (Richardson, 2006). Further research may help explain why such supplements appear to work in some contexts for some individuals with ADHD (Richardson and Puri, 2002) and not in others (Voigt et al., 2001). A recent study has added to the evidence supporting such a role for these supplements, with parental ratings of ADHD behaviour showing a medium to strong improvement (Sinn and Bryan, 2007).

Despite the lack of any rigorous trials looking at improvements in cognition and/or school performance among the general population of children, there has been a flourishing of 'clever' products on supermarket shelves providing supplementary Omega-3. Undoubtedly, current findings suggest we might look for evidence linking such supplements with improved brain function and academic achievement among the general population. The neuromyth, suggested by the enthusiasm with which these foods are being marketed and consumed, is that we already have such evidence. And it may be difficult to find, judging by the results of a recent study in Taiwan. In this research, over 500 of the 2,417 children in the families surveyed reported that they took supplements (Chen et al., 2007). These were usually just one of five types: multivitamins and minerals, calcium, vitamin C, cod-liver oil (a source of Omega-3) and bee propolis. Supplement taking was associated with higher school performance, irrespective of the supplement taken, and also with parental education and household income. This tends to suggest that supplements come with wealthier and better educated home environments, but also that the home environment is the key factor in any associated school success, rather than the supplement. Also, whereas related evidence for a link between Omega-3 supplements and improved brain function does appear to be growing, such effects are unlikely to match the known impact of good overall and regular dietary habits (such as having breakfast) which is probably the most important nutritional issue influencing educational performance and achievement (Bellisle, 2004).

Sugary snacks and drinks

The consumption of sugary snacks and drinks is commonly associated with subsequent inattentiveness and hyperactivity in children. Ironically, however, the research shows that confectionary snacks tend to increase children's ability to remain focused on a task for an extended duration (Busch et al., 2002). This tends to confirm previous research suggesting reports of poor behaviour may be due to expectations rather than the effects of sugar (Hoover and Milich, 1992), which appears not to have any negative effects on cognition or produce hyperactive behaviour (Roshon and Hagen, 1989; Wolraich et al., 1995). There may be other, strong arguments for reducing levels of sugar-intake among children and adults. For example, its effects on dental health, of course, are undisputable but these are beyond the scope of this chapter.

Although the educational suspicions around sugar appear unjustified, there is evidence that some food additives, or combinations of food additives, can increase hyperactivity in children. McCann et al. carried out a study in which two age groups (3 yrs and 8/9 yrs) were given daily drinks containing sodium benzoate combined with different types of other additives (McCann et al., 2007). The doses were similar to 2–4 bags of sweets a day, and increases in hyperactive behaviour were observable for both age groups. Despite action at European and UK levels, many sweets and drinks still contain the suspect additives (see www. actiononadditives.com) although more research is needed to understand the extent of their individual contribution to hyperactive behaviour.

Why are there (so many) neuromyths in education – and how do you spot one?

Writing this chapter has been difficult, because examining each neuromyth has unearthed another and it has been a struggle restricting the review to a few major issues. How has the neuromythology within education become so broad, deep and institutionalized?

Stitch identified four contexts that promote unfounded ideas (Stitch, 1990). The first of these is explicit fraud. However, there are very few examples of education being the victim of those who have promoted ideas, knowing them to be false, although some writers have used words like 'fraud' and 'scam' to describe their distrust of unscrutinized 'brain-based' interventions (Jorgenson, 2003; Novella, 1996). In contrast, Beyerstein characterizes the pseudoscientist, a key figure in the promotion of neuromyth, as a victim of self-deception (Beyerstein, 1999a). The pseudoscientist often holds a 'sincere but deluded fixation on some eccentric theory that the holder is absolutely sure will revolutionize science and society' (p. 60). However sincere their beliefs, the techniques used by some individuals to promote them in the educational arena can be quite strategic and manipulative, taking full advantage of the vacuum of understanding between education and the relevant sciences. One feature of that vacuum is educators' impatience with the technical debates and the sometimes obfuscating language of science. While scientists argue and theorize, educators are stuck with the task of implementing solutions today. The author recently watched a 'motivational speaker' expertly warm up an audience of 800 teachers with over 20 jokes, increasingly aimed at poking fun at the authority of traditional science and then asking 'shall we leave education to the scientists?!!' After the audience gave a resounding 'no', the speaker began successfully promoting their own home-grown ideas about the brain, ironically laced with associations of the same scientific authority he had just denigrated. The audience appeared blind to this inconsistency. Here they appeared to have someone who understood the science but was not detached like a scientist. This was a charismatic member of their own community who had gained the authority to pick and choose the concepts that were most appealing, presented in the fashion that exactly fitted educational sentiments. The teachers left the hall buzzing with positive excitement and enthusiasm, but also with some very strange concepts about the brain.

The second context described by Stitch is when there is distortion of sound evidence by anxieties or wishful thinking. There is a strong desire within education for immediate 'quick fix' solutions, and many of the stranger ideas created to satisfy this need, as we have seen above, began their life connected to genuine scientific understanding. In the terms used by Beyerstein, this 'nonsense piggy-backing on reliable knowledge' (Beyerstein, 1992) provides a powerfully attractive cocktail. A classic example of this arises from ideas of hemispheric dominance discussed above. One danger in disavowing educators of left-brain right-brain learning theories is discrediting the reliable knowledge from which they grew unchecked, e.g. that some functions such as language are usually left lateralized. This can generate confusion. More than purely psychological explanations, research shows non-specialists gain additional satisfaction from explanations that feature neuroscience, to the extent that this effect can mask otherwise salient flaws in these explanations (Weisberg et al., 2008). The researchers involved with this study suggest their results demonstrate the seductive nature of neuroscientific details, but admit that it is not clear why such details should possess this property. One possible explanation, tentatively proposed here, is that all of us, including non-specialists, possess a sophisticated theory of mind, whereas our theory of brain is more naive. That may result in non-specialists possessing greater confidence to scrutinize ideas about the mind than the brain. If a non-specialist is presented with a psychological theory that is incomplete or irrelevant, we may be more automatically sceptical than if it is a neurobiological one.

Stitch's third context is the absence of sound evidence. In line with Beyerstein's description of pseudoscience, many current neuromythologies have ideas at their heart that are difficult or impossible to falsify – such as the notion of multiple intelligences, or ideas about neural repatterning in response to exercise. This can arise as a quality of the theory itself, as with the undefined number of multiple intelligences, or from limits of current imaging technology, as in our present inability to image neural function at the level of the synapse. However, there are also examples of evidence arriving somewhat late in the day, as with VAK learning styles (Kratzig and Arbuthnott, 2006), despite no such methodological barriers. And where are the experimental studies of Brain Gym (other than in the *Brain Gym Journal*)? It would appear that the scrutiny of educational ideas claiming to have a brain basis is not a high priority for the brain sciences, if these ideas are not part of any current debate within those sciences themselves.

The final context identified by Stitch is when sound evidence can easily be ignored. This is relevant in terms of educational neuromythology, as when the evidence questioning a theory is published in highly technical language in specialist journals. Such reports can become even easier to ignore when there appears any lack of consensus among the specialists. As we have seen, there have been several, often contradictory, articles published about Omega-3. Information about the ambivalence of these findings, and their restricted relevance to developmental disorders, has been lost in the fog created by strong commercial forces and their unambiguous marketing messages for clever milk, clever bread, etc.

Summary

Many myths have proliferated within education about what neuroscience tells us, from the need for enriched environments in the early years, to the existence of multiple intelligences and the effectiveness of teaching to learning styles. Sometimes its language has been 'borrowed' by entrepreneurs when using pseudo-science to promote ineffective or unevaluated educational approaches. In addition to these education-specific neuromyths, other misconceptions abound in the education, as elsewhere in public domains, about the effects of different foods and drinks upon brain function.

However, we have also seen that neuromyths often feature, in their present or past form, some semblance of scientific fact that adds to their potency. They also thrive on the vacuum created by educators' desire to know more about the brain and the lack of accessible expertise and scientific information available to teachers. The arguments involved in picking apart common neuromyths are diverse and sometimes complex. Classroom teachers' professional interest in the brain is natural and justifiable but they lack the time to make their own individual investigations of ideas they are suspicious of. At the moment, that makes teachers a soft target for unscrupulous entrepreneurs and attractive ideas designed to resonate with their own sentiments. However, there appear to be three simple but crucial questions that should always be asked of someone trying to promote an apparently 'brain-based' idea:

- What are the scientific principles?
- How was the idea evaluated in educational terms?
- Where were these principles and evaluations published?'

An awkward silence to any, or all, of these questions can be helpful in confirming suspicions.

Chapter 3

Educators on the brain, neuroscientists on education

The construction of knowledge at the interface of neuroscience and education will require collaboration. When two professional areas meet to collaborate, each brings a set of preconceptions about the other's domain. This chapter will explore educators' ideas about the brain, and neuroscientists' ideas about education, as these may crucially influence collaborative outcomes. Ideas about brain function can be expected to diverge between these communities since the two previous chapters provided a sense of two separate worlds with little communication between them. As a result of this isolation, educators have been exposed to a set of concepts about the brain that differ from those established in science. How might this influence their professional practice? Similarly, since most neuroscientists are trained as scientists rather than school teachers, how might this influence their constructions about education?

One caveat should be provided from the outset of this chapter. The author has deliberately emphasized differences, rather than similarities in perceptions, because it is the appreciation of these differences that is most challenging and most critical for researchers in this field. So, in some of the research reported below, teachers were often asked questions about the brain where the worst misconceptions were anticipated to exist. Similarly, some of the quotes from scientists are from scientific specialist journals and were not always intended to convey meaning to an educational audience. Other quotes have been reproduced from transcripts and summaries of discussions at meetings, which may have provided insufficient opportunity for scientists to reflect and word their opinions as carefully as they might. The selective nature of these approaches is not intended to provide a fair overall appraisal of teachers' and scientists' knowledge of the others' fields. Instead, these quotes illustrate some of the typical misconceptions made by scientists and educators, helping to sketch some 'first impressions' of each other's domain – the type that might typically characterize discussions at the beginning of an interdisciplinary project. The danger here is that such an approach can exaggerate differences between both communities and even caricature them in a negative manner. That is certainly not the author's intention. The growing discourse between education and the sciences of mind and brain is powered by the intelligent curiosity of those who want to know more about each other's work. Indeed, given the increasing level of dialogue in this area, the distance to be travelled by both parties is never likely to be greater, and it is a distance that can close rapidly with increasing collaborative activity.

Educators on the brain

Educators do not usually have professional training in neuroscience or, in most cases, psychology, but they can still be expected to develop constructions about the brain. Research suggests a 'theory of brain' is informed by three sources: from integrating reflections upon our own and others' cognitive processes, from assimilating relevant culturally specified popular conceptions, and from information derived from technical sources such as books and documentaries. From as early as 4 years old, we think of the brain as an internal body part linked to mental acts but, throughout the early school years, we tend not to consider concepts of mind and brain as distinctly different. We think of them both as internal and material parts of our head that perform mental acts. Concepts of mind and brain become increasingly differentiated as we progress through our school years, with the mind becoming a less material entity and more closely associated with conscious mental activity. By the age of 10 or 11, we realize some cognitive functions of the brain are related to most sensory-motor acts, with a realization by adulthood that the brain is essential for all behaviour, including noncognitive involuntary responses such as fear and laughter (Johnson and Wellman, 1982). In this way, we gather a common-sense awareness that mind and brain may be different, although we are not provided with any simple understanding of the relationship between them. Instead, analysis of everyday language and text reveals that trustworthy but non-specialist sources, such as our friends and family around us, implicitly transmit notions of a mind–brain relationship that ranges from them being separable entities (as in 'my brain made me do it' legal arguments) to them being the same thing (as when the terms 'mind' and 'brain' are used interchangeably) (Rodriguez, 2006). Thus, even in regard to this fundamental relationship, all non-specialists, including teachers, are confronted by confusing messages about the brain from influential sources, and these messages can only impede progress towards a more sophisticated understanding (Bloom and Weisberg, 2007).

However, some researchers consider evidence exists that teachers resist such popular messages in the press and even those predominant in the texts of their own professions, when they consider the role of biology in issues of educational interest. A survey received replies from 667 UK teachers asked to what extent nature (genes) or nurture (environment) was responsible for various pupil outcomes (Walker and Plomin, 2005). The percentage of teachers who perceived that genetics accounts for at least half of the influence, was 87 per cent for personality, 94 per cent for intelligence and the same figure for learning difficulties, 43 per cent for behaviour problems and 91 per cent for mental illness. Walker and Plomin use their results to suggest that most teachers, despite a lack of formal genetics in their training and the frequent use of misleading phrases in the media (e.g. 'dyslexia gene'), possess a balanced view of the importance of both genetics and environment as influences upon outcome. The survey did not ask what remaining proportion of environmental influence derives from formal education, although the authors of the study claim that teachers are undaunted by their perceptions of the role of genetics. Indeed, contrary to such concerns, Walker and Plomin suggest that teachers want to know more about such biological influences, believing this knowledge can support their teaching, with 82 per cent of teachers in their survey claiming they would change their method of tracking and instructing a child if they knew he/she suffered from a genetically influenced learning difficulty. (While such findings sound heartening, research will be reported below that disputes these findings, and suggests teachers' sense of agency is significantly influenced by their constructions around the role of genetics in educational outcomes.)

A survey in Rio de Janeiro found that public knowledge about the brain appeared strongly related to general level of education (Hurculano-Houzel, 2002). This bodes well for the way teachers might view brain development and function, since they have usually been educated to graduate level. However, in the Rio de Janeiro study, even 30 per cent of graduates did not know learning was related to neuronal connectivity, and almost a quarter did not know it corresponded to modifications in the brain at all. Several other predominant misconceptions about learning and the brain were also revealed by this survey. These included the belief, held by almost half (48 per cent) of graduates, that we use only 10 per cent of the brain at any one time (we use the entire brain), the belief of most graduates (53 per cent) that mental practice does not improve performance (it does) and the conviction held by 41 per cent that memory is stored in the brain like a computer (when, in fact, it is distributed).

Teachers, of course, continue to learn after their initial training, and they place a high value on in-service training and educational conferences as a key source of knowledge about the brain (Howard-Jones et al., 2007). But, as mentioned in Chapter 2, such training often features the type of so-called 'brain-based' learning programmes that promote unsound concepts, such as the need to balance hemispheric dominance or the existence of neuroscientific evidence for the usefulness of learning styles.

In a world where everyday language promotes contradictory ideas about the mind–brain relationship, and even professional development cannot be relied upon to deliver valid neuroscientific concepts, it can be expected that teachers' ideas about the brain diverge from conventional scientific thinking. So how do teachers think and talk about the brain, and how might this influence their attitudes and practice?

Researchers at NEnet began investigating this issue with some informal interviews with a primary school headteacher, 6 teachers (3 primary, 3 secondary) each with several years experience, and 6 trainee secondary teachers about to embark on their career. These were informal conversational affairs. We started by asking them what sort of ability range they had encountered as teachers, and what they thought produced such a diverse range of achievement. Some of our group, as might be predicted from the survey by Walker and Plomin, were convinced that genetics should be considered as the key factor or, as one primary school teacher put it: 'I believe it's about genes, I believe you do see intelligent children from intelligent parents'.

Our headteacher also put forward genetics as the key reason for such diversity, but suggested home environment was the next big factor:

> It is genetically inherited. If I try to do calculus, high math, with some children it wouldn't matter how much I try they wouldn't understand it and then their motivation would decrease … I think it's genetics … genetics is a very high one and motivation and the environment at home is another one.

Indeed most of our group considered there was a balanced influence between genetics and environment on brain development, with a secondary school teacher explaining:

> …. you've got the combination of nature and nurture because … it's a horrible kind of a sweeping statement and generalization … but often more educated parents would have more resources to help their children when they are young.

It was also clear, however, that when different teachers discussed 'environment', they rarely used the term as scientists do, i.e. as an umbrella term that covers all influences derived from social and physical settings. It could sometimes refer to just influences derived from the home:

Interviewer:	Why do you think there is this range between students in the classroom?
Primary school teacher:	I think it has a lot to do with the environment.
Interviewer:	Environment – what exactly?
Primary school teacher:	Kind of their home environment. Perhaps the way they have been brought up and the area that they live in, perhaps, but then also, I think, it could be genetic as well in their families. So it could be to do with the make up of the family.

Or, when used in the educational sense, the word 'environment' could mean the influence or stimulus provided by the teacher and classroom, as in this comment by a trainee teacher:

> I think maybe in a very enriched environment probably the brain will be bigger and heavier ... lots of different kinds of stimuli, lots of changing activities very rapidly, a really good mixture of conventional grammar and spelling, at the same time doing fun stuff like music, images, sound.

Ideas around the plasticity of the brain were diverse and sometimes complex, with the same trainee expressing how mental ability can develop, but uneasy about how such changes might be reflected at biological level:

> I think the brain must be able to change to be honest. You see people who don't have hands so they (learn to) use their toes to be able to paint. So you work about the problem, not getting rid of it but you are certainly working about it ... It is like a car and you have the engine and you can supe it up and rewire it and polish it but it is the same car.

Ageing of the brain was mentioned by some as providing a limitation on learning arising from lack of brain plasticity, although, again, our teachers were unclear about how this worked. Explanations often touched upon neuromythology:

Interviewer:	Do you know how the brain grows?
Secondary school teacher:	I know that after you're 18, as far as I know, you don't regenerate brain cells anymore, so people shouldn't hit you on the head.
Interviewer:	If you're not hit on the head, can you learn new skills? For example, if brain cells are not regenerating, would that hinder your learning and your skills?
Secondary school teacher:	I don't think so, no, I mean we only use 10 per cent of our brain anyway apparently, that's what I've been taught.
Interviewer:	Why don't we use the other 90 per cent?
Secondary school teacher:	I have no idea.

The extent to which brain development was open to educational intervention proved an interesting area for discussion. On the one hand, as above, teachers tended to agree with direct questions about whether an improvement in ability might correspond to physical brain changes. On the other hand, when learning difficulties were associated with differences in brain function, teachers appeared unclear about the effectiveness of educational solutions and thought more in terms of 'coping', as in this exchange with another secondary school teacher:

Interviewer: Does knowing this (a learning difficulty) has something
                        to do with the brain change the way you're looking at the
                        student?

Secondary school
teacher: It certainly I suppose changes how you deal with it
                        because, if you were told that it's entirely to do with
                        the brain then you're kind of looking at ways to cope
                        with them that would make things easier for them in the
                        classroom.

There appeared to be a type of 'all or none' theorizing about problems being either biological in nature or not:

Interviewer: What are the options in front of you do you think?
Secondary school
trainee teacher: I think … I suppose yes … if there's a biological problem,
                        things like diet, drugs. I don't really like the idea of drugs,
                        but I think some people do see them as a readily good
                        option for some children.
Interviewer: What exactly do you mean by diet?
Secondary school
trainee teacher: I mean avoiding colourants, avoiding fizzy drinks, avoiding
                        too much sugar. So, you know, trying also I suppose fish
                        oils as well, I am real believer in all of that.

A medicalization of learning difficulties occurred in some interviews, linked to a reduced sense of agency and the use of medical words such as 'cure', 'symptoms', 'diagnosis':

Interviewer: What do you think causes pupils to have special needs, other
                        than the environment?

Secondary school
trainee teacher: It is a diagnosable condition so it must be very physiologi-
                        cal, neurological as well and related to the brain … I don't
                        know if you can cure kids with symptoms, by giving them
                        strategies to get around it. If teachers have dyslexic students
                        they may cope with it but you cannot cure it.

Our headteacher explained that a sense of reduced agency might be why explana-tions involving the brain, which he perceived as deterministic, were less popular with some educators. He suggested that factors perceived to be less amenable to their influence might feature less in teachers' discussions of cause (note that this respondent, like several others we spoke to, had previously used the word 'environment' to refer to home environment):

> As a teacher you are faced with classes of children and you do your very best, I think teachers have an understanding that the environment and the emotional responses of children have to do with things outside their control but they have to try to work it out. It's not much use if you are faced with a child and say it has to do with a dysfunction of the brain because if you are a class teacher that wouldn't help.

Teachers sometimes associated the amelioration of brain-referenced learning difficulties with controlling diet and this may be due to a belief that 'fixable' brain issues involved some type of biological intervention. This was expressed more explicitly by one teacher in relation to dyslexia. In fact, although claims are circulating that sufferers of dyslexia can be helped by supplements of unsaturated fatty acids, empirical evidence does not support them (Kairaluoma *et al.*, 2009). Our respondent, however, referred to the possibility of chemical intervention in more general terms, suggesting a strong association of problems involving brain function with the need for medication:

Interviewer:	When we were talking about dyslexia, we were saying that the working memory of the brain might not be functioning well. If we know the reasons, can we fix it?
Secondary school teacher:	I guess it would depend if it's a chemical imbalance.
Interviewer:	What do you mean by a chemical imbalance?
Secondary school teacher:	Well … if what's there in the brain is more of a certain chemical or less than a certain chemical then yes you can fix it. But if it's a structure in the brain then I would imagine you can't fix it.

When asked what foods were good for the brain, the issue of fish oils came up regularly, but also some more surprising ones:

Interviewer:	Can you improve this connectivity in the brain?
Primary school teacher:	Probably there is some food.
Interviewer:	Like what?
Primary school teacher:	There are lots of traditional recipes to neuralize the brain.
Interviewer:	Like what?

Primary school
teacher: Like walnut ... it has the shape of the brain ... and also
                          I think there are some components of walnut that kind of
                          help to improve the neurons in your brain or to kind of ...
                          moisturize it.[1]

More predictably, our teachers also referred to the effects of too much sugar and
not enough water on children, as in these comments by two trainee secondary
school teachers:

> When they have too much sugar in breaks, they come to class very active.
> If they are dehydrated – dehydration is a serious issue.
> Sugary food .... after break time they are a bit lively.

A survey of teachers' neuroscience literacy

Our initial interviews had revealed a mixture of ideas strongly influenced by
those in public and educational domains, and also raised questions about how
constructions around brain function and development might influence teachers'
sense of their own agency. To understand more, NEnet carried out two surveys
of trainee teachers to assess their neuroscience literacy (Howard-Jones *et al.*,
2009). The first survey was carried out in 2008, when 158 trainees were in the
closing stages of a Post Graduate Certificate in Education (PGCE) course to
train as secondary school teachers in a variety of different subjects. Like most
PGCE students, they had received no formal training about the brain, but were
likely to have picked up information informally from the popular press and
media, and also from the schools where they had been doing their teaching
practice. The latter influence was suggested by the numbers of respondents who,
by the end of their one-year course, had already encountered concepts of
Multiple Intelligences, Learning Styles and Brain Gym in schools (56 per cent,
83 per cent and 58 per cent respectively). Another study had already confirmed
that many practising teachers commonly associate these ideas with the brain, and
generally consider them to be useful (Pickering and Howard-Jones, 2007). This
speaks of the extent to which these ideas have flourished in UK state schools,
despite their scant scientific basis.

We asked trainees to express their agreement with sets of assertions linked to
the brain. There were six assertions about the mind–brain relationship that had
been used in the Rio study (Hurculano-Houzel, 2002). This allowed comparison of understanding among UK teacher trainees with the sample of neuroscientists and public surveyed by Hurculano-Houzel – as bench marks of specialist
and non-specialist opinions (although South American, rather than British).
Additionally, prompted by some of the comments of the teachers above, we
provided an assertion intended to explore attitudes about learner agency. This
was 'Individuals are not responsible for behaviour associated with a developmental difference in brain function'. Responses to assertions about the mind–brain
relationship and our assertion regarding learner agency are shown in Table 3.1.

Trainees' responses revealed considerable uncertainty in these areas. Around three-quarters did not consider that consciousness was possible without a brain, and only about 15 per cent wished to consider the mind as arising from the action of a spirit or soul on the brain. This might suggest some sense of mind–brain relationship. However, beyond this, most did not agree that a 'state of mind' reflected brain state, or that the mind is a product of brain function, or that mind can be studied through studying brain activity. This contrasts not only with current scientific opinion, including the opinions of the thirty-five neuro-scientists sampled by Hurculano-Houzel (2002) but also the majority opinion of their sample of the South American public with graduate level education (see Table 3.1). It may be that many of these trainee teachers had been recently impressed by the social complexity of behaviour in the classroom and, therefore, had become less certain than other non-specialists about the role of biological function in mental activity. However, particular caution is required here, as in all comparisons with the Hurculano-Houzel study, due to the potential influence of general cultural differences. The majority of trainees were also undecided about how responsible students should be for behaviours associated with their developmental disorder (55 per cent).

Table 3.1 Responses of trainee teachers to assertions of subjective opinion about the mind–brain relationship and learner agency, the former shown with responses of the graduate sample of the public studied by Hurculano-Houzel (2002) for comparison

	Trainee teachers			Public with graduate education (from Hurculano-Houzel, 2002)		
	Agree	d.k.	Disagree	Agree	d.k.	Disagree
The mind is the result of the action of the spirit, or of the soul, on the brain	15	49	36	18	51	31
'State of mind' is a reflection of the brain state in a given moment	48	40	12	48	27	25
If there are ways to study brain activity, the mind can be studied through them	22	56	22	50	34	16
The mind is a product of the working of the brain	43	45	11	72	22	6
Without a brain, consciousness is not possible	77	12	11	82	8	10
Intuition is a 'special sense' that cannot be explained by the brain	24	44	32	25	39	36
Individuals are not responsible for behaviour associated with a developmental difference in brain function	14	55	31			

The rest of the assertions could be judged correct or incorrect, according to established scientific understanding. These included sixteen of the correct/incorrect assertions adapted from the Hurculano-Houzel study and selected according to their potential relevance to education (e.g. memory, emotional behaviour). The mean number of correct responses of trainee teachers to these assertions was 9/16. Generally, trainees' general knowledge about the brain was similar to the sample of the public reported by Hurculano-Houzel, but with a few exceptions (Table 3.2). More members of our trainee sample correctly disagreed with 'Keeping a phone number in memory until dialling, recalling recent events and distant experiences, all use the same memory system', but this may have been due to our survey including examples to clarify this assertion, since we judged the assertion in the Hurculano-Houzel survey as ambiguous. A high number in our sample also agreed with the statement 'Learning is not due to the addition of new cells to the brain'. However, although Hurculano-Houzel included this as an incorrect assertion, recent findings provide support for a weaker form of this assertion, i.e. that learning can be accompanied by neurogenesis (Shors et al., 2001). This makes subjects' responses to this assertion more difficult to interpret

Table 3.2 Responses of trainee teachers to a selection of the general assertions

	Trainee teachers			Public (from Hurculano-Houzel, 2002)		
	Agree	d.k.	Disagree	agree	d.k.	Disagree
One's environment can influence hormone production and, in turn, personality (C)	61	30	8	64		
We use our brains 24 hours a day (C)	89	5	6	92		
To learn how to do something, it is necessary to pay attention to it (C)	43	13	43	73		
Learning occurs through modification of the brain's neural connections (C)	50	44	6		30	
Performance in activities such as playing the piano improves as a function of hours spent practising (C)	78	12	10	82		
It is with the brain, and not the heart, that we experience happiness, anger, and fear (C)	76	11	13	97		
Hormones influence the body's internal state, and not their personality (I)	25	34	42	24		
Memory is stored in the brain much like as in a computer. That is, each memory goes into a tiny piece of the brain (I)	36	38	26	41		
Memory is stored in networks of cells distributed throughout the brain (C)	50	42	8	60		

Table 3.2 Continued

	Trainee teachers			Public (from Hurculano-Houzel, 2002)		
	Agree	d.k.	Disagree	agree	d.k.	Disagree
Keeping a phone number in memory until dialling, recalling recent events and distant experiences, all use the same memory system (I)	12	45	44	49		
When we sleep, the brain shuts down (I)	0	7	93			80
Learning is not due to the addition of new cells to the brain (C*)	52	35	13	82		
Brain activity depends entirely on the external environment: with no senses stimulated, we don't see, hear or feel anything (I)	11	22	66	33		
Emotional brain processes interrupt those brain processes involved with reasoning (I)	69	23	8	70		
Cognitive abilities are inherited and cannot be modified by the environment or by life experience (I)	3	10	87			91
We mostly only use 10% of our brains (I)	52	38	10	48		

*See text for discussion of the correctness, or otherwise, of this assertion.

Note
(C = correct assertion, I = incorrect assertion) about the brain intended to assess levels of neuroscience literacy. Results of the Hurculano-Houzel survey of those members of public who had been educated at graduate level are provided for comparison (Hurculano-Houzel, 2002), with blank cells where results were not reported.

as a measure of general neuroscientific awareness, although conventionally it has been assumed by scientists that changes in neural connectivity are sufficient to explain learning. Indeed, most trainee teachers in our sample either disagreed or were undecided about the more conventional explanation based on neural connectivity. This suggests some basic uncertainty about conventional neuro-scientific understanding of learning, and it is this uncertainty that may underlie the increased agreement with the neurogenesis explanation rather than any over-interpretation or confusion arising from the latest scientific findings.

Perhaps the most surprising response of our trainee teachers to these general assertions was that most did not agree (43 per cent), or did not know (13 per cent), whether it was necessary to pay attention to something in order to learn it. In the sense of learning that is commonly used in education, it is difficult to imagine how learning without attention can occur. It may be that teachers interpret the word 'attention' in a more educational sense (i.e. paying attention to the teacher), although the assertion said clearly 'attention to *it*'. Alternatively, this response may indicate the rise of a new misunderstanding about the brain related to implicit learning. Work with artificial grammars, in which participants are able to acquire grammatical rules by observing examples of artificial language, demonstrates our ability to learn unconsciously (Johnstone and Shanks, 2001). Such experiments have prompted calls to consider the 'enormous' implications of implicit learning for education (Claxton, 1998). However, there are considerable barriers to the practical application of such ideas, making their usefulness to education questionable and causing some scientific authorities to label them a new source of neuromyth (Goswami, 2004). A non-specialist interpretation of the phenomenon of implicit learning might assume information and concepts can be absorbed from the environment without attending to them, but attention is still needed. For example, in the artificial grammar scenario, formal rules may be acquired without the learner consciously formulating them, but the learner must pay considerable attention to the examples of artificial language in order to facilitate this. In a more real world context, we may also develop understanding unconsciously about, for example, the motivations of people around us, without being able to articulate how we have achieved this. Again, however, this is only possible by paying attention to the behaviour of those people; 'implicit learning' does not equate to 'learning without attention'. Even given the popular rise of ideas about unconscious learning, it seemed somewhat surprising that 43 per cent of our sample of trainee teachers, towards the end of their training, appeared to consider that their pupils might learn without paying due attention. This finding may suggest the need for some further research.

Also included in the survey were fifteen additional assertions (see Table 3.3) that were labelled educational neuromyths, due to their presence in educational discourse. These were drawn from ideas promoted by popular brain-based educational programmes, the neuromyths discussed in Chapter 2, other concepts identified in the preliminary interviews, and issues arising in previous research with teachers, e.g. Pickering and Howard-Jones (2007). The mean score for the number of correct responses to these common educational neuromyths was 5/15.

In some instances, trainees' opinions about the fifteen assertions involving educational neuromyth showed a majority in agreement with present scientific opinion. For example, 62 per cent were aware that 'extended rehearsal of some mental processes can change the shape and structure of some parts of the brain', a fact which has been demonstrated in at least two well-reported instances (Draganski *et al.*, 2004; Maguire *et al.*, 2000). Additionally, 63 per cent considered (correctly) that the production of new connections in the brain can continue into old age, a fact which can be assumed as correct on the basis that learning relies on synaptic plasticity, and learning can be shown to continue throughout life. There was also a majority (55 per cent) in agreement with current opinions in neuroscience that sensitive, rather than critical, periods exist for learning. There appears no clearly defined time window of opportunity for

Table 3.3 Responses of trainee teachers to a selection of assertions drawn from educational neuromyths

	Trainee teachers		
	Agree	d.k.	Disagree
Children are less attentive after sugary drinks and snacks (I)	63	24	13
Omega-3 supplements do not enhance the mental capacity of children in the general population (C)	23	54	23
Environments that are rich in stimulus improve the brains of preschool children (I)	89	10	1
Individuals learn better when they receive information in their preferred learning style (e.g. visual, auditory, kinaesthetic) (I)	82	11	7
Short bouts of co-ordination exercises can improve integration of left and right hemispheric brain function (I)	65	31	4
Regular drinking of caffeinated soft drinks reduces alertness (C)	33	45	22
Differences in hemispheric dominance (left brain, right brain) can help explain individual differences among learners (I)	60	35	5
Learning problems associated with developmental differences in brain function cannot be remediated by education (I)	9	41	49
There are no critical periods in childhood after which you can't learn some things, just sensitive periods when it's easier (C)	55	30	15
Vigorous exercise can improve mental function (C)	63	29	8
Individual learners show preferences for the mode in which they receive information (e.g. visual, auditory, kinaesthetic) (C)	79	16	5
Exercises that rehearse co-ordination of motor-perception skills can improve literacy skill (I)	35	56	9
Production of new connections in the brain can continue into old age (C)	63	25	12
Extended rehearsal of some mental processes can change the shape and structure of some parts of the brain (C)	62	31	6
Drinking less than 6–8 glasses of water a day can cause the brain to shrink (I)	18	39	43

Note
(C = correct assertion based on scientific evidence, I = incorrect assertion, or an assertion for which there is no scientific evidence).

learning outside which progress is impossible, just periods during our development when learning can be more efficiently achieved (Blakemore and Frith, 2005, p.26). Even those periods that have been identified tend to involve primary sensory or motor functions, rather than the higher types of learning process that are usually the subject of formal education. Misconceptions did abound elsewhere, however, and the fact that most trainees had already come into contact with approaches such as learning styles and 'Brain Gym' may explain the large numbers of trainees suffering some types of misconceptions. For example, 82 per cent of trainees considered that 'individuals learn better when they receive information in their preferred learning style', even though there is little evidence to support this idea. It is, of course, true that individuals often show preferences for the mode in which they receive information (as agreed by 79 per cent of trainees) but there is no convincing evidence that identifying learners' preferences improves their learning (Coffield *et al.*, 2004; Kratzig and Arbuthnott, 2006). Most trainees (60 per cent) also believed in the usefulness of hemispheric dominance (left brain, right brain) as a means to explain individual differences amongst learners. This belief is also used as a learning style approach to categorizing learners and as a means to differentiate teaching strategies accordingly (see Chapter 2). However, no part of the brain is ever normally inactive, with everyday tasks requiring both hemispheres to work together in parallel. Dividing people into left-brained and right-brained learning styles makes no sense in terms of what we know about the brain, and has not been demonstrated as educationally helpful.

Although most trainees (63 per cent) were correct in believing that vigorous exercise can improve mental function, there was also a majority in favour of the concept that co-ordination exercises can help integrate the functions of left and right hemisphere (despite the lack of scientific evidence for such ideas), and over a third of trainees (35 per cent) felt this type of exercise could contribute to development of literacy skills, with most (56 per cent) expressing uncertainty as to whether this might be possible or not. This latter belief contributes to the theoretical approach of programmes such as 'Brain Gym', but is not supported by scientific evidence (Hyatt, 2007). Approaches such as 'Brain Gym' also promote the drinking of water as a way to support learning. Apart from circumstances involving vigorous exercise, ill health or unusually hot weather, the previous chapter found no evidence of children suffering from voluntary dehydration in the classroom or the cognitive effects associated with it. However, the prevalence of myths around the health-giving properties of water (Valtin, 2002) and those that now associate it with learning, may help explain why 39 per cent of trainees were not sure if their brain would shrink if they drank less than 6–8 glasses a day, with a further 18 per cent thinking (incorrectly) that it would. In other nutritional areas of potential interest to educators, most trainees were unaware or unsure about the established understanding that habitual use of caffeine suppresses cognition rather than enhances it. Despite the current lack of studies on the effects of Omega-3 supplements in the general population, and the mixed results among samples of children with developmental disorders, 23 per cent of our trainees already believe it can enhance the cognitive abilities of children in the general population. The majority (54 per cent) were unclear about this issue. Most trainees (63 per cent) also believed in the myth that children are less attentive after sugary drinks and snacks.

Clearly these results attest to widespread misunderstandings about the brain among teachers entering the profession, and in many areas likely to influence practice. But might such misunderstandings be ameliorated by better training, if this conflicts with neuromyths being promoted within schools and public domains? What influences resistance to such neuromyth? Good information about the brain is available in many quality scientific newspapers that might help. However, Herculano-Houzel reported that it was the general level of education that contributed more to scores of correctness than the reading of newspapers and scientific magazines. Indeed, we found that whether trainees read popular science magazines and/or newspapers, and the number of books they read per month, had no significant effect on scores. All our trainees, of course, were educated to graduate level, but we did find a clear association between scores for general assertions about the brain and for correct understanding of concepts involving educational neuromyths. This suggests a link between a basic knowledge of brain function and some protection against the most prevalent misconceptions currently influencing educational thinking and classroom practice. In other words, a modicum of general understanding about brain function in teachers' training might help immunize against neuromyths.

Perhaps, however, the most worrying result of our first survey was that most trainees did not dispute the statement 'learning problems associated with developmental differences in brain function cannot be remediated by education', with 40 per cent undecided and 9 per cent believing this was true. This suggests that a teacher's knowledge of a pupil's developmental difference from a biological perspective may diminish their belief in the potential for positive change, as if some biologically determined barrier has been exposed. This contrasts with current perspectives in developmental cognitive neuroscience which avoid predictive mechanisms of biological cause and effect. Modern science emphasizes the complexity of interrelation between biological systems and environments such as those provided by education, and highlights the enduring possibility of mitigation (Morton, 2004). In Walker and Plomin's survey of UK teachers, 82 per cent of teachers claimed they would change their method of tracking and instructing a child if they knew he/she suffered from a genetically influenced learning difficulty. Walker and Plomin interpreted this in a positive sense, but our findings raise doubt about this interpretation.

Walker and Plomin's survey also found that 'teachers view nature to be at least as important as nurture', although our preliminary discussions with teachers had also raised questions about how teachers interpret the word 'environment'. More specifically, although Walker and Plomin asked teachers about the role of 'genes (nature)' and 'environment (nurture)', it seems plausible that teachers might interpret 'environment (nurture)' as not wholly inclusive of education. The term 'environment' can have a range of disparate meanings in education, most of which are narrower than those within the field of genetics, and many of which might not even include the teacher's efforts. To further investigate this issue, we asked our trainees to indicate the mean per cent contribution to educational outcomes that they would attribute to education, genes, home environment and other (see Fig. 3.1).

Our sample of trainee teachers considered, on average, that only 25 per cent of educational outcome was due to genetic issues. Fourteen trainees responded in the 'other' category, but all naming influences that might easily be placed under educational environment and/or home environment ('experience', 'social status', 'community'). Only 8 per cent thought genetics was at least as important as other factors in determining general educational outcome, which contrasts considerably with Walker and Plomin's figure of 94 per cent who thought this was the case for outcomes such as intelligence and learning disorders. Clearly, Walker and Plomin's finding that 'teachers view nature to be at least as important as nurture' does not seem likely to hold in the general case. Furthermore, our low score may be explained by teachers' unwillingness to attribute outcomes to factors they consider immune to educational intervention. Indeed, although the small sub sample was unamenable to statistical analysis, the 8 per cent minority who placed great emphasis on the role of genetics in educational outcome showed less (than average) confidence that learning problems associated with developmental differences could benefit from educational remediation. And yet, such an explanation is at odds with Walker and Plomin's reassurance that genetic beliefs do not relate to a teacher's sense of agency.

A brief second survey was devised that followed up on this issue. As before, it asked a new cohort of 166 trainee teachers to estimate the mean per cent contribution to educational outcomes that they would attribute to education,

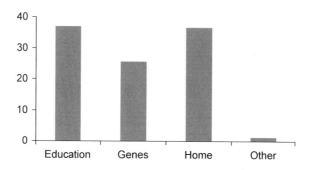

Figure 3.1 The mean per cent contribution to educational outcomes that 158 trainee secondary teachers attributed to education, genes, home environment and other.

genes, home environment and 'other'. It then asked them to rate their agreement with two statements on a 5-point Likert scale:

1   There is a biological limit to what some individuals can achieve in their education.
2   There is no biological limit to what any individual can achieve in their education.

Trainees' responses to these statements were scored for their belief in a biological limit to a learner's achievement (i.e. level of agreement with the first and level of disagreement with the second). Trainees' beliefs in the influence of genetic factors were significantly correlated with believing in a biological limit to what a learner can achieve.

Neuroscientists on education

In our preliminary interviews with teachers, most of our participants made it clear they knew little about the brain and, indeed, it is unusual to hear educators offering their opinions about it. On the other hand, as those in the profession know, almost everyone has an opinion about education, whether their own, their children's or about education in general. Neuroscientists are no exception. Yet, given the highly scientific nature of their daily business, the views and attitudes expressed by scientists about education might differ from those of educators in some important ways. Might they, for example, consider education in scientific terms, or even as a science itself?

In their popular book written by neuroscientists for educators, Sarah Blakemore and Uta Frith express their own view of education: '... education changes your brain and not just your mind. ... Education is to the brain what gardening is to the landscape'.

Educators may find the 'teacher as gardener' an appealing idea. It suggests the richness and individual nature of each educational context, the important role of the teacher in promoting brain function and development, and the potential usefulness, as well as limitation, of understanding factors influencing these processes.

Blakemore and Frith's well-chosen metaphor may reflect the long-standing interest that both authors have shown in developing a dialogue with educators. However, just as teachers can be naive in their conceptions of the brain, some neuroscientists can lack awareness about educational issues, including, it would seem, of the many political and moral sensitivities within the field. For example, consider the article in *Science Mind* written by the renowned neuroscientist Michael Gazzaniga, about cognitive enhancing drugs (Gazzaniga, 2005b). Gazzaniga sums up his position in the last paragraph: 'The government should stay out of it, letting our own ethical and moral sense guide us through the new enhancement landscape'. His appraisal of possible moral objections to such pills is chiefly restricted to these few lines:

> Why do we resist changes in our cognitive skills through drugs? The reason, it seems to me, is that we think **cognitive enhancement is cheating.** If, somehow, someone gets ahead through hard work, that's okay. But popping a pill and mastering information after having read it only once seems unfair. This position makes no sense. Among the normal population are men and women with incredible memories, fast learners of language and music, and those with enhanced capabilities of all kinds. Something in their brains allows them to encode new information at lightning speed. We accept the fact that they must have some chemical system that is superior to ours or some neural circuitry that is more efficient. So why should we be upset if the same thing can be achieved with a pill? In some way, we were cheated by Mother Nature if we didn't get the superior neural system, so for us to cheat her back through our own inventiveness seems like a smart thing to do. In my opinion, it is exactly what we should do.

Neuroscientists are most used to considering behaviour on an individual basis. From Gazzaniga's 'individual' perspective, popping a pill to enhance one's mental capacities may, arguably, seem a fair way to cheat nature. However, educational assessment has the task of characterizing individuals on the basis of their academic achievement, such that they are inevitably compared with each other. Attitudes to educational assessment are intertwined with the values of our society, with many stakeholders in assessment beyond the individual being assessed. Academic assessment provides information to the individual about the outcomes of their efforts and contributes to self-perception, but also to their educational institution about the impact of its teaching and support for learning, and to potential employers regarding each individual's relative suitability for a particular professional role. It appears unlikely that introducing any component of artificial enhancement would not raise some complex issues involving all these stakeholders, each with their own different perspective. Additionally, the fact that socio-economic status is likely to mediate access to cognitive enhancers will make the issues surrounding them even more inflammatory (see also Chapters 7 and 10).

Discussions of the potential value of bringing together neuroscience and education have often promoted the possibility of developing a new science of learning, or even a science of education. Some scientists discuss education as if it can already be considered as a science. A paper published in *Trends in Cognitive Sciences* by cognitive neuroscientists Daniel Ansari and Donna Coch eloquently promotes the case for a two-way collaborative approach to such a venture (Ansari and Coch, 2006). But the article begins in a way that many educators might find controversial 'Education is quintessentially a cognitive science ....'. Can educational research be reduced to determining and building a progressive body of scientific knowledge? Certainly, as acknowledged by Ansari and Coch, past efforts to achieve this have not been successful, possibly because of the highly situated nature of educational practice.

Indeed, given the epistemological differences existing between the social and natural sciences, scientists may find some of the methods by which pedagogic knowledge is constructed in education surprisingly different to the highly focused and sometimes reductive laboratory studies they prefer themselves. However, such surprise can also reflect a lack of understanding regarding the reasons for these differences (see Chapter 5). Manfred Spitzer is a psychiatrist working at the University Clinic in Ulm, but is also heading Ulm's Transfer Centre for Neuroscience and Learning. In an OECD symposium hosted at Ulm in 2003 (OECD, 2003), he noted 'there are hardly any randomised placebo controlled studies in education'. Spitzer explained his preference for natural science epistemology by referring to animal-based research using Randomised Controlled Trials (RCTs): 'when one changes the cages of the rats they forget about what they learned in the previous cage because the new cage is so interesting. Translated into the school setting you would get the following scenario: we allow kids to learn fresh vocabulary and then send them to the movies. There are no such informed randomised studies on such effects on kids to date' (p. 4). As a quasi experimental study with children, such a proposal appears a fair way to test a hypothesis and, thus, the scientific concept behind it. However, it reveals naivety about the educational usefulness of such findings and the moral and ethical dimensions of educational decisions. Would diminished recall after the cinema produce a recommendation that lessons should be followed by dull activities? Leaving aside the uncomfortably close association here between experiments with children and animals, the use of RCTs within education is highly contested, not least because control is very difficult to achieve. This attraction to evaluating ideas in controlled situations may also account for the interest shown by some neuroscientists in developing and evaluating educational software rather than pedagogical principles (e.g. Wilson *et al.*, 2006).

Neuroscience has a seductive allure and promises to have profound effects on many different areas of society. Some would claim that it is increasingly able to explain our behaviour in purely material, and therefore concrete, terms. Although these claims are questionable, such ideas are prominent and appear to reflect the special status that neuroscience enjoys within our society. Brain science feels real and important, and its findings have impact within other highly respected professions such as medicine and the law. Media portrayals of our education system, on the other hand, are often characterized in terms of problems that must be solved. Perhaps this imbalance is partially responsible for suggestions that, rather than sustained interdisciplinary communication between neuroscience and education, all is needed is some system which serves to transmit appropriate interpretations of neuroscientific knowledge to education. Goswami (2006) has suggested that neuroscientists are too concerned with the rigour of their experiments to provide the broad brush messages required by teachers, who prefer simply to be 'told what works'. (Goswami, 2006) proposes neuroscience should communicate with education via middle men/women, rather than through the neuroscientists responsible for creating the knowledge. This would relieve neuroscientists of the considerable challenge provided by such communication and allow them to get on with what some may do best, i.e. produce new fundamental knowledge about the brain. However, educators may consider that developing new pedagogical approaches involving the brain may need a more judicious synthesis of neuroscience with understandings from other domains, including their own. A simple transmission model, in which teachers are told 'what works' via communicators attached to education departments, may not support the type of two-way dialogue with neuroscience required to achieve this. Furthermore, when it comes to applying such knowledge, many teachers may feel they are best placed to decide what is working in their particular classroom contexts.

After a discussion between educators and neuroscientists, described by the authors as 'heated', Szucs and Goswami (2007) expressed in more detail their vision for the role of research involving neuroscience and education. This vision appears more heedful of the limits of the authority of neuroscience, although does not directly deal with how boundaries should be negotiated or integrated concepts constructed. They refer, in scientific terms, to teaching as 'the shaping of individual brains via targeted experience in the classroom' and education as aiming to 'discover the optimal ways of shaping and enriching the cognitive system of the individual'. But their proposal is sensitive to the importance of social implications, including the need to evaluate interventions at this level. Also, it is clear that they are not suggesting neuroscience should displace existing educational understanding but augment it instead. Towards the end of the article, they refer to Skinner's comment that learning is a science and teaching is an art, and express the hope that a science of learning can contribute to this art. Unlike Ansari, they stop short of suggesting that education is itself a science or, with the help of neuroscience, can be transformed into one.

As implied by Szucs and Goswami, it is helpful to consider education and learning as different concepts and perhaps, in some contexts, this can allow the term science to be more freely applied to the latter. However, the Japanese neuroscientist Koizumi suggests it possible to go further and to consider them as conceptually separable. Koizumi suggests they are closely related but can be 'essentially' distinguished on the basis of whether concepts are being externally provided (education) or internally generated in response to external stimuli (learning). Based on this conceptual distinction, Koizumi claims both can be studied from a natural science perspective. Koizumi proposes 'education is a process of optimal adaptation such that learning is guided to ensure proper brain development' (Koizumi, 2004, p. 435). Questions such as what is meant by 'optimal' and 'proper' are left open, but the emphasis upon brain function is clear. Such emphasis may reflect the professional preoccupations of neuroscientists, but any discussion of learning and education in these terms does, inevitably, sound narrow to educators. This is, not least, because what we currently understand about brain function is derived chiefly from individuals carrying out laboratory tasks.

It is no more fair to generalize teachers' understanding of neuroscience as based on enthralment and delusion than it is to conclude neuroscientists are always naive about the complexities of education. There are many teachers who have developed their knowledge of the brain through previous educational or professional experience, appropriate training and individual effort. Similarly, the perspective of neuroscientists can also change as a result of their contact with education and also as a result of becoming a parent. Eveline Crone leads research at Leiden University (Netherlands) into the development of cognitive control and decisionmaking in school-aged children and adolescents. In 2008, at a meeting of expert neuroscientists and educational researchers in Amsterdam, the author asked her opinions of what she thought education was about. Her candid response (recorded and transcribed with her permission) illustrates how challenging this experience of 'broadening' can feel:

> It's a difficult question. Yesterday I asked my husband. We are expecting a child, so we have had all these discussions about learning and how you can increase your knowledge. Then I asked 'do you feel it' most important that our child leaves school as someone who has a lot of knowledge about the world and can use abstract rules – or do you feel it's more important that our child can function well in groups and enjoy good socioemotional development?' And he said 'oh definitely – that's the more important aspect'. So we both think it's important you should learn your stuff but also that that isn't the only domain education should focus on. And I notice that, as scientists, we are very much focusing on how can we improve the brain and how can we make things better. But apparently that's not what education is about ... and that makes it so complex. I think in terms of what we do as scientists, we can figure out how certain problem solving is represented in the brain but the education problem is much bigger. So it's a difficult question and I don't have a clear-cut answer.

Summary

Educators' ideas about the brain are influenced by misconceptions in public circulation, as well as by popular ideas and neuromyths within education that claim to be brain-based. Educators, or at least those about to enter the profession, place equal importance on home environment and education as determinants of educational outcome, with genetics a significant but smaller influence than either. Beliefs in strong genetic influence are linked to stronger ideas about biological limits to learners' achievements.

Most of the trainee teachers in our survey did not accept, or were unsure, about whether mental activity derives from biological brain function. Apart from conflicting with modern scientific concepts, this also contrasts with a sample of the public surveyed in South America, who generally accepted the conventional scientific position. In other respects, however, trainees' general knowledge about brain function was comparable to this sample of the public, although knowledge scores were predictably low on topics that are frequently misrepresented in educational neuromyth.

Neuroscientists' views on education may not always attend to the ethical, political and social complexities of the field. Despite emerging consensus regarding the need for two-way collaboration, some scientists can still tend towards characterizing education as a potential natural science that can be enriched, through a transmission model, by neuroscience.

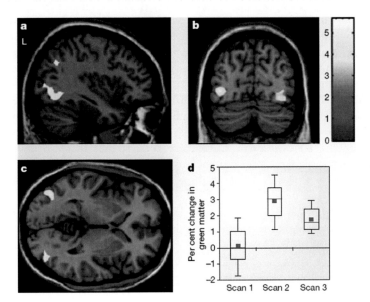

Figure 1.1 When adults spent three months learning to juggle, the size of some brain regions (shown as hot spots) changed relative to a non-juggling control group. The graph shows the percentage difference in size of these regions for jugglers compared with non-jugglers, with a clear increase (from scan 1 to scan 2) after training. These regions shrank back closer to their original size (scan 3) after three months of not practising their skills.

Source: Draganski, B., Gaser, C., Busch, V., Schuierer, G., Bogdahn, U. and May, A. (2004) Changes in grey matter induced by training. *Nature,* 427, 311-312. Reprinted by permission from Macmillan Publishers Ltd. Copyright © 2004.

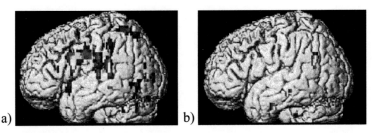

a)   b)

Figure 1.2 (a) Hot spots show where brain activity *decreased* after participants undertook mathematical training – reflecting a decreased demand on working memory; (b) A different analysis of the same participants, this time with hot spots showing areas where brain activity *increased* after mathematical training – reflecting an increase in automatic processing.

Source: Delazer, M., Domahs, F., Bartha, L., Brenneis, C., Lochy, A., Trieb, T. and Benke, T. (2003) Learning complex arithmetic – an fMRI study. *Cognitive Brain Research,* 18, 76–88. Reprinted by permission from Elsevier. Copyright © 2003.

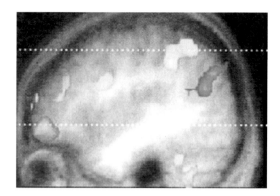

Figure 1.3 Sagittal view (between the ears, eye socket visible in bottom left of image) of left hemisphere activities when participants were asked to carry out exact calculations (in blue) and approximations (in yellow).

Source: Dehaene, S., Spelke, E., Pinel, P., Stanescu, R. and Tsivkin, S. (1999) Sources of mathematical thinking: behavioral and brain-imaging evidence. *Science*, 284, 970–974. Reprinted with permission from AAAS. Copyright © 1999.

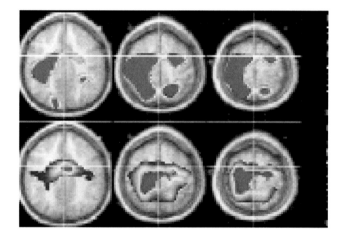

Figure 1.4 Sleep is not just about resting but also about consolidating what we have learnt during the day, as can be seen in these transverse (horizontal) cross-sections of brain activity. The sleeping brain (images below, each section from left to right is closer to the top of the head) appears to reproduce the neural activities resembling those recorded during preceding hours of wakefulness (images above).

Source: Maquet, P., Laureys, S., Peigneux, P., Fuchs, S., Petiau, C., Philips, C., Aerts, J., Del Firoe, G., Degueldre, C., Meulmans, T., Luxen, A., Franck, G., Van Der Linden, Smith, C., Cleermans, A. (2000) Experience dependent changes in cerebral activation during human REM sleep. *Nature neuroscience*, 3(8), 831–6. Reprinted by permission from Macmillan Publishers Ltd. Copyright © 2000.

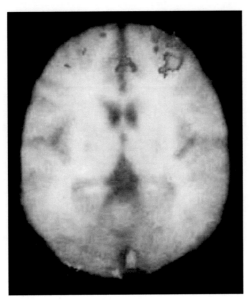

Figure 2.1 Horizontal cross-section of the brain (front at top of image) showing a widely distributed set of additional 'hot spots' in the right hemisphere when participants generated an unusual verb to follow a noun, rather than the first one that comes into our heads (e.g. 'the cat painted', rather than 'the cat purred'). However, such images show where the difference in activity between two conditions is exceeding a statistical threshold – not where the brain is, and is not, active. Since language is involved, regions in the left hemisphere would also be increasing activity in both types of task. In the absence of a serious medical condition, the brain is always active everywhere.

Source: Seger, C. A., Desmond, J. E., Glover, G. H. and Gabrieli, J. D. E. (2000) Functional magnetic resonance imaging evidence for right-hemisphere involvement in processing of unusual semantic relationships. *Neuropsychology*, 14, 361–369. Copyright © 2000 by the American Psychological Association. Adapted with permission. The use of APA information does not imply endorsement by APA.

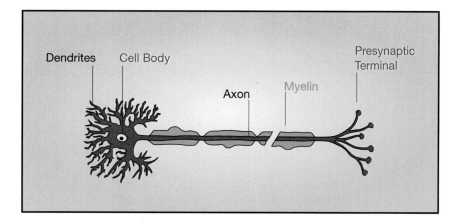

Figure A.1 Each neuron in the brain consists of cell body, from which are connected dendrites and an axon. The axon ends in presynaptic terminals that form connections (synapses) with the dendrites of other neurons.

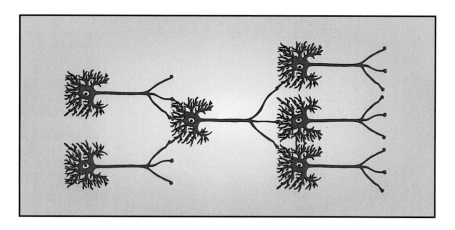

Figure A.2 Neurons connect together to form networks.

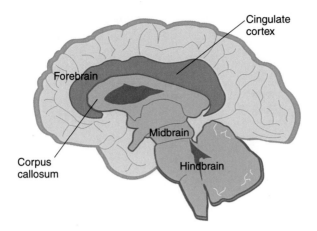

Figure A.3 Section through the brain showing division into forebrain, midbrain and hind-brain regions. This diagram also shows the position of the corpus callosum which connects hemispheres, and the cingulate cortex.

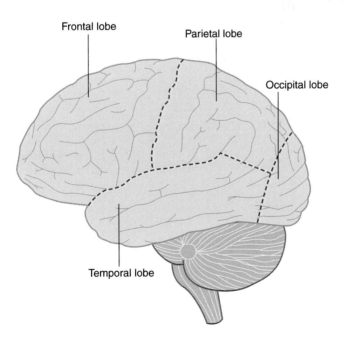

Figure A.4 Each cortical hemisphere is divided into four lobes.

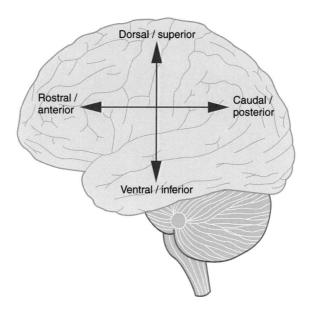

Figure A.5 There are two commonly used terms for each of the four directions required to identify brain regions. So, a phrase such as "posterior superior temporal sulcus" means the rear part of the valley at the top of the temporal lobe.

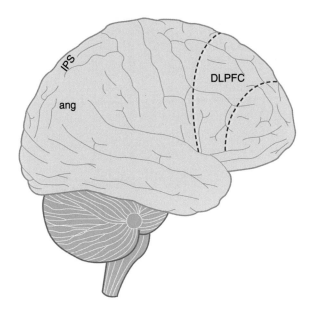

Figure A.6 Some sulci and gyri have special names. Shown are the positions of the right angular gyrus (ang) and intraparietal sulcus (IPS). Also shown on this diagram is the region known as the Dorso-Lateral PreFrontal Cortex (DLPFC).

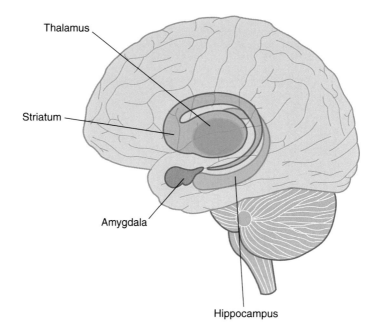

Figure A.7 Some important sub-cortical (below the cortex) structures include the thalamus, hippocampus, amygdala and striatum.

Chapter 4

Neuroscience and education in dialogue

Previous chapters have revealed education and science as two separate worlds separated by a gulf of communication, and whose inhabitants possess two different sets of constructs about the brain and mind. So, if educators and neuroscientists inhabit such different worlds, what happens when they sit down face-to-face and consider working together? This chapter draws on discussions during the 2005–2006 ESRC-TLRP seminar series (and related consultations) to identify the types of issues that surface when educators engage with neuroscientists and psychologists with a view to collaboration. This chapter does not seek to appraise any particular research ideas that arose, but to report the issues characterizing this type of discourse. Many of these will be examined more critically in later chapters but here prominence is given to the voices and thoughts of the participants themselves as, for many of those involved, they experience 'first contact'. As such, it provides a useful introduction to the arguments and concerns that researchers may encounter at the interface between these two diverse domains of understanding.

Early discussions between neuroscience and education

Around the beginning of this decade, a small number of neuroscientists began persistent and active efforts to suggest that education could benefit from greater awareness of our understanding of the brain. Most notably, in the UK, Sarah-Jayne Blakemore and her colleague Uta Frith were commissioned by the Teaching and Learning Research Programme (TLRP) to carry out a review of neuroscientific findings that may be of relevance to educators (Blakemore and Frith, 2000). This review attacked a number of neuromyths, including those concerning critical periods, and highlighted some new areas of potential interest to educators such as the role of sleep in learning. Rather than point out areas where neuroscience could be immediately applied in education, the review sought to highlight neuroscientific questions that might be of interest to educators, thus making an important initial step towards defining an interdisciplinary area of collaborative research. In January 2001, to promote further discussion about a possible research agenda, the TLRP wrote to 439 institutions, including 233 scientific institutions and 193 education departments in higher education, asking for comments on the report by Blakemore and Frith. In addition to identifying any omissions, respondents were particularly asked to provide 'identification of key research questions ... their priority ... and estimate of their tractability (in terms of return on research effort)'.

Only fourteen education departments responded to the request. In their comments, one can identify some of the issues that would be debated more fully in the seminar series to come. These included doubts expressed by some respondents about whether they had sufficient expertise to comment usefully on the document, which may also help explain the low response rate. There was also anxiety that the inclusion of neuroscience in educational thinking might result in the transfer of educational research funding to neuroscience. Other respondents were more positive and identified areas mentioned in the report that they also felt were potentially interesting, such as developmental disorders, long-term and working memory, gender and plasticity. Some of the most positive comments appeared hopeful that neuroscience would legitimize teachers' existing understanding with a new level of compelling evidence: 'teachers recognise a truth when they read it ... the relevance of all this to neurological research is that evidence is badly needed to show which is the most effective way of teaching our young people'. In addition to areas identified by Blakemore and Frith, educational respondents also suggested other areas for interdisciplinary research, including learning styles and emotional intelligence which, as we saw in Chapter 2, were later recognized as being problematic as robust scientific concepts suitable for orientating research efforts. Although the report on the consultation concluded that no collaborative research agenda had yet emerged (Desforges, 2001), it also emphasized how both the education and scientific communities were complimentary about the contents and timeliness of the review.

In 1999, around the same time as the Blakemore and Frith report was being commissioned in the UK, a supranational project on 'Learning Sciences and Brain Research' was being launched by the OECD's Centre for Educational Research and Innovation (CERI). The first phase of the project (1999–2002) brought together international researchers to review potential implications of recent research findings in brain research for policymakers. The second phase (2002–2006) channelled its activities on three main areas (Literacy, Numeracy and Lifelong Learning) within three transdisciplinary and international networks co-ordinated in collaboration with three leading institutions (Sackler Institute-USA, INSERM-France, RIKEN Brain Science Institute-Japan). These international meetings focused chiefly on discussing concepts arising from neuroscience that might be of benefit to education, rather than dealing directly with the issues that might arise in attempting collaboration. However, once again, the meetings provided early indicators of issues that would characterize this type of transdisciplinary discourse. These included concerns about the seductive attractiveness of neuroscience for educators, the gulf between concepts of learning in the two fields and doubts about the willingness of scientists to cross it. At one point, the coordinator of the project (Bruno della Chiesa) wondered how many of the neuroscientists attending would have done so if ten minutes of each presentation had to be devoted to human education, adding that the project was not concerned with educational policy for rodents. Scientists had to be assured that their existing research pursuits would not be interrupted by their involvement, that web-site summaries would not oversimplify conceptual complexities and would not 'betray' their work. Teachers, it was reported by Denis Ralph,[1] were enthusiastic about neuroscience, but often their ideas could be described as 'neurobabble' (OECD, 2002a). Summing up at the same meeting, Bernard Hugonnier observed that scientists' time was limited and they were not necessarily interested in applied research. Therefore, he suggested, some sort of interface was needed between neuroscience and its application in education. At the same time, however, he also noted the need for scientists to be made more aware of the potential educational significance of their work and asked how it was possible to raise their awareness in this way. At a later meeting (OECD, 2004) a call was made to create a 'lingua franca' that would unify the terminology between the two camps of educators and neuroscientists, and facilitate better discussion.

One of the final meetings highlighted concerns about transferring knowledge from controlled laboratory settings to complex educational contexts, and considered the need for laboratory experimentation using tasks that better represented these contexts (Hinton, 2005). Partnership in research, the possibility of new career paths and the need for multimethod approaches were considered. The strategic and cautious communication of scientific information to non-scientists was also considered as critical. The meeting ended positively, with an awareness that progress towards tractable and valuable research questions had arisen from educators' provision of relevance and scientists' accurate assessment of the feasibility of potential studies.

The ESRC-TLRP seminar series and related consultation

In 2005, the TLRP launched its second initiative in this area, by funding a major seminar series 'Collaborative Frameworks in Neuroscience and Education'. This brought together experts and stakeholders from education and neuroscience to discuss the issues and opportunities from collaborative research between neuroscience and education. Rather than just identify potential areas for research, the series was to identify the means by which this type of research capacity could be developed, to examine the theoretical, practical and strategic issues involved. Six one-day events were held in locations cross the UK. At each event, teachers, psychologists, neuroscientists and policymakers heard scientific presentations and then took part in interdisciplinary discussions. These were held in small groups (each with a representative range of stakeholders) and were guided by provocative questions such as 'What sort of evidence from neuroscience should inspire educational change?'. After each event, discussants contributed to producing summaries that helped clarify the issues arising.² By the time of its conclusion in June 2006, over 400 teachers, educational researchers, psychologists and neuroscientists had attended one or more of the events. The series successfully highlighted the potential value of dialogue and research such that, on 6 March 2006, Susan Greenfield raised questions in the House of Lords about how the UK government would assess the outcomes of the series, and what plans existed to foster interdisciplinary research in this area. Lord Adonis, parliamentary under-secretary of state (DfES) solicited a response from the UK research councils suggesting such research could, in principle, be funded under existing schemes.³

Soon after this seminar series was underway, a parallel consultation was undertaken. This was designed to support discussions with a general profile of educators' current views on the role of the brain in education. The consultation involved 200 educators and took the form of a large-scale questionnaire study followed by a series of in-depth interviews with classroom teachers (Howard-Jones *et al.*, 2007; Pickering and Howard-Jones, 2007). In seeking to learn more about the views of educators in the UK, the questionnaires were distributed to participants in contexts where the potential relationship between neuroscience and education was to be discussed. Specifically, seventy-one respondents were attending the 'Learning Brain Europe' (LBE) conference at Manchester in June 2005 and seventy-nine were at the 'Education and Brain Research' (EBR) conference at Cambridge University in July 2005. The first of these samples consisted of teachers arriving at an event that was compulsory training for all staff from a small group of local schools. This sample should have received only typical exposure to ideas about the brain before arriving at the conference and might be considered as most representative of the general population of UK teachers. The second sample consisted of teachers who had given up personal time to voluntarily attend an academic conference on the brain and education (part of the seminar series). To gain some sense of how the views of these teachers compared with international perspectives, we also received responses via a discussion forum for educational practitioners interested in the brain hosted on the OECD web-site between September 2005 and June 2006. The fourty-eight OECD respondents were based in eighteen different countries across the world. Interview participants included teachers from the EBR conference and local teachers recruited from the south-west of England. The comments and discourse arising from these two complementary initiatives are here considered with respect to nine key themes that characterized seminar discussions.

Theme 1: Positive interest and mutual respect

Much of the rest of this chapter will highlight the challenges, potential barriers to progress and areas where particular caution will be required for researchers and communicators at the interface between neuroscience and education. So it is important to emphasize here that all the seminar events generated a genuine enthusiasm from scientists and educators for interdisciplinary dialogue and, overall, there was a cautious optimism about the possibilities for collaborative research. The prevailing mood during discussions was far from cynical. There was a general perception that greater collaboration between neuroscience and education could be mutually beneficial. This enthusiasm was also reflected by the views expressed in the survey of educators' views carried as part of the related consultation exercise. When we asked educators if an understanding of the workings of the brain was important in their educational activities, the answer was resoundingly positive. Apart from curriculum content, the majority of participants rated the role of the brain as important, or very important, in all educational areas (including the design and delivery of teaching, provision for special needs and the role of nutrition). There was, however, some general difference in enthusiasm between attendees at the two conferences, with 87 per cent of participants at the LBE conference and a more modest 67 per cent at the EBR conference providing an average rating of important or very important in these categories (curriculum excluded) across adults and children. The participants attending the EBR conference were exposed to a considerable amount of myth-busting, and this may have produced a more sceptical and cautious attitude. Such an effect was illustrated by the remarks of one primary school teacher at this conference:

> There isn't one person here who doesn't know about visual learners, auditory learners, Brain Gym, and it's because I guess it's something easy to understand and I don't mean that in a patronising way. It's the sort of thing that you can grab onto and you can run with – but – we've been a bit misguided about that sort of thing haven't we – not having the time to verify it for ourselves – we have no choice.
>
> (from Howard-Jones *et al.* 2007, p. 43)

The enthusiasm of OECD respondents fell somewhere between that of EBR and LBE respondents (80 per cent). A similar pattern between conferences applied to curriculum content, but there was also a notably lower general enthusiasm for involving the brain in decisions about curriculum content in all groups, with only 57 per cent of participants across the three groups considering this as important or very important. In relation to the differences between the three groups, it would appear that an active pursuit of academic knowledge about the brain was associated with more guarded views. Indeed, interviews revealed that teachers' views can be very unstable and open to influence in either direction, as expressed by this teacher of Key Stage 2 (7 to 11 years):

> And I've gone from one extreme to the other, from not thinking about it at all to suddenly thinking, oh my God, its crucial for everything, its really,

really important ... the impact that it might have on our thought processes, and then also our physical actions.

(from Howard-Jones *et al.* 2007, p. 32)

Educational issues involving learners with special educational needs (SEN) appeared most strongly associated with the brain. 94 per cent respondents at the LBE conference gave a high rating to the importance of neuroscience in matters involving children with emotional/behavioural difficulties, while 76 per cent of respondents at the EBR conference rated its relevance highly in regard to issues involving the cognitive processes of adults with special educational needs. This perception of neuroscience as strongly related to understanding SEN was also reflected in interviews with teachers. When asked whether teachers would view what goes on in the brain as important as the other factors affecting a child's learning, one special needs teacher working in a secondary school answered:

I think that they'd consider it amongst everything else, probably as equally important. Particularly now, because if you have an inclusive setting and you've got lots of people with differences and difficulties ...

(from Howard-Jones *et al.* 2007, p. 41)

The implications of neuroscience for SEN appears almost undisputed amongst educators, but interviews also confirmed our survey results showing it was perceived as relevant for mainstream learners too. Our LEA adviser suggested our understanding of the brain should be used to enrich the education of all learners:

I'd like to see it focussing on what typical learners do and how they learn, because there's a lot of children in our schools that aren't learning as effectively as they could be doing and I think that it's important to focus on them as well as the special needs kids ... And I think that teachers will be very interested in what they can do for the majority of children.

(from Howard-Jones *et al.* 2007, p. 40)

Scientists were strongly represented in seminar discussions, with a particular and natural interest shown by educational psychologists whose profession involves illuminating educational issues with an understanding of mind. There was some surprise expressed by educators at the extent of the humility and positive interest shown by neuroscientists who made very modest claims for the educational significance of their own field, but were clearly motivated to seek out educators and discuss with them the potential relevance of their work.

There appeared, then, a convergence of interest from educators, scientists and policymakers for work in this area but, as we shall now see, some serious challenges were also recognized.

Theme 2: Seduction: fame and images

Some educators felt it was informative to explore their own expectations – what were they hoping for from neuroscience? Some suggested teachers' enthusiasm arises from a notion that neuroscience can contribute to their existing under-standing of the classroom, rather than provide an alternative and/or complete panacea. Fascination for the processes of learning was cited as a key motivation for teachers wishing to develop their own practice, and this may lead to a natural openness and curiosity about concepts involving the brain. Teachers' interest in neuroscience may also be growing with the number of children in their classroom experiencing developmental difficulties and receiving psychoactive medication.

The potential dangers of this enthusiasm were clear. Guy Claxton, from an educational perspective, suggested '... education has always been an insecure discipline, which has always had to ask itself "Where do we get our warrant? How do we justify and rationalise what we do?" And now, particularly when the means and ends of education are hotly contested, this insecurity can make us somewhat credulous as a profession, and vulnerable to the claims of a discipline that comes along and says: "I'm proper scientific knowledge, I'm based on hard data, I can tell you what to do". This creates a problematic relationship between neuroscience and education'.

Alongside the concerns of some educators, scientists also felt the need to moderate optimism with a sense of caution. Two neuroscientists warned of the seductive nature of a venture combining neuroscience and education, for both educators and scientists: Mark Johnson, a specialist in developmental cogni-tive neuroscience, drew attention to the excitement created by pictures of the brain among non-specialists. 'There is a danger that neuro-myths can arise from attractive publishable pictures of apparently static activation of a small number of regions rather than, more accurately, as a complex interaction ...'. Scientists can also be seduced by the lure of publicity, encouraging them to adopt roles and make statements that compromise their science. Daniel Wolpert, a specialist in how the brain controls movement, pointed out the 'real danger of education seeking answers from neuroscience since it is inevitably an attractive and very seductive opportunity for individual fame and attention, when such answers may be exposed as "nonsense" 30 years later'.

Theme 3: Professional aims and levels of authority

One primary school teacher during the consultation feared that scientists might not be sufficiently grounded in their understanding of the classroom and sug-gested that '... before [researchers] go about applying information, I think [they] should visit [schools] and see what it's like ... because otherwise [their] sugges-tions just might not be suitable at all'.

This point was taken up by John Ashby (General Teaching Council of England) in seminar discussions, who reminded colleagues that 'one of the big shifts in the last couple of years is the realisation that you must factor in the reality of the classroom from the onset of research. So from the beginning of the thinking, when planning a research project, teachers should be involved at the onset of articulating the problem. Although this may not be practical in every project, this should be the principle of it. It has been shown that this collaboration works, in that the outcome of educational research is used and usable in the classroom'. He emphasized that, in research involving collaboration with neuroscience, this involvement of teachers would be particularly important because neuroscience appears one step further removed from the classroom than conventional educational research. This type of mixed research community involving teachers would be an important factor in producing research that was applicable and relevant. Realistically, for educational and neuroscientific research to come together, individuals in both camps might need to learn and to change, in order to work towards a common endeavour. Ashby identified one barrier to producing such a community as the perceived difference in the status of the two fields (as also observed by Claxton), which he caricatured as the soft stuff (education) versus rigorous and 'hard' factual science. This echoed issues arising from the OECD project. If it was necessary for scientists to become involved with the classroom, how would this meet with their professional aims of carrying out laboratory-based research? Would the power difference between neuroscience and education make this classroom involvement even more unlikely?

Anxieties about power differences also fed more generally into the way some educators spoke about neuroscience. Almost all the teachers and educators in the consultation survey had responded to the question 'What do you understand by the term "neuroscience"?' with a very simple description of it as the study, science or understanding of the brain. On the other hand, more complex and value-based perceptions of neuroscience were also revealed when educators exchanged views with the scientists. Some aspects of these perceptions were negative, in terms of the potential influence of neuroscience on educational thinking. Words such as 'reductionist' and 'un-naturalistic' arose, with anxieties that the inclusion of neuroscientific concepts would produce ideas overly focused on the biological and measurable at the expense of the social and educationally valuable. There were concerns about the concept of mind being influenced by the concept of 'brain as machine', a tendency for neuroscience to draw potentially general implications from studies that average over individuals, and a focus on neuroscientific questions rather than educational ones. There was caution about being involved with an incomplete science whose authority was exaggerated, via the media, by the impression it can always provide coherent 'hard' facts. Would such authority, with a professional status that might be perceived as higher than teachers', help further displace teachers' intuitive and professional judgements? Would there be a 'medicalization' of learning through, for example, the transformation of 'problems with maths' into the disorder of dyscalculia?

Neuroscientists' and educators' aims orientate them towards different types of evidence. In neuroscience, evidence serves to validate a fairly narrow component of understanding which has a very well-defined place as part of a larger body of progressively built knowledge. In education, evidence is used to promote values and ideas on a much larger scale, and yet value can be granted to evidence on the basis of 'resonance' with teachers' existing ideas. Evidence can be seen as valuable if it supports and guides these ideas within the specific contexts of their own teaching. In education, evidence is often described as powerful or valuable, suggesting it needs to cover distance in terms of its effect, and that it has association with value-laden issues. Evidence that provides explanation, as one teacher in our consultation pointed out, may not be enough:

> If you go into schools and say, right, we've identified that this is happening within the brain and it affects children in this way, we now know why children are having problems with, say, literacy or numeracy, because such and such is occurring in the brain, we've scientifically proved that its happening in all of them .... I don't think that that's enough for teachers, because what they're looking for you to say is ... what do we have to do to make sure we can help the children to overcome that problem?
>
> (from Howard-Jones *et al.* 2007, p. 39)

Educational applications may be a key priority for educators, but they are not a priority for scientists more often involved in determining, rather than applying, new fundamental principles. On the other hand, these two sets of objectives are clearly related, and the development and testing of brain-mind-behaviour relationships in more complex social environments than the laboratory has also been gathering scientific interest. This may be of particular interest in the new field of social cognitive neuroscience, which appears to have rapidly developed in recent years (Blakemore *et al.*, 2004).

Theme 4: Two philosophies

Such interdisciplinary collaborations may founder on the differences in how neuroscientists and educational researchers collect and use information. Jonathan Barnes, a lecturer in primary education, pointed out:

> ... there is a big difference between the paradigms that neuroscientists and educationalists are working with. Neuroscientists use primarily quantitative evidence, but research in education is highly qualitative, and has to do with meaning and interpretations. These are very different ways of providing evidence, and there may be a need to tackle and discuss these differences.

Phil Bayliss, a specialist in special education, saw the difference as even more fundamental, with the two areas separated by '... different sets of philosophical understandings about the object of study. Part of the problem with neuroscience is that those philosophical conditions aren't challenged ... It's also important to remember that we're all talking about the same thing, children, not brains or social institutions'. It was suggested that, otherwise, any initiative in this area might quickly draw a negative response from educators such as 'I believe in children, I don't believe in neurons'.

Although the interests and questions asked by educators and scientists sometimes appear very different, Ann Dowker pointed out that educational and scientific perspectives on learning are not necessarily conflicting. She discussed the benefits arising from her own long-standing collaborative dialogue with teachers. As a developmental psychologist, she had collaborated directly with teachers on numeracy intervention work and had conducted research with them in their schools. She suggested there may be basic similarities between what teachers and neuroscientists are looking for, and that these can inform one another. Her research on individual differences in specific mathematical components had not only been informed by findings in neuroscience and experimental psychology, but by teachers' own observations of pupils' performance. Ann Dowker drew attention to teachers' strong intuitive awareness of their children's performance, their strengths and weaknesses and how interventions could be targeted. She proposed that, although the methods and techniques of researchers and teachers may be different, the fundamental viewpoints of researchers and teachers may be much closer than is often thought.

Theme 5: Need for scrutiny and improved communication

A vacuum was recognized to exist between educators' enthusiasm to know more about the brain and the availability of reliable sources of relevant information that could be understood by non-scientists. It was felt that teachers needed information about brain in a form that could be quickly reached and digested. As Lynn Knapp, a primary headteacher, suggested: 'accessibility is key'. Educators described an established industry of entrepreneurs that exploited the present vacuum to sell unscientific ideas, with these often promoted even through in-service training days (INSET), including those arranged through Local Education Authorities (LEAs). It was noted that the lack of access to sound educational concepts involving the brain was likely to extend beyond teachers, headteachers and LEAs, and to include many educational researchers and also the Office for Standards in Education (Ofsted). The basic need to develop a stronger capability within education to make informed decisions about educational 'brain-based' ideas was uncontested. Chrystal Widdeson, a teacher of infants, suggested that without such capability within the educational system:

> Teachers who want to know how to get their children concentrating and remembering better would be left with the conclusions of the snake oil sellers, or left to make their own conclusions – which they currently don't have the tools to do properly.

The extent to which teachers should be informed about the mind and brain in their training was debated. Given the highly contextualized nature of learning situations, there appeared a strong argument for teachers to be better supported as their own empirical assessors of programmes claiming to be brain-based. One deputy headteacher suggested that this was in line with an increasingly critical and scientific approach being taken by Ofsted, who often ask 'Why we do what we do? Does it make an impact? And, if not, why not?'. Anne Cooke, research facilitator for the Bristol Neuroscience network, agreed, and suggested that perhaps 'the aim should be to give teachers the tools to make an informed judgment about the science for themselves'. A frequent call during formal and informal discussions during the seminar series was for a greater focus on mind and brain in initial teacher training. It was felt this would help teachers' ability to critically examine some of the programmes and ideas about the brain they are faced with. As one Key Stage 2 teacher explained during interview:

> I think that as a start it should be more of an important issue in terms of teacher training, because ... I just find with the education system that you're ... almost like a rat in a wheel once you get into the system, because there's never enough time for anything ... Whereas I think if it's something that is kind of embedded at teacher training level, so when people start on their career at that stage, they think 'oh yes, this is really, really important and this is something which needs to have an impact throughout my teaching career, because it's something that's always going to be influential in terms of maybe how children are learning and responding to what I'm doing'.
>
> (from Howard-Jones *et al.* 2007, p. 37)

Certainly there appears the potential for educational misunderstanding about the brain. Speaking at the EBR conference, after a neuroscientist had warned against making unwarranted conclusions for practice, one teacher of Key Stage 1 (5 to 7 years) commented:

> I did a few of those conclusions myself listening to [academic researchers'] results, I'd say, oh well, that must mean that I can do this in the classroom, when actually they concluded it in a completely different way because ... I'd misread the result, or misinterpreted it, or overgeneralised it.
>
> (from Howard-Jones *et al.* 2007, p. 36)

Theme 6: Who should communicate?

Neuroscientists already produce evidence-based non-specialist explanations, often to publicly communicate their work – which is sometimes called 'transfer work' in science. However, it was agreed that carefully formulating information and explanations (for teachers, learners, parents and the many other stake holders in education) would become an especially critical determinant of success in ventures interfacing neuroscience and education, and more so than in conventional scientific work. Neither would such construction be simple. For example, how would scientists be involved in producing advice for teachers, drawing on understanding of the mind and brain? Presently, even texts by respected neuroscientists aimed at educators (Blakemore and Frith, 2005) tend to stop short of this. However, the role of provisional truth in producing such explanations proved controversial. Usha Goswami expressed concerns about the diluting of scientific findings, and that diluted findings could more easily be misinterpreted, polarizing debates. It was suggested that the careful composition of such provisional ideas might chiefly be a role for education faculties.

As we have seen, those already peddling uninformed ideas about the brain were frequently referred to as 'snake-oil sellers'. However, there was also debate about the potential value of such a 'middle person' in communication. For example, this might be the motivational speaker who is neither teacher nor scientist, but often a private consultant hired to deliver INSET. Some suggested that the term 'snake-oil seller' was unhelpful – as these were often very good speakers with no evidence suggesting they were insincere in their beliefs and motivations, merely unscientific in their understanding. One LEA adviser, attending the EBR conference at Cambridge University, proposed that communication about the brain might require a broad partnership that included such middle parties:

> ... the neuroscientists ... some of them have got a fantastic wealth of knowledge, but it's difficult for them to translate that knowledge ... they're not seen as communicators always, whereas the snake oil sellers often are gifted communicators and they're the ones that the teachers pay to come and talk to them on their INSET [in-service training] days ...
>
> (Pickering and Howard-Jones, 2007, p. 112)

Theme 7: How should messages be constructed?

Whatever the processes by which messages needed to reach teachers, the construction of the messages themselves would need careful attention. At the most fundamental level, meaningful discussion benefits from some sense of shared meaning for the terms used to progress it. However, on frequent occasions, it was clear that the same word was being used in different ways (e.g. evidence, behaviour, learning), prompting John Geake to suggest there were 'two languages with one lexicon'. This appears true even within education. The first question on our teacher survey asked what they felt the terms 'neuroscience' and 'education' meant. As mentioned, educators defined neuroscience in fairly straightforward ways. On the other hand, being asked to explain their understanding of the term 'education' elicited many diverse and extended responses. Less than a third made reference to learning, using phrases such as 'Giving people the opportunity to learn effectively', or 'all experiences of learning and engagement'. The rest mostly referred to developing a person's potential (e.g. 'every child achieving their academic and social and emotional potential'), a preparation for life in society, a life-long experience of some type of enrichment or some interaction with knowledge. Others did not fit easily into any category, e.g. 'a preschool and school based provision as regulated by government policies ...'.

Some other differences in the use and meaning of words may be more subtle but are still associated with important shifts in values as one travels between scientific and educational perspectives. For example, despite its negative connotations within science as a confounding factor, the term 'placebo effect' may not be viewed in quite the same way by educators. If a placebo effect can be maintained over time, some discussants speculated about its status as a positive and authentic educational outcome. Also, some basic terms can become emotive in the politically sensitive arena of education. For example, it was considered how the emotional response to ideas about cognitive enhancers might be influenced by calling them drugs, supplements, 'cogs' or foods.

Part of the communication problem may derive from teachers being poorly situated to receive concepts about the mind and brain, since they usually possess little grounding in psychology and there is no inclusion of the brain in initial teacher training. Teachers' time is very pressured and attempts to retrieve appropriate information can also be hampered by an apparent lack of consensus among scientists. This was a point picked up by Daniel Wolpert, who suggested the need for scientists to sometimes commit to a definite view in order to inspire confidence. It was a point echoed by some of the teachers we interviewed, including a primary special needs co-ordinator, who found the lack of consensus frustrating:

> I think that possibly one of the biggest hurdles, though, is where there isn't a consensus amongst researchers ... whatever one group says, somebody else says something different.
>
> (from Howard-Jones et al. 2007, p. 42)

Therefore, as well as careful attention to language and meaning, as understood by the educational audience, it was felt that scientific information should reflect the present state of consensus among scientists. In short, messages involving neuroscience and education would need to be constructed through integrating expertise from both fields.

Theme 8: What should be communicated – limits and complexity

There were two issues that many scientists and educators felt deserved special attention in communications about the brain: complexity and the current limitations of scientific understanding.

Language can be an imperfect tool of communication that encourages, for example, overly simplistic dichotomies. A variety of these were identified during discussions, including mind/brain, learning/development, nature/nurture.

Discussants drew attention to how even associating a learning difficulty with a neurological correlate has potentially diverse social influence and educational implications. These can include a more strongly perceived case for additional special support, the perception of a permanent and innate 'broken brain' or even a sense of relief among parents and learners that a low level of achievement is not their 'fault'. Care should be taken to avoid 'all or none theorizing' that seeks to identify particular developmental trajectories as biologically determined when, in fact, all trajectories come about through a complex interaction of genes and the environment, including the educational environment. An additional point was also raised that the biological systems involved with cognition extend beyond the brain. There is a need to include the peripheral nervous system and many other aspects of body function, and most especially the endocrine system and the role of hormones, including in emotional responses.

Related to this, there were suggestions that any venture involving neuroscience and education might need to emphasize what neuroscientists do not know, given that some simple claims, or their interpretation, can have significant social and educational implications. For example, areas of research involving consciousness cannot provide indisputable proof that we do or do not possess free will, yet the authors of some research would have us believe one argument or the other. This has implications for the sense of students that they are 'in control of their brain', and their sense of themselves as potentially autonomous learners.

Some areas of research linking neuroscience and education will inevitably be controversial. Part of the potential for this controversy arises from the great range of imagined possibilities in this area, fanciful or otherwise, some of which can be associated with well-known science fiction themes (e.g. smart drugs, brain control and computer-brain interaction). It is these more sensational possibilities that seem likely to attract the greatest publicity and may have a disproportional impact on perceptions. This may also reflect a lack of public awareness about what neuroscience can presently achieve. Similarly, some discussants also expressed a view that neuroscientists can be naive in terms of the political and social significance of their own science. Given the social and political sensitivity of education, messages would need to emphasize the limitations of neuroscience in terms of what is technically possible and the extent to which scientific findings can provide recommendations for what *should* be done. It was felt that such recommendations would require drawing on a broader set of perspectives than those constrained by a natural science approach.

Annette Karmiloff Smith, a specialist in developmental neurocognition, drew attention to a range of technical issues likely to limit the role of neuroscience in educational terms. There are a number of fundamental 'gaps' in neuroscientific understanding, some important limitations of imaging techniques and, in some vital areas, a lack of data. For example, due to the nature of the BOLD signal used in fMRI, there is difficulty in distinguishing when an increase in intensity in a particular region arises from a heterogeneous distribution of highly active individual neurons or whether it arises from a general increase in neuronal activity across the region. This is particularly important when comparing different syndromes with typical controls. There is also a focus on pre-test/post-test group studies rather than the effect on a single individual as measured by multiple measurements over time, a lack of normative data (templates used to normalize atypical brains are usually from a normal brain) and a tendency for neuroimaging data to be from adults rather than children. Adult data is sometimes inadvisably used to make inferences about processes in children, despite known differences in functioning of the developing brain.

Despite such limitations, educators maintained a hope that neuroscience could become a new 'theoretical anchor' and/or a source of new inspiration. This met agreement with the views of Sashank Varma (a specialist in educational psychology), who described his own positive view on the role of neuroscience in education, while also suggesting the possible limits of its authority:

> Neuroscience is not the saviour of education – it's better perceived as an interesting source of hypotheses ... Neuroscience cannot provide top-down answers – it tackles low level problems and comes up with insightful explanations of what's going on in the mind and brain. Educators need to learn from these explanations and come up with ways to translate the science into meaningful ways to improve learning during lessons – neuroscientists don't think that way.

Theme 9: Neuroeducational research

Despite goodwill and interest from scientists and educators, and a wealth of neuroscientific insights that appear relevant to education, there appeared to be few findings that experts on both sides felt were immediately applicable in the classroom. Indeed, Uta Frith, a specialist in cognitive neuroscience, summarized the important point that no ready-made educational solutions are likely to come off shelves marked 'neuroscience' with the simple statement: 'neuroscience does not have answers'.

Educational researchers may find insights into learning processes interesting, but chiefly as a means to develop and explore new educational interventions. An interdisciplinary neuroscience/education venture might need to apply scientific expertise in developing both the understanding and the application. As one of our interviewed teachers commented after a lecture on the brain:

> ... as interesting as the information is, for a teacher you have to have some practical implication and it has to be deliverable and manageable ... and I think previously that's what's caused difficulties ... people don't suggest how you might go about it. And I think that it's important to think about that.
>
> (from Howard-Jones et al. 2007, p. 41)

Thus, the translation work that Sasank Varma refers to was not merely an issue of communication, but also a need to formulate, test and evaluate ideas linking neuroscience to educational outcomes. This research-based translation work appeared, at the time of the seminar series, to be missing from the picture, although there was some discussion about how such work should proceed. Should it be done by educators to ensure educational relevance and effectiveness? Or, in order to ensure the survival of scientific validity, should this work be carried out by scientists? Both scientific and educational inputs appeared necessary, suggesting a need for shared enterprise, with two-way dialogue and ideas that are constructed and explored jointly. Discussions identified potential scientific and educational value in such work, suggesting a field of enterprise with two interrelated goals of improving understanding in both fields. Discussants had quickly moved away from looking for 'here and now' answers to the idea of developing such interdisciplinary research, and the generation of concepts combining insights from neuroscience with those from other perspectives, including psychology (with its understanding of mind, as linking brain and learning behaviour) and education itself. Alison Price, a specialist in early mathematics education suggested: 'It is the responsibility of neuroscientists, educational psychologists, researchers and teachers to develop something that has long-lasting application and can be tested'. Such 'neuroeducational' research was seen as crucial, if the time and money required to communicate and promote such ideas were to be justified, and if confidence in educational approaches involving the brain was to be fostered and maintained.

Some teachers interviewed during the consultation considered that, in addition to nurturing collaborative discussion and research, there was benefit in encouraging the development of hybrid professionals, i.e. individuals with expertise in both areas. As one teacher of infants put it, these could help 'bridge the gap ... people that understand the educational terms and the scientific/technical terms to be able to see how it sort of translates from one to the other to make it useful ... you need someone to be really picking holes in things and really getting the essence of what that experiment has or hasn't found out and then how that translates into layman's terms or teacher's terms to help in the classroom'.

One Key Stage 1 teacher suggested that that the concept of 'hybrid professional' might be helpful not just within research projects but, perhaps in the future, at school level, as '... somebody within the school who is perhaps given responsibility for keeping updated on all sorts of recent developments ...'.

Given the highly contextualized nature of different learning situations, informed dialogue within school may be an important element in the chain of communication, so that individual educators are able to, as another interviewee put it, 'actually talk about the evidence that there is to support these new things, so that teachers can make their own mind up about how they fit into the classroom'. Hybrid professionals may also be needed to help orientate educators towards sources of evidence that are reliable since, as several educators pointed out, at the moment teachers are simply not told *who* to trust.

With or without the help of such hybrid professionals, members of collaborative interdisciplinary teams would need to work closely with each other, despite some of the attendant problems already mentioned (e.g. two sets of professional aims, different sets of philosophies). But several scientists suggested ways in which science could learn and benefit from a two-way dialogue with the educational community. For example, Sashank Varma considered education might be a fruitful source for neuroscience of well-honed tasks for experiments that were more complex and potentially interesting than the traditional low level tasks provided by cognitive psychology.

Summary

Face-to-face discussions, and the consultations that supported them, have revealed a broad base of positive interest and enthusiasm for interdisciplinary dialogue and research spanning neuroscience and education. However, a range of issues have been identified that may provide particular challenges for researchers in this area. These include:

- the dangers of producing more neuromyth;
- differences in professional aims and levels of authority;
- differences in the underlying philosophies and methodological approaches.

Agreement also began emerging on a variety of issues, such as:

- the vital importance of scrutiny and good communication in such research, such as the need to ensure scientifically valid and accessible information about concepts and research involving the brain for educators;
- the important role of both scientists and educators in such communication;
- the need to make clear the current limits of scientific understanding and the complex interrelation of factors influencing educational outcomes.

Perhaps most of all, the discussions highlighted the inappropriateness of directly applying concepts from neuroscience in the classroom, and the need for interdisciplinary neuroeducational research aimed at filling the gaps in our current knowledge. The author would argue that the challenges identified do not present insurmountable problems but, as will be set out later, they do require careful deliberation and attention if a secure bridge is to be developed between these two fields of understanding. In Part II, it will be shown how critical consideration of such challenges can help develop theoretical and practical approaches to knowledge construction at the interface of neuroscience and education.

Part II

Neuroeducational research

Chapter 5

A multi-perspective understanding of learning

In the previous chapter, the point was made that neuroscience and education appear to associate different meanings with the same words. One important area of divergence is the meaning of the word 'learning'. This chapter will begin by comparing how neuroscience and education view learning, revealing some fundamental differences of underlying philosophy. However, it will also be argued that the frequent occurrence of 'non-sense' in some dialogues involving neuroscience and education does not indicate an essential incompatibility between these two areas, but reflects the need for an improved understanding of the brain and better appreciation of the philosophical issues that surround it.

One such issue is the mind–brain relationship and we will see that cognitive neuroscience can provide helpful guidance here. However, neuroeducational researchers may need to extend the existing brain-mind-behaviour model of cognitive neuroscience to include emphasis upon processes of social interaction and construction – processes more amenable to investigation using interpretative approaches. The chapter builds towards providing a simple theoretical framework for thinking about how different approaches to thinking about learning may be combined to provide an enriched and multiperspective understanding.

What is learning? The view from neuroscience

Learning and memory

In neuroscience, the noun 'learning' can often be used interchangeably with the word 'memory'. For many decades, psychologists tried to classify memories in terms of simple dichotomies such as declarative/procedural (Cohen and Squire, 1980), explicit/implicit (Graf and Schacter, 1985), and memory and habit (Mishkin *et al.*, 1984). However, due largely to research on the biology of memory, it is now accepted that we have multiple memory systems and these operate both independently and in parallel with each other. Each of these can be classified as one of two types: declarative and nondeclarative. The declarative memory system is closest to the everyday meaning of 'memory' and also closely related to many educational concepts of learning. Defined as our capacity to recall everyday facts and events into consciousness, Squire (2004) suggests this system is most dependent on structures in the medial temporal lobe (e.g. the hippocampus) and the diencephalon (e.g thalamus) (see Fig. 5.1 from Squire, 2004). The forming and recalling of declarative memories activates a variety of other regions in the cortex, whose location appears influenced by other characteristics of the memories, such as whether they are episodic (the re-experiencing of events) or semantic (facts). Nevertheless, it appears semantic and episodic memory do arise from essentially the same system, with models now being created of how the hippocampus operates in facilitating these different types of declarative memory (Shastri, 2002). Whereas declarative memory is representational and provides us with the means to model the world, and to explicitly compare and contrast remembered material, nondeclarative memory is expressed through performance rather than recollection. Declarative memories can be judged as either true or false, whereas nondeclarative memories appear only as changes in behaviour and cannot be judged in terms of their accuracy. 'Nondeclarative memory' is actually an umbrella term for a range of memory abilities arising from a set of other systems. One type of nondeclarative memory of interest to educators helps us acquire skills and habits, and is related to changes in activity in the striatum. Another type supports conditioned emotional responses and is associated with activity in the amygdala. Nonassociative learning responses, such as when our response is diminished by repetitive exposure to a stimulus, appear linked to reflex pathways located chiefly in the spinal cord. Priming, a fourth type of nondeclarative memory, refers to our capacity to use part of a representation in our

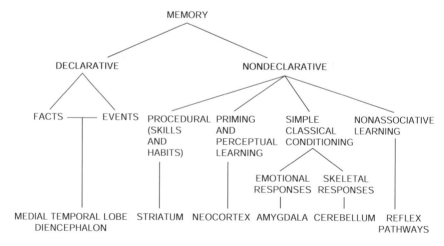

Figure 5.1 A taxonomy of mammalian memory systems listing the brain structures thought to be especially important for each form of declarative and nondeclarative memory.
Source: Squire, L. R. (2004) Memory systems of the brain: A brief history and current perspective. *Neurobiology of Learning and Memory*, **82**, 171–177. Reprinted by permission from Elsevier. Copyright © 2004.

memory to retrieve the rest of it, such as when the first one or two letters of a word allow us to recall it in its entirety. This capacity depends on a number of cortical regions but, again, is thought to arise from an essentially different system to that serving declarative or other types of nondeclarative memory.

Connectivity

Knowing that memory is distributed and involves multiple systems is important, but how is memory achieved in biological terms – what processes are involved?

Among neuroscientists, there is a common acceptance that human learning, as in the formation of memory, occurs by changes in the patterns of connectivity between neurons – or 'synaptic plasticity'. There are two key ways in which this can occur, known as long-term potentiation (LTP) and long-term depression (LTD). LTP refers to an enduring increase (upwards of an hour) of the efficiency by which a neuron relays electrical information, as a result of a temporal pairing (coincidence in time) between the incoming and outgoing signal. By being able to change its efficiency in response to temporal pairing, LTP allows a neuron to adjust its connectivity, according to what other neurons are doing, an ability celebrated in the expression 'neurons that fire together, wire together'.[1] This may seem a modest ability but, as can be seen in simulations involving artificial neurons, it affords even small networks the possibility of organizing themselves to produce a type of 'learning' with human-like qualities and a range of cognitive functions (Arhib, 2003; McClelland and Rogers, 2003). Such networks can 'learn' to identify patterns, make useful guesses and exhibit a graded decrease in functionality when connections are lesioned, as do biological neural networks – so called 'graceful degradation'. The role of LTP within the hippocampus, a region key to formation of memory, has been of particular interest to scientists. LTD refers to an enduring decrease in synaptic efficiency. This is a mechanism thought to explain, for example, how neurons in some regions of the brain can decrease their output as a stimulus is repeatedly presented, underlying our ability to recognize familiarity.

At present, neuroscience does not possess the methods needed to directly observe the role of synaptic plasticity, or its mechanisms, in human learning. Instead, less direct evidence is sought. One example of this evidence arises from treating animals with a particular protein-synthesis inhibitor, which is known to diminish the retention of memory. Animals treated in this way are shown to suffer a slow onset of amnesia (over a period of hours), which coincides in time with a decreasing ability to maintain LTP. Such studies are typical in their provision of compelling evidence as opposed to a firm proof of the role of LTP. Present data suggests we should be confident that such mechanisms are necessary for learning, but we cannot be sure that the plasticity required for learning rests on these alone (Martin et al., 2000). Or, as warned in a recent review of this evidence, 'establishing a causal connection between a specific form of synaptic plasticity and the behavioural consequences of specific experiences remains a daunting task'

(Citri and Malenka, 2008), p. 30). Indeed, in recent years, there has been increasing criticism within neuroscience of the synaptic plasticity hypothesis. It appears theoretically problematic that stable declarative memory formation, lasting over decades, is founded on such an unstable phenomenon as synaptic plasticity. This has prompted calls for a genomic hypothesis of memory, in which DNA modifications serve as carriers of elementary memory traces (Arshavsky, 2006; Crick, 1984; Davis and Squire, 1984).

Working memory

There is one other type of memory that should be reviewed here, because it is essential to the type of learning promoted by education. Working memory is the ability to temporarily hold information in consciousness, and this ability is limited to only a few chunks of information at any one time. We came across it in Chapter 1, where it was seen to be strongly linked to individual differences in educational achievement. Activity associated with working memory has been observed in many different parts of the brain, but particularly in a region of the frontal lobes known as the Dorso-Lateral PreFrontal Cortex (DLPFC). Rather than being supported by mechanisms of synaptic plasticity and the production of new connectivity, it would appear that the DLPFC supports working memory by controlling a temporary increase in activity within pre-existing networks that are either within the DLPFC itself or in other regions of the brain where the information is stored (see Curtis and D'Esposito, 2003).

Structural change

In addition to producing micro changes at the cellular level in terms of connectivity, learning can also produce gross structural changes in the brain. For example, the type of declarative memory required for visuo-spatial tasks appears strongly dependent on particular regions of the hippocampus (Burgess and O'Keefe, 1996). London taxi drivers are generally accomplished in their visuo-spatial learning, as demonstrated by their ability to rapidly and accurately recall complex street plans and routes. In a well-known study, it was shown that the posterior part of the hippocampus in a sample of taxi drivers was larger than those of non-taxi drivers. One must always be careful in making cause–effect inferences in regard to brain differences and behavioural differences. However, the evidence is quite compelling here, since the growth was proportional to the number of years they had been driving a taxi (Maguire *et al.*, 2000). Brain volume, of course, is constrained by the skull. So these increases must have been accompanied by decreases in other regions. In this case, there was an associated shrinking of the anterior part of the hippocampus. More recently, research has shown that learning can produce detectable changes in brain structure over periods of months rather than years. We saw in Chapter 1 how some regions in the brains of adults increased their size by the end of a three-month training course in juggling (see Fig. 1.1 in colour plate section). After three further months of rest, these regions had shrunk back and were closer to their original size (Draganski *et al.*, 2004). At the moment, we do not understand how these structural changes come about and whether, for example, they are due to increased connectivity or the birth of new cells such as glial cells or even neurons.

Functional correlates

When learning happens, we can often observe associated changes in biological function. For example, in the fMRI study described in Chapter 1 (Delazer *et al.*, 2003), we saw what happened when adults attempted to perform long multiplication. This generated increased blood flow in the frontal regions associated with working memory load, as these learners worked consciously through new routines step-by-step. However, after practising for a week (25 minutes per day), performance had improved and imaging showed increased activity in those posterior regions associated with more automatic processing demands. At the same time, frontal activity had decreased in a way indicative of reduced load on working memory. This provides a clear demonstration of how learning is often accompanied by a shift in patterns of activity within brain networks, rather than an increase or decrease *per se* in a single region of the brain. Since we draw on different mental resources when we are first attempting a task, compared with when we are proficient, one may expect a changing relationship between regions of brain activity and learning over time. Thus, any changes in biological activity need to be interpreted in relation to a clear dynamic cognitive model of the learning processes involved and a clear, if often hypothetical, understanding of how different brain networks may be supporting these processes (for discussion see Kaufmann, 2008; Schwartz, 2008).

What is learning? The view from education

Educational ideas about learning are diverse and eclectic in their origins (see Chapter 3 for some typical examples of these). They are the product of a variety of different processes and forces, including those arising from theoretical educational and psychological traditions, and other culturally transmitted ideas from within and beyond the teaching profession. The lack of consensus within educational thinking ensures that individual teachers' beliefs about learning play a critical role in their practice. Teachers' personal beliefs develop through an accrued professional understanding and do not usually require empirical validation. A teacher's beliefs may not always be reflected in their practice or their justification for it, and neither of these is immune from pragmatism and the pressures of political expediency.

A recent study in the US (Snider and Roehl, 2007) supported previous research in revealing a generally atheoretical approach among teachers (Pinnegar and Carter, 1990), but with beliefs more consistent with the traditions of constructivism than explicit instruction. At the heart of constructivist learning theory is the belief that learners construct knowledge based upon their own experiences and prior understanding. Successful learning requires opportunities for meaningful and authentic exploration, engaging activities, interactive group work and student ownership of the learning process.

Teachers' personal beliefs may, in reality, be diverse but those wishing to influence educational thinking and policy must present a coherent message about learning. The executive of Britain's most recent programme of educational research (Teaching and Learning Research Programme, TLRP) published such a message in *Principles into Practice: A Teacher's Guide to Research Evidence on Teaching and Learning* (TLRP, 2007). A review of this text provides some further indication of the types of ideas about learning that are favoured by educators in the UK. The pull-out centre pages list ten principles. Principles 1 and 6 expand the concept of what learning can achieve beyond factual recall, emphasizing that it must 'equip learners for life in the broadest sense' and promote learners' independence and autonomy such that they have 'the will and confidence to become agents of their own learning'. In their indication of how such learning is achieved, Principles 3, 4, 5 and 7 reflect strong constructivist leanings, recognizing 'the importance of prior experience and learning', emphasizing the need to assess meaningful understanding and to foster 'both individual and social processes and outcomes'. Indeed, Principle 4 states directly that 'effective teaching and learning requires the teacher to scaffold learning'. 'Scaffolding' is a term well known to educators that describes how a teacher can control elements of a task that are initially beyond the learners' capacity, thus permitting him/her to concentrate their attention on those elements that are within the learner's range of competence (Wood *et al.*, 1976). Principles 2, 8, 9 and 10 encourage an understanding of learning that extends beyond the school pupil, emphasizing the importance of teachers' continuous professional development, the significance of informal learning such as that occurring out of school and policy at institutional and system level. The report from which these principles were drawn likens educational innovations to a pebble being thrown into a pond (TLRP, 2006). The first ripple may be a change in classroom processes and outcomes, but this may have implications for teachers' roles, values, knowledge and beliefs. This may require a change in professional development and training that may, in turn, influence school structure and even national policy. The key point here (illustrated in Fig. 5.2) is that changes at any one of these levels may have implications elsewhere.

The UK and US educational reports discussed above make no mention of the biological processes involved with learning. Instead, there is an emphasis on social construction, learning within groups and communities, and the importance of context. Additionally, there are issues of meaning, the will to learn, values and the distributed nature of these and other aspects of learning beyond the level of the individual.

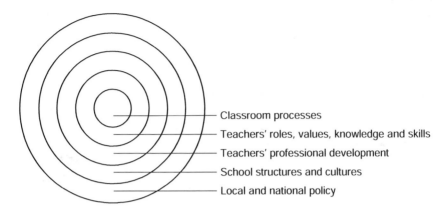

Figure 5.2 Levels of educational change as proposed in a recent commentary by the Teaching and Learning Research Programme (TLRP, 2006).
Source: Adapted with permission from TLRP (2007) *Principles into practice: A teacher's guide to research evidence on teaching and learning*, London: Teaching and Learning Research Programme. Reprinted with permission from TLRP Copyright © 2007.

Concerns about the incompatibility of neuroscientific and educational perspectives on learning

Studying the discourse between neuroscience and education reveals tendencies by some commentators to stray into 'non-sense', i.e. to use words and language that conflict with established understanding in one or both domains. These errors can give rise to misunderstandings about what neuroscience can provide evidence for and, more broadly, they might be symptomatic of what happens when two fields interact that are essentially incompatible or irrelevant to each other. However, it can also be shown that these errors revolve around some quite old but important philosophical issues. Indeed, such misunderstandings merely demonstrate the need for a more sophisticated understanding of the brain in education. One type of misunderstanding is an extreme form of *dualism*: in which the mind and brain are considered as separate and distinct. The reverse point of view, that they are one and the same, is described here as *monism*.

Monism: Does brain = mind?

The very different perspectives on learning within neuroscience and education have prompted some commentators to make objections in principle to any claim that neuroscience can be relevant to education. For example, one author has explored the possibility that such claims involve a fundamental 'category mistake'(Davis, 2004). To illustrate this possibility, Davis refers to an article in

Educational Leadership in which the author discusses learning something new by speaking of the brain looking 'for an existing circuit or network into which the information will fit' (Wolfe, 1998, p. 64). In this article, the author goes on to discuss how reading about quantum physics cannot make meaningful sense without previously stored information about physics. Davis correctly identifies the author's implicit suggestion that she has empirical evidence for a conceptual truth. Further, Davis suggests this is a typical category mistake, in the sense that connections between psychological items are being confused with neurophysiological connections.

In terming this a category error, there is the suggestion that the writer considers the mind, or our 'mental domain', as a category distinct from the brain, but that she has made a mistake in using these two categories – a type of dualism gone wrong. An alternative explanation is that the writer is applying a simplistic brain–mind model that appears to inappropriately conflate the two concepts as one – a type of neurocognitive monism. If we consider the mind and brain as the same thing, we can use terms usually associated with the mind to describe the brain, e.g. 'my brain is confused'. In the instance described by Davis, if Wolfe has made a category mistake, this could be an accidental error. Alternatively, she may be deliberately conflating mind and brain in order to provide some provisional truth that is more digestible and more clearly supports the pedagogic advice being promoted. Suggesting one-to-one correspondences between connections in the mind and synaptic connections in the brain is typical of the type of folk cognitive neuroscience used to promote many commercial 'brain-based' educational programmes. But, as is often the case, there is also some grain of truth upon which her explanation is founded. As we have seen, a connection between two concepts in the mind is commonly considered by scientists to involve the making of neuronal connections, or a change in the connection strength between neurons. As described by Mel (2002): 'pull the average neuroscientist off the street and ask them how learning occurs in the brain, and you're likely to get a reflex response that includes such pat phrases as "activity-dependent changes in synaptic strength, LTP/LTD"....'. However, as described above, there are some worrying flaws in arguments promoting such mechanisms as a sufficient basis for learning. Therefore, given this state of affairs, Davis may be correct in suggesting that neuroscience should not be used to provide any additional support for the promotion of psychological concepts of meaning-making. These concepts should be sold on the basis of the psychological and educational evidence that supports them, rather than promoted on the basis of proposed neuroscientific processes that have not been scientifically studied in this context. Returning to the philosophical issue that underlies such misleading promotions, it could be argued that neuroscience itself is policed well enough to avoid monistic confusions. In the author's view, these are quite rare, if only because there are experts in both the brain and the mind who are defensive of their territory being misappropriated by the other. Monist statements, then, appear most dangerous within education, where they often support the impression of conclusive and concrete biological evidence for a psychological idea about how our minds work (or even that a previous biological observation can now be given psychological relevance) when, in fact, no such evidence exists.

Some, however, might disagree that neuroscience is immune to this type of conceptual conflation. Bennett and Hacker (2003) suggest modern neuroscience itself, rather than just those wishing to interpret it in educational terms, is also beset with confusions arising from attempts to portray our emotional, cognitive and perceptual mental states as states of the brain. The claim here appears to be that scientists are prone to their own type of absolute monism, i.e. a belief that the mind can be fully described by states of the brain. In the sense that our mind's contents is influenced by a variety of other external and internal factors beyond the brain itself, Bennett and Hacker suggest that ascribing our mental states to brain states is no more sensible than ascribing them to an immaterial soul. Bennett and Hacker accuse scientists of contributing to the impression that our minds are our brains through unrelenting efforts to use metaphors in describing *representations* in the brain (e.g. 'maps', 'symbols', 'images') when these, as commonly understood, cannot possibly exist there. There is no map to be found in the brain, and no pictorial representation that follows conventions easily read by a map-reader. So, Bennett and Hacker conclude, neuroscience is clearly using 'old' terms in new ways. However, the fluid use of such metaphors can also be viewed as a standard scientific tool. It helps prompt investigations that test and formulate hypotheses that are, at least in an absolute sense, already known to be false but whose investigation reveals deeper understanding of the underlying reality (Churchland, 2005). For example, few scientists would ever have imagined there are two-dimensional maps in the brain that use easily under-stood conventions, but attempts to find something similar have been revealing. And these metaphors still retain some meaning: there is, for example, a complex, interactive but essentially topographical mapping of sensory information at dif-ferent levels of the sensory pathway. The meaning of 'map' in this context is thus contingent, and emerges and develops with the conceptual progress made by testing the hypotheses the metaphor generates. That said, Bennett and Hacker (2003) correctly point out that the 'original' meanings of such words often have their basis in a folk psychology that is not policed by the sorts of revisionary pressures within science. That makes it easy to understand how the meanings ascribed to the same vocabulary within the neuroscientific and other communi-ties, including education, have been rapidly diverging.

Dualism: Are brain and mind distinct concepts?

The extreme dualist confusion also affords the promotion of other misunder-standings. If the mind is entirely separate from the brain, then one can make statements about brain-behaviour relationships without considering the mind (and vice versa). If we consider the mind and brain as separate entities, then the mind has no efficacy upon the brain, or the brain upon the mind. Indeed, if such a case holds, it is difficult to imagine any possibility of mind-brain interaction. Again, like monism, few would express such a dualistic view explicitly, but it is not hard to find its implicit influence. Partly, this can arise because many neuroscientists have an understandable desire to publish their work without becoming embroiled with issues that psychologists and philosophers feel more comfortable with. It can seem wise to avoid explicit consideration of how the biological processes they are studying might be related to complex cognition, particularly of the types associated with such problematic areas as consciousness. Unfortunately, this can ultimately result in almost a denial of the mind-brain relationship.

For example, consider the quotation from a scientist that Davis uses to defend his position. This is suggestive of mind and brain as two distinct concepts: 'Our brains do not understand. They do not assign or contemplate meanings. They are only electrical and chemical processes in brain activity which would have no meaning except insofar as they are the working of cognitive tools that *people* use to think with' (Harre, 2002). Such a statement, suggesting that the brain may reflect the mind but does not contribute to mental meaning, brings us close to a dualistic sense of mind as a concept that should be considered entirely separately from the physical world, including the brain. To lend sense to the statement that a living brain cannot possess some understanding, it must be possible to separate entirely the concepts of mind and brain (or, alternatively, the brain in question has some serious problems). It is not difficult to find evidence of a dualist approach existing implicitly in matters connected with the brain, including among scientists. Degrandpre conducted a scathing analysis (Degrandpre, 1999) of what he called the rise of a 'new scientific dualism'. He reviewed several studies to support this view. One of these claimed differences in brain function between two samples of children, with and without Attention-Deficit Hyperactivity Disorder (ADHD), might provide the basis for 'biologically valid criteria' for diagnosis (Vaidya *et al.*, 1998). This study implied these biological differences were causal and led to headlines such as 'Test found to identify attention disorder'. As pointed out by Degrandpre, however, the results might equally be the physiological correlates of a behavioural disorder caused by some other factor. This extra factor might be an environmental one, such as their education. The tendency to ignore such factors, as in this confusion between correlation and causation, may arise from an assumption, implicit or otherwise, that the brain can be considered independently of the mind and the external influences upon it.

Another example demonstrates the dangers of such dualism, covert or otherwise, for education. In a local newspaper (Parkinson, 2006), a headteacher discusses the challenge provided by a child suffering from ADHD: 'He is uncontrollable and we do not have the facility or resources at the school to cope with his intolerable behaviour ... this is a medical problem and we need to find a solution that is best for everyone'. Here, it appears that the biological aspects of ADHD have surfaced as its most salient feature just when all educational efforts to support the child have failed. This may be because medicalization of a problem effectively shifts the focus of professional responsibility. If brain can be conceptually separated from the mind, cause can be attributed in totality to the biology of the brain, leaving the educator's domain of influence.

Brain processes, however, are clearly more than just a *reflection* of our mind's attempt to assign and contemplate meaning, since their suppression (through trauma or experimental techniques such as transcranial magnetic stimulation, TCMS) reduces such abilities. In reality, then, brain processes appear intimately bound up with our mental abilities. Indeed, our personalities, values and recall of what we have learnt and experienced can all be influenced by the biology of our brains. Furthermore, and as discussed above, we know that our mental life, as stimulated by our experiences, can influence our brain development at a number of different levels. So, although slipping into dualism can be, for purely pragmatic reasons, attractive for educators and scientists alike, it seems unwise and nonsensical to consider the mind and brain in separation from each other.

Returning to the example of ADHD, the prevalent use of drugs in its treatment does not make it a wholly a medical problem beyond the influence of the school environment. On the contrary, there is growing evidence that teachers following informed strategies have an important role in improving the well-being and academic performance of students suffering from ADHD (Corkum *et al.*, 2005; Gureasko-Moore *et al.*, 2006; Miranda *et al.*, 2002). Successful interventions have included the application of cognitive and instructional approaches to managing children's behaviour, the inclusion of parents and teachers in such interventions, and the training of students themselves in self-management. This research emphasizes the importance of teachers' understanding of the disorder, its medication and management. It also reminds us of the practical benefits of avoiding dualist notions.

Mind and brain together: cognitive neuroscience

Understanding the dangers of monism and dualism leads to a desire to understand mind and brain as concepts under constructions, words we use to describe the mental and biological aspects of our behaviour, aspects which are intimately related in some way, which is often still to be determined. For one thing science has certainly learned is that the interrelation between mind and brain is not straightforward. Indeed, a whole field of scientific research, cognitive neuroscience, has been founded on efforts to achieve this understanding. Cognitive neuroscientists believe that mind and brain must be explained together (Blakemore and Frith, 2000). Cognitive neuroscience, with its interest in the mind, is the field of neuroscience of most interest to educators. In this field, the notion of mind is regarded as a theoretical but essential concept in exploring the relationship between our brain and our behaviour, including our learning. Seen in this way, the study of cognition is a vital part of the neuroscience-education bridge, since it links our knowledge of the brain to our observations of behaviours involving learning. Indeed, it has been pointed out that without sufficient attendance to suitable cognitive psychological models, neuroscience will have little to offer education (Bruer, 1997).

Figure 5.3 shows a well known model used by cognitive neuroscientists to combine environmental, biological, cognitive and behavioural levels of description (Morton and Frith, 1995). Invisible cognition is portrayed as sandwiched between behaviour (which is usually observable and measurable) and biological processes (which can sometimes be scientifically observed and recorded), with environmental factors influencing outcomes at each stage. For example, we have seen that activity in the DLPFC (brain level) can increase with increased working memory load (a cognitive concept) which can occur when an individual carries out a mathematical process (with a behavioural outcome – i.e. producing an answer). Note that, in this brain–mind–behaviour model, the term 'environment' must be considered in terms of the level being described. For example, at the brain level, the environment is characterized by biological factors that include oxygen and nutrition. At the level of the mind, the environmental cognitive factors include educational, cultural and social influences, whereas behavioural environmental issues include physical opportunities and restrictions.

There are two arrows leading from the brain to the mind, and from mind to behaviour. These arrows indicate the directions in which causal connections are most often sought. The issue of cause, as understood by those working within developmental cognitive neuroscience, is potentially complex and will be returned to again. For the moment, it can be said that behaviour is most often explained in

Examples of Environmental factors	Examples of Intra-individual factors	Factor affected
Oxygen Nutrition Toxins	Synaptogenesis → Synaptic pruning Neuronal connections	BRAIN
Teaching Cultural institutions → Social factors	Learning Memory Emotion	MIND
Temporary restrictions e.g. teaching tools →	Performance Errors Improvement	BEHAVIOUR

Figure 5.3 A model of the brain/mind/behaviour interrelation from Morton and Frith (1995). The notation in the diagram uses arrows to indicate causal influences (dotted lines are the author's–see text). Interactions of external factors with factors that are internal to the individual contribute to causal explanation. 'Facts' are situated at a behavioural and biological level, theories at the cognitive level. The notation can be used to think about links between biology and behaviour via the inferred cognitive level that bridges the gap between them.
Source: Adapted from Blakemore, S. J. and Frith, U. (2000) The implications of recent developments in neuroscience for research on teaching and learning. Exeter: TLRP, adapted with permission from TLRP Copyright © 2000.

terms of the contents of the mind, and cognitive neuroscientists usually attempt to understand the mind by drawing upon our understanding of the brain. Hence, there are arrows leading from brain to mind, and from mind to behaviour. However, these arrows might also be drawn as bi-directional. For example, environmental influences (such as being able to access new stimulus) can influence our behaviour that also, in turn, influences our mental processes. If these processes produce learning, this learning can be assumed to have some neural correlate at a biological level, such as the making of new synaptic connections in the brain. We have also seen that continual rehearsal of mental processes can even produce changes in the brain in terms of its structure, i.e. the shape and size of its component parts. These directions of influence have traditionally been of less interest to cognitive neuroscientists and this may explain their omission in this model. However, they are, of course, of considerable interest to educators – who often attempt to enrich minds (and brains) by organizing the behaviour of learners, and so these directions of influence are represented here (with dotted arrows). This is one important way in which a model of description for neuroeducational researchers may differ from that currently used in cognitive neuroscience.

Leaving behind biologically privileged learning – a 'levels of action' model for neuroscience and education

Another criticism, in principle, of efforts to include the brain in educational understanding is that neuroscience cannot provide the types of explanation required for improving instruction. Schumacher suggests neuroscientific studies may inform psychological understanding about learning but its biologically privileged explanations are of no direct interest to educators (Schumacher, 2007). Biologically privileged learning is described by Schumacher as occurring if 'biological programmes determine which learning processes are initiated by which environmental influences, at which developmental stage, and taking which way of execution' (p. 387). In particular, Schumacher (2007) and Davis (2004), emphasize the importance of social and cultural factors in learning which cannot be excluded from such explanations. However, there is no conflict here with current neuroscientific thinking which has a strong appreciation of environmental influence on development. On the contrary, one leading developmental cognitive neuroscientist has commented: 'Cause is not an easy word. Its popular use would be laughable if it was not so dangerous, informing, as it does, government policy on matters that affect us all. There is no single cause of anything and nothing is determined' (John Morton in Howard-Jones, 2007). Of course, although cause is a problematic construct, it is a helpful tool in trying to alleviate the difficulties faced by many children. The important challenge for those reflecting upon cause is to resist being seduced by explanations exclusively privileging factors of one type, be they biological, social or whatever.[2] This will be particularly true for those involved with research at the interface between brain, mind and education, who have much bridge-building between perspectives ahead of them.

In this sense, then, the model of individual development depicted in Fig. 5.3 may be unhelpful in its emphasis upon the individual.

Given the role of social processes in education, the representation of learning in terms of two individuals interacting (as in Fig. 5.4) becomes more appropriately suggestive of the complexity of interrelating brain processes with behaviour (including learning behaviour) within educational contexts. The two individuals may be two learners or, perhaps, a teacher and learner. In this diagram, the space between the individuals is filled by a sea of symbols representing human communication in all its forms. The lines separating brain, mind, behaviour and this sea of symbols are shown as dotted, to emphasize their somewhat indistinct nature and the difficulty in clearly defining concepts lying close to them.

Travelling across 'levels of action'

In this conceptual framework, neither natural nor social science, on its own, offers sufficient traction to travel across all levels of description. In Fig 5.4, the

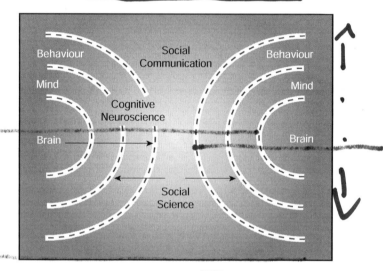

Figure 5.4 To interrelate the most valuable insights from cognitive neuroscience and the social science perspectives of education (represented by arrows), the brain-mind-behaviour model may need to be socially extended. Even two individuals interacting, as represented here, is suggestive of the complexity that can arise when behaviour becomes socially mediated. Such complexity remains chiefly the realm of social scientists, who often interpret the meaning of such communication in order to understand the underlying behaviour. Cognitive neuroscience has established its importance in understanding behaviour at an individual level but is only just beginning to contemplate the types of complex social domains studied by educational researchers.
Source: Howard-Jones, P. A. (2007) Neuroscience and education: Issues and opportunities, London: Teaching and Learning Research programme. Reprinted with permission from TLRP Copyright © 2007.

arrows attempt to indicate the most frequently (but not exclusively) travelled pathways of investigation associated with different epistemologies. Cognitive neuroscience is marked by an arrow extending from the brain to behaviour. This natural science concerns itself with relating measurable neurobiological systems to the behavioural responses of individuals, via a construction of the mind represented by cognitive models. Experiments usually consist of highly controlled procedures involving the production of simple and quantifiable responses. For example, in a study of reading acquisition, Turkeltaub *et al.* (2003) used an implicit reading task (in which reading happens automatically) so that all ages could perform equally well, to overcome the problem that developmental imaging studies require equal performance across age groups. In their task, participants were presented with words and strings of meaningless symbols, and were asked to detect whether a feature (a tall symbol) was present. The additional activity when detecting features in words, compared with symbols, provided the neural correlates of reading in this task (see fMRI method of contrasts in the next chapter). Studying reading activity in this way, researchers found a gradual disengagement of right hemisphere regions (involved with visual memory) and increased activity in left language regions (involved with phonological processing) as children's reading ability improved. This is important, since it supports an existing psychological model of reading in which early readers move from a reliance on visual features of letters to developing a phoneme-grapheme correspondence. When biological and cognitive concepts of development resonate in this way, one can feel more confident about the validity of both. These results might also, for example, help explain how trauma in a particular region of the brain may influence reading development. It does not, however, provide an entire explanation of how we come to read, since many other factors, including our education, influence this outcome. Neither can it prove that reading begins as a result of activity shifting from right to left regions. It could as meaningfully be said that the shift has occurred because reading has developed. Dyslexic readers show decreased activity in left-hemisphere regions associated with phonological processing. Again, this indicates a potential link between their reading difficulties and their ability to process phonological information, without necessarily proving any causal link (it may, instead, be due to less rehearsal of phonological processing due to some other source of reading difficulty, exacerbating reading problems further). This type of evidence does, however, suggest interventions based on improving auditory and oral language skills, and these have been shown to help remediate both the reading difficulties and the associated brain activities (Shaywitz *et al.*, 2004). At the associated levels of action (which appear at an individual level of brain-mind-behaviour), this natural science investigation has proved very valuable.

However, when it comes to a fuller understanding of how such interventions are applied, individual differences in teachers' interactions with children may need to be explored. Here, meaning-based interpretations of the discourse between teacher and pupil are useful in understanding the factors influencing pupils' progress. The meanings ascribed to our actions, including our use of language, are multiple, ambivalent and transitory. The production of language has been a fruitful area for scientific research, but the interpretation of meaning within everyday contexts is essentially a problematic area for experimental scientific paradigms. Interpretations of meaning that cannot be judged by the methods of natural science may be considered beyond its jurisdiction. Leaving aside issues of interpretation, the difficulties in using current imaging technology to study everyday social interaction also provides a barrier for neuroscientists approaching the sea of symbols – at least at present. The recent flourishing of journals focusing on social cognitive neuroscience demonstrate the beginning of efforts in this area, but interpretation of social complexity remains chiefly the realm of social scientists, who are accomplished in interpreting the meaning of such communications in order to understand their fuller significance.

A neuroeducational researcher wishing to carry out a classroom study of an intervention to remediate dyslexia based on neuroscientific research might, therefore, face the task of integrating insights from the perspectives of both natural and social science, and in ways that are mindful of the different epistemologies that gave rise to them. Although challenging, this is very different from a wholesale commitment to a biologically privileged approach to learning divorced from all considerations of context, such as that feared by Davis (2004) and Schumacher (2007). Historically, it may be true that ideas linking learning and development have often emphasized the constraining nature of our biology and our biological development upon our learning. Piaget was criticized for suggesting that learning 'merely utilizes the achievements of development rather than providing an impetus for modifying its course' (Vygotsky, 1978, pp. 79–80) and even Bruner, though acknowledging that learning can lead to development (Bruner, 1974, p. 417) discussed the psychobiology of pedagogy chiefly in terms of the *constraints* provided by the human nervous system (Bruner, 1972, pp. 118–31). However, in the proposed framework, boundaries with bi-directional permeability emphasize the role of the educational social environment, and to an extent that it influences our biological development. Such an approach discourages notions of biological privilege, reflecting more accurately present notions of development within cognitive neuroscience.

What about the free will of the individual?

As discussed above, effective teaching and learning is considered by many to depend upon the promotion of learners' independence (TLRP, 2007, p. 9). Educators believe they are striving to produce autonomous learners, personally motivated and able to learn in response to their own free will. Neuroscience, on the other hand, is presently unsure how, and even whether, free will comes into existence. Studies suggest that the experience of a conscious action often departs from processes more likely to be causal and so might not reflect direct perceptions of any conscious thought that may have caused the action. For example, when TCMS was applied to influence respondents' movements of their fingers, they reported that they were consciously willing their fingers, even though this was clearly not the case (Brasil-Neto *et al.*, 1992). In spontaneous intentional finger movement, another study showed electrical brain activity preceding action by at least 550 ms, with participants' awareness that they had made a decision *following* some 350-400 ms after this signal (Gazzaniga, 1995). Some scientists suggest, therefore, that our sense of free will is a trick, just the mind's way of estimating its own *apparent* authorship by drawing causal inferences about relationships between thoughts and actions (Wegner, 2003). Unsurprisingly, this has been identified as another type of biological privilege likely to cause conflict for those working at the interface between neuroscience and education (Giesinger, 2006).

However, educators can feel reassured that denying the existence of free will brings neuroscience into conflict not just with education but also with the entire legal system (Burns and Bechara, 2007). Since discussions about the existence of free will are bound up with those about consciousness, these are unlikely to be resolved in the near future (Tancredi, 2007). In the meantime, we most of us share, to a greater or lesser extent, some existing construction about free will as a highly prized causal factor in our behaviour.

Despite the popularity of educational concepts such as the 'independent learner' and the 'autonomous learner', free will has never been a serious focus of educational research, possibly because of the conceptual and methodological difficulties associated with studying it. Given the debates within neuroscience around the concept of free will, there is a danger that researchers at the interface of neuroscience and education may find convenience in excluding its consideration, despite this being antithetical to many educational aims. To understand how such concepts may be included, it may be useful to consider the field of social psychology, where similar potential conflicts between perspectives exist. In the context of personal growth and development, the role of free will is highly valued and frequently a focus for humanitarian psychologists employing experiential research techniques. One such psychologist is Richard Stevens, who has reflected on how experiential insights involving issues of free will and autonomy may be interrelated with concepts from the natural and social sciences. Stevens' 'Trimodal' theory interrelates perspectives in a practical manner based upon 'mode of action' (Stevens, 1998). Although originally intended to describe social behaviour, the trimodal approach will be illustrated here in terms of learning. In trimodal terminology, the *primary* mode of learning arises from the physical embodiment of the learner. This provides a basis for learning that is best described in terms of biological and neurophysiological processes whose scientific study can help explain our thinking and learning mechanisms in terms of causal models that may be informed by, and inform, our understanding of brain function. In trimodal theory, it is these primary mechanisms that support the emergence of symbol systems and the use of language, thus facilitating a *secondary* basis for learning. It is the use of symbol systems that makes it a meaning-based mode of learning that involves interpretation by those participating in it and by those attempting to investigate it. Thus, as discussed above in the context of teacher–pupil interaction, Stevens suggests this basis for learning is often best explored through the perspectives of social science, with a perspective that is appropriately sensitized to the unique and complex nature of meaningful social contexts. According to Stevens, it is our ability to use such symbols that crucially supports our formation and manipulation of concepts, including those that describe ourselves. Thus, from the secondary symbolic mode of action emerges a third basis for action – our reflexive awareness. This *tertiary* mode involves self-awareness and reflective choice. Here, our actions are less determined solely by primary biological and cognitive processes and/or by secondary meaning-based processes. This is the level at which the learner generates some autonomy through a capacity to reflect upon his/herself and the events in his/her life. At the tertiary level, investigation becomes something of a moral science. It is concerned with the choices we make and how things, including ourselves, *could* be. Of course, such investigation can still be informed by knowledge of learning processes at the primary and secondary levels, as provided by the natural and social sciences.

Many educational issues involve free will, and this reminds us of the importance of experiential 'insider' perspectives in education, i.e. from the accounts of the learner themselves. Figure 5.4 is suggestive of an 'outsider' model of learning involving processes that can be studied socially and biologically from observers standing on the outside and looking in, but there is no tertiary level of action representing the learner's reflections and freely-willed choices here. Perhaps reflective of our lack of understanding of consciousness, it is not easy to represent a tertiary level of action in such a diagram. However, given the growing emphasis on learning autonomy in education, neuroeducational researchers need to remain mindful that, in some ways, Fig. 5.4 is a poor representation of what can be a dynamic scenario of personal change and transformation. In the real world, tertiary processes such as those involving free will and reflexive self-determination, are making powerful contributions to learning that are likely to interact with all the levels of action described in this diagram.

Finally, let us return to why all this philosophy is important. Philosophy investigates the 'bounds of sense: that is, the limits of what can coherently be thought and said' (Bennett and Hacker, 2003, p. 399). Those who attempt to work at the interface of neuroscience and education will find themselves straddled across at least two, very different, philosophies (even if many members of both communities tend not to concern themselves with philosophy!). This has one very clear implication: great care is needed to generate messages that retain coherence, in terms of their meaning within both these communities. In this and previous chapters, we have heard several everyday statements being made by scientists and educators that sound like sense to most within their own community, but are 'non-sense' to the other. The 'levels of action' framework described here reminds us of the interrelation of the different perspectives that can contribute to our understanding of learning, and thus provides a basis for 'sense' to be constructed that preserves meaning across perspectives.

Although it does not provide any immediate solution to the philosophical gap that exists between perspectives, it may be helpful to those working to close that gap, by suggesting the value of a multi-perspective approach and by supporting the interrelation of different types of findings.

Summary

Neuroscience and education currently understand learning in diverse ways. However, common transgressions in sense-making at their interface do not reflect any fundamental incompatibility between these two areas. Rather, they reflect the need for an educational understanding that includes the cognitive neuroscience perspective.

To support the interrelation of different perspectives on learning, a brain–mind–behaviour model from cognitive neuroscience has been extended to include a greater emphasis on social interaction and construction. This provides a helpful 'levels of action' framework for examining the potentially complex inter-relationships between the different learning philosophies, concepts and types of finding that will contribute to neuroeducational research. This theoretical framework reminds us of the value of natural science approaches to understanding primary biological processes, and social science approaches to understanding secondary social processes that require meaning-based interpretation. It is, however, less effective at highlighting tertiary 'insider' perspectives (including that of the learner his/herself) that are of considerable importance in education, especially in respect of transformative experience and change. Neuroeducational researchers should remain particularly mindful of the experiential perspective, to ensure concepts that are valued in education, such as free will, are not ignored, despite their problematic history within biological approaches to learning.

With this 'road map' in hand, it is possible to travel across levels of action to imagine how different insights combine to provide a more integrated understanding of specific educational issues. The next chapter will build upon this theoretical framework. It will examine more closely its implications for developing and applying methods of data collection in attempts to construct knowledge spanning neuroscience and education.

Chapter 6

Methodology in neuroeducational research

In Chapter 4, the notion of a field of neuroeducational research was suggested that might further both scientific and educational understanding. It is proposed here that the two goals of such a field are:

1   To further educational understanding and practice, through the inclusion of insight derived from the sciences of brain and mind.
2   To further scientific understanding of the complex interrelationship between mind, brain and learning, through the engagement of natural science with the context of education.

These goals emphasize the need for two-way dialogue between neuroscience and education in order to construct knowledge that draws on both disciplines. They also draw attention to how their professional aims may complement each other.

Szucs and Goswami (2007) point out that this new field will be founded, in part, on methodological foundations. This is undoubtedly true, although the nature of the methodological foundations appears still open to debate. For example, reviewing the limitations of current neuroscience methods in meeting the field's new demands, Szucs and Goswami focus chiefly on the need to acknowledge the technical limits of current imaging techniques, particularly in terms of poor ecological validity and constrained temporal and spatial resolution. They propose that 'complex educational tasks must be analysed and translated into simple tasks within the neuroscience laboratory and placed within a framework of meticulously designed experimental procedures which together may shed light on an educational question' (p. 122). However, the task of producing the knowledge required to implement educational insights derived from neuroscience is likely to extend beyond such experiments. This knowledge must take account not just of primary biological and cognitive processes that can be studied in the laboratory, but also how these processes involve themselves in the social world of the classroom, including the experience of the learner and teacher. Neuroeducational scientific studies will, undoubtedly, be important in developing scientific insights that are closer to educational understanding. However, 'bridging' studies are also needed in order to investigate the relevance and potential implications of these insights in the classroom, and practice-based studies will be required for the development of educational practice that includes them.

Such reflection suggests neuroeducational research may involve three categories of studies:

1 *Scientific studies* aimed at revealing new scientific knowledge about the mind and brain more closely related to issues regarding educational intervention, thus supporting conceptualization across perspectives.
2 *Bridging studies* aimed at further scrutinizing the potential educational relevance and effectiveness of concepts about learning that span educational and neuropsychological understanding.
3 *Practice-based studies* aimed at developing pedagogical concepts, language, understanding and transfer of good practice based on the above.

It will be important that these studies are not done in isolation from each other. Both goals of neuroeducational research individually demand education and the sciences of brain and mind should inform each other. So, if the above types of study are to serve neuroeducational goals, the concepts, findings and direction associated with each of these three types of study should be open to influence by one another, even though it may involve collecting an entirely different type of evidence and/or analysing it in an entirely different way. We will see that this need to relate concepts and findings associated with different forms of evidence has a significant impact on the methods and techniques used to produce this evidence. This chapter aims to explore the impact of neuroeducational goals on research methodology in more detail, beginning with a look at the disparate types of evidence involved. It then examines a small sample of the techniques used to collect these types of evidence and some of the methods that employ them. This provides a basis for examining how such methods and techniques are influenced by the need to interrelate different types of study, which is an important challenge in neuroeducational research.

EVIDENCE

There are three fundamental types of evidence that can help us understand learning. Two of these sources of evidence (biological and social) derive from consideration of Fig. 5.4 in the previous chapter. However, as was discussed, Fig. 5.4 is a representation of learning from the outside, and does not include the experiential perspective which provides a valuable third source of evidence in respect of, for example, our constructions relating to free will and autonomy. Secondly, note the absence of anything we could describe as direct 'cognitive evidence' since, if we consider the mind as an intangible and theoretical concept, we cannot produce thought as evidence itself. (Even self-reports of our own thoughts are subject to constraints of language and mediated by our own personal interpretations, and so are better described as an important type of experiential evidence.) That leaves us with social, biological and experiential sources of evidence for understanding the wide range of environmental factors, behaviours and other phenomena we presently associate with learning (see Fig. 6.1). Whatever methods we presently use to unravel learning, they usually include techniques for recording evidence we associate with learning, or assume to be of the learning itself, and these always derive from one or more of these three fundamental types.

We will now consider some of the techniques used to mine these three sources of evidence, before looking at some examples of the methods that have employed them, and how these can be implemented in the three types of study described above. (The word 'technique' refers here to means of gathering data, whereas 'method' refers to how such techniques are used, and often combined, to answer research questions). It should be noted from the outset that there is no simple one-to-one correspondence between the three types of study and the three types of evidence they draw on. As this chapter develops, it will be clear that how the different types of study draw on these three types of evidence depends upon, among other issues, the educational topic of interest. However, it will also become clear that an investigation with neuroeducational goals can benefit from researchers being mindful of all three types of evidence when pursuing each type of study, to the extent of adapting the methods and techniques of a study in order to collect all three types.

The interdisciplinary nature of neuroeducational research makes it impossible to review all the techniques and methods that may be employed. The selection below has been chosen to help the reader appreciate the case studies in later chapters, but is pitifully small in relation to the full range that might be use-fully involved. However, this selection still gives some sense of the diversity of

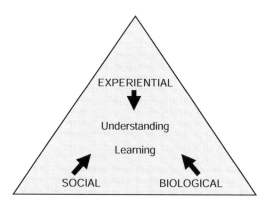

Figure 6.1 There are three fundamental types of evidence to draw upon when attempting to understand the wide range of environmental factors, behaviours and other phenomena we associate with learning: social, biological and experiential.

methods and techniques that may be required, and emphasizes the unique challenge of neuroeducational research in practical terms.

NEUROEDUCATIONAL TECHNIQUES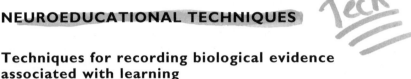

Techniques for recording biological evidence associated with learning

Functional magnetic resonance imaging (fMRI)

Perhaps the technique known as functional magnetic resonance imaging (fMRI) has produced the most highly publicized images of brain activity in recent years, thanks to the high quality spatial resolution this technique provides.

In this method, the participant is placed with a strong magnetic field (about 10,000 times the strength of the Earth's magnetic field). The hydrogen nuclei (or protons) in the participant's body respond to this field by aligning themselves with it. A secondary magnetic field produced by a coil around the head is then pulsed at radio frequency and this causes the protons to temporarily change their alignment again. It is the way in which the protons relax back that produces the important signal, which can be picked up by the coil. Hemoglobin has different magnetic properties depending on whether it is oxygenated or not and, in the brain, this depends on the activity of local neurons. Thus, by computerized analysis of the relaxation signal, it is possible to determine a blood-oxygen-level dependent (or BOLD) signal in different parts of the brain.

The chief advantage of fMRI, compared with other brain imaging techniques, is a spatial resolution that allows identification of activity within 3 mm. However, due to the time taken for the blood to respond, its temporal resolution is a few seconds. This is a long time in cognitive terms (bearing in mind how quickly we can recognize a word, or attend to an image). fMRI is referred to by medical experts as 'entirely non-invasive' because no physical material passes into the body (Detre and Floyd, 2001), but the participant may not always find it a comfortable experience. Participants must lie in the narrow bore of the magnet, with their head strapped inside a secondary coil and their vision restricted. Additionally, the technique produces considerable noise so ear protection must be worn.

Changes in BOLD signals associated with undertaking a particular task are very small and tasks in different conditions often have to be repeated many times in order to produce meaningful images displaying statistically significant activity. As with other imaging and experimental techniques, attempts are made to control extraneous variables that add additional variance, or noise, to the BOLD signal. This provides an experience for the participant which may depart considerably from anything resembling a classroom or 'everyday' learning experience. Nevertheless, well-designed experiments using fMRI have provided invaluable insights into the neurocognition of many learning processes of educational interest, including the remediation of dyslexia and the learning of complex arithmetic.

Positron emission tomography (PET)

In this technique, the participant may be injected with compounds such as glucose that are 'labelled' with a small dose of radioactivity. Since neurons that are more active will demand more glucose, radioactivity (in the form of positrons) temporarily collects in regions of the brain where activity is greatest, and this radioactivity can be located and measured by external sensors. This allows a 3D construction of brain activity to be computed (a process known as tomography) from BOLD activity. Due to the minor risk associated with the dose of radioactivity, this technique can be carried out only a few times on a single participant. Its spatial resolution is inferior to fMRI and its temporal resolution is also poor. However, by using compounds other than glucose, it is possible to target processes involving specific neurotransmitters, and this has helped maintain PET's prominence as a useful research technique.

Magnetoencephalography (MEG)

It is possible to circumvent the temporal issues involved with the BOLD signal and measure neural activity more directly. One way of doing this is by measuring the magnetic field produced by electrical firing of neurons. These changes in field strength are very small, with an estimated 10,000–100,000 neurons required to fire in temporal synchrony in order to produce a detectable signal. However, through careful measurement and calculation, it is possible to work backwards and estimate the level of electrical neural activity that would have produced the magnetic field change. Spatial resolution is still not good, partly because the signal from an individual neuron depends upon its orientation within the cortex, but very rapid changes of neural activity in time can be revealed. Although it is currently the most expensive imaging technique in common use, there is increasing interest in MEG's potential to image changes in activity in brain regions from moment to moment.

Electroencephalography (EEG)

It is also possible to make measurements of electrical field changes due to neural activity. An array of small electrodes attached to the scalp can be used to measure the tiny voltage changes at different points on the scalp, producing an electroencephalogram, or EEG. Temporal resolution, as with MEG, is extremely good, and frequency analysis of the waveforms recorded reveals delta, theta, alpha, beta, gamma wave patterns that are each associated with particular cognitive functions and different regions of the brain. It is possible to build a spatial map from such signals, although spatial resolution is very poor. Compared with MEG, EEG is more sensitive to tissue conductivity differences and calculations are more complex, which can lead to a further decrease in localization accuracy (Rampp and Stefan, 2007). When used to detect responses to particular events, such as the presentation of an acoustic stimulus, the event-related potential (ERP) can be recorded as a slow wave that is either negative (N) or positive (P). For example, the P200 is a standard 200 ms positive ERP regularly observed after many different types of stimulus presentation, making it easier to identify and compare it across experimental conditions. Used in this way, temporal resolution is excellent and it is the cheapest and most portable of the techniques reviewed here. It is also the most comfortable and least intimidating, with the possibility of using it in more everyday settings with children of all ages able to wear the 'hair net' of electrodes (including babies). This has allowed many valuable insights into early language development, such as the fact that children as young as 4–5 months are sensitive to the rhythmic characteristics of language (Weber et al., 2004), supporting the development of new theories about dyslexia (Goswami et al., 2002).

Simpler body-based physiological signals

There are other physiological signals beyond brain activity that can be helpful in understanding cognition, and particularly with respect to emotional response. A now famous experiment by Antoine Bechara and colleagues showed that participants started generating anticipatory skin conductivity responses when pondering choices that turned out to be risky, even prior to explicitly knowing they were risky (Bechara et al., 1997). This prompted the development of the 'somatic marker' hypothesis, in which emotion-related signals can precede conscious decision-making (Bechara et al., 2005).

Although very cheap, non-invasive and portable, one problem with such simple physiological measures (heart rate, skin conductivity, skin temperature, breathing rate) is that, although they may tell us that some sort of emotio-cognitive processing is occurring, it is often difficult to be more specific. Insofar as these are bodily responses, they are often further removed from mental processes than brain-based measurements. However, bodily responses are considered to have a close association with some processes involving emotions, and research involving response to emotional pictures has suggested that a combination of such measures can be effective in distinguishing between the basic emotions of happiness, surprise, anger, fear, sadness and disgust (Collet et al., 1997).

Techniques for recording social evidence associated with learning

The term 'social evidence' is used here in the broader sense, spanning all forms of data collected within social contexts, from quantitative measurements of behaviour that can be collected and statistically analysed to records of dialogue and text that require qualitative interpretation in order to derive their meaning. It includes the type of behavioural responses collected during an experiment in the laboratory (even button pressing reflects a social discourse between participant and experimenter, particularly in respect of the instructions provided). It also includes field notes regarding the behaviour of learners in more naturalistic settings such as the classroom, including spoken dialogue and other vocalizations (e.g. laughter, sighs), gestures, facial expressions and written text. It does not include biological measurement, or data that is alleged to capture someone's personal experience or reflections.

Typical laboratory techniques collecting quantifiable behavioural data can involve the electronic measurement of response times and responses via response boxes or computer keyboards. In more naturalistic settings, highly structured observation of social behaviour, aimed at accurate and objective measurement of precisely defined and operationalized concepts, can also produce quantitative data in the more positivist traditions of the social sciences. Thus, the research setting itself does not decide whether social data is collected qualitatively or quantitatively, but it is does influence the acceptability of the assumptions underlying the researcher's choice. In quantitative data collection subject to statistical testing, considerable assumptions must be made about meaning *before* the data is collected. In the confines of controlled experimentation in the laboratory, where initial assumptions are embodied in the predefined hypotheses under test, it can appear reasonable to make these assumptions. In 'real world' settings such as the classroom, where behaviours are likely to be more complex, it becomes difficult to ignore the wide range of social, cultural and political influences upon them. In the social sciences, an appropriately diverse range of qualitative interpretive techniques have developed to study such contexts and how we behave in them. These techniques usually allow meaning to be a major focus of investigation in itself, allowing it to emerge through the process. Typical data collection techniques include the keeping of field notes and still photography, video and audio recording of naturalistic situations and semistructured interviews, and the collection of texts. After collection, qualitative data is often coded (i.e. categorized), although the way in which this occurs can vary according, again, to basic assumptions about meaning.

Techniques for recording experiential evidence associated with learning

Experiential evidence is data which is intended to reflect a person's experience (e.g. a learner or a teacher). There are no perfect ways to record experiential evidence. Where researchers are intending to reveal the authentic experience of a participant, the choice of techniques and how they are implemented considerably influence the value of the data collected. For example, data collected hurriedly from learners about their experiences at the end of a lesson, using a highly structured multiple-choice questionnaire is likely to be considered low in authenticity. In contrast, conversation-like interviews can provide a participant with the opportunity to reflect and interpret their own thoughts and feelings about issues they consider (rather than the researcher) pertinent to the research question. This approach is likely to provide a more authentic representation of the participant's personal views and constructions. As with other types of qualitative evidence, meaning is derived from the data according to interpretation but, if presented as experiential evidence, such interpretation should be validated by the participant's own reflections.

Participant observation is another method of collecting experiential evidence, this time drawing from the researcher's own experiences. It is derived from the technique used by ethnographers when seeking to describe social contexts in the terms used and understood by its members. Here, the researcher participates in the situation and becomes a member themselves, in order to see the world more from the point of view of those being studied.

In some types of practitioner research, the researcher's own perceptions, in terms of their own understanding and its application in practice, can become the chief focus of the research. Techniques of data collection that support participant-researchers in reflecting upon their own experiences and constructions can include keeping records such as text-based or video diaries. This type of data collection is commonly used in action research methods discussed later in this chapter.

Experiential evidence (as with qualitative social evidence) often resists statistical analysis, because the assumptions upon which such analysis is carried out are often not applicable in 'real world' environments. However, this does not mean that number is necessarily redundant. Just as interpretative observations of social behaviour can be explored with counting, quantity can also be usefully involved in experiential data gathering techniques. For example, in the repertory grid technique, participants are supported by the researcher in exploring their personal constructs around a topic (Kelly, 1955). Together, researcher and participant devise constructs that differentiate between elements (or examples of the topic) and then express these constructs as contrasts on a numerical scale, thus allowing the elements to be characterized in quantifiable terms. George Kelly, who devised the repertory grid technique, did not intend such contrasts to be statistically analysed. Instead, the technique remains a good example of how number can be used to allow more detailed differentiation between personal constructions, providing a stimulating basis for personal reflection and growth.

Techniques for recording evidence of learning

The above techniques can be useful in collecting data thought to be linked in some way with learning. But what of the learning itself – how do we collect evidence of that? We have seen that learning is considered in a variety of different ways in neuroscience and education, from changes in the synaptic connectivity of neurons to the social construction of knowledge in the classroom. It follows that evidence for what we broadly call learning can also be collected using a wide variety of techniques, and all the above have been used to provide it. For example, biological evidence of learning has been derived from brain images of learners before and after educational intervention (Shaywitz *et al.*, 2004), social evidence of learning has been derived from classroom dialogue (Mercer and Wegerif, 1999), and experiential evidence (albeit sometimes lacking in authenticity) is frequently derived from course evaluations that ask students if they feel they have benefited from the course.

In conventional educational terms, however, learning is most often assessed on the basis of highly structured forms of social evidence. That is, we place greatest emphasis on performance in public examinations (written or oral, formal or informal) of knowledge and understanding, as judged against socially derived norms. Perhaps the most closely researched techniques related to these are the paper-based types of laboratory or classroom tests sometimes designed by researchers to measure increases in factual knowledge and/or demonstrable ability to apply understanding in new contexts.

NEUROEDUCATIONAL METHODS

Methods

The above techniques can be used to collect evidence of different types, but their usefulness will depend on their contribution to carefully designed methods aimed at understanding learning and how it comes about. These are methods, or means, by which we can journey across the map in Fig. 5.1, as discussed in the previous chapter. To help illustrate the broad range of the types of methods commonly available, and how these draw on the techniques above, following are a (very) few examples of journeys along some of the best-travelled routes.

Experimental methods of cognitive neuroscience

Cognitive contrast using fMRI

All of our brain is active all the time, but we can find out which parts are more associated with a particular cognitive function than others. We can do this by using the simple method of cognitive contrasts and an imaging technique such as fMRI. Here, at least two experimental conditions are designed that differ only in the cognitive function of interest. The difference in activity between the two conditions, produced by subtracting the data in one condition from data in the other, can be assumed to approximate to the activity produced by the cognitive function of interest.

In this type of experiment, it is important to have a cognitive model (i.e. how we believe the particular learning behaviour we are studying may be represented at the cognitive level of mind) and an anatomical hypothesis (where and how we expect brain activities to change if this cognitive model is correct). A successful prediction allows more confidence in our general understanding of the learning behaviour at both the levels of brain and mind. An unsuccessful prediction may cause us to rethink the cognitive model and/or our understanding of brain function.

Cognitive contrast experiments are the simplest way of using fMRI in cognitive neuroscience. In one such example, Simon *et al.* (2002) investigated the fine organization of activities produced by a range cognitive processes, all of which had been associated with very similar brain regions in the parietal lobe (Simon *et al.*, 2002). Analysis of previous studies suggested these tasks might produce some of the same parietal activations, but it was difficult to be sure because the studies had been produced by different labs using different participants. Here, the cognitive model and anatomical hypotheses were, in effect, quite simple: these are considered as different cognitive processes and may, therefore, be associated with different regions of the parietal lobe. This was an important hypothesis to test because it would shed light on the role of the parietal lobe in these different tasks. If not true, the shared parietal regions would be implicated with some generic mechanism (such as attention) rather than suggesting they hosted a range of different functions in different, but closely organized, parts. Simon *et al.* (2002) asked ten adults to perform six tasks: grasping, pointing, saccades (eye movement), attention, calculation and phoneme detection. In each case, a control task was also used, which differed only in respect of the behaviour of interest being absent. So, in the experimental pointing task, subjects fixated their gaze on a box in the centre of a screen while pointing their finger at wherever another box appeared, while in the control pointing task they kept their finger pointing at the centre box, ignoring the other appearances. Data collected using the control task was subtracted from that collected using the experimental task to create an image of the activity associated with pointing only. A similar contrast analysis for other tasks showed a systematic organization of activations across tasks, but with some regions where these were shared or closely organized. For example, a 'four corners' region was identified in the intra-parietal sulcus in which four regions of activation are juxtaposed, including activity associated with calculation and manual (pointing and grasping) tasks. It has been suggested that this proximity of functionally distinct regions for manual and mathematical tasks gives advantage to the use of fingers in calculation.

The method of cognitive contrast is still used with imaging techniques, but increasingly methods have become more sophisticated. More modern approaches include designs that attempt to identify correlations between changes in the BOLD signal and behavioural parameters (parametric modulation designs). Dynamic causal modelling approaches are also becoming popular. These allow inferences about connectivity, i.e. how different brain regions are coupled and how that coupling is influenced by experimental variables that the experimenter is manipulating (Friston *et al.*, 2003).

Experimental methods of cognitive psychology

The fMRI methods above can use physiological measurement to provide insight into biological processes that may be related to learning. To be educationally meaningful, such biological information must be associated with notions of the learning process at cognitive and behavioural levels. Knowing that there is an increase in blood flow in a certain region of our brain (or, in the case of EEG, a change in the electrical field above it) is not, in itself, helpful to educational understanding. It has to be related to how we think and behave (i.e. to processes at cognitive and behavioural levels of understanding). A neuroeducational experiment involving fMRI (or any other biological method) would usually be designed to explicitly explore this link, by testing hypotheses relating changes in biological measurement with changes in learning behaviour. These hypotheses might be predictions derived from current understanding of how biological function and measurable behaviour are related, via some theoretical cognitive model of what is happening at the level of mind – which, of course, cannot be observed or measured. We have seen that these experiments either support understanding of the brain–mind–behaviour relationship in a particular context or, otherwise, cause it to be modified, allowing understanding to be continuously and progressively developed.

Consideration of what is known about one part of this relationship, between mind and learning (the cognition of learning) is, therefore, essential to the successful design of such experiments. This also makes measurement at the behavioural level alone, without biological measurement, potentially valuable to neuroeducational research in its own right, as a means to test and develop cognitive-behavioural models. Although cognitive-behavioural experiments may not include any measurement directly related to the learners' brains, or even their physiology, they may reflect current understanding at all levels, and the insights they provide about the relationship between mind and brain may provide an improved theoretical basis for further studies at the biological level. It is, therefore, appropriate that they should be included here.

Further, such experiments, insofar as they may be testing cognitive behavioural relationships based on understanding of biological brain function, can represent a particular type of neuroeducational bridging study – i.e. an experiment that tests more explicitly the potential educational effectiveness/relevance of an idea derived from neuroscience.

One example of such a bridging study was based on increasing evidence from brain imaging experiments that a link may exist between numbers and fingers. This has been used to suggest a special cognitive role for fingers in the learning of mathematics. Such ideas prompted Gracia-Bafalluy and Noel (2008) to carry out a cognitive-behavioural study in a school to test this idea. Following the experimental method, they divided forty seven school children into 3 groups: children with poor finger gnosis, high finger gnosis, and a control group (Gracia-Bafalluy and Noel, 2008). After an eight-week intervention consisting of two weekly half-hour sessions of finger training, the children with poor finger gnosis improved on mathematical tests, in contrast to the control group who did not receive the intervention, or the group who were already very competent with their fingers. These trends, confirmed as statistically significant, support the hypothesis for a functional link between finger gnosis and numerical skill development. In this way, they help interpret brain imaging studies, i.e. that association of activities due to finger use and calculation is probably not just due to the proximity of brain regions subserving these representations; it also prompts more questions: is there a sensitive period for this relationship that influences when we are most able to grasp the foundations of mathematics? Perhaps more importantly for educators, however, it brings the theoretical model closer to being useful in the classroom, by demonstrating the relevance of this brain–mind–behaviour relationship in a school environment. Of course, as a controlled experiment, this is not likely to get educators as excited as the successful evaluation of an educational programme based on such ideas, developed and delivered by educators in a variety of different schools as part of the curriculum. It lacks such authenticity. But it is an example of how scientists are beginning to study more 'real world' contexts, as a means to test and modify concepts around brain–mind–behaviour relationships in studies that mutually benefit laboratory based measurement of biological processes and educational understanding.

Interpretive methods of investigation

The potential importance of finger gnosis is one of many insights arising from neuroscience that suggests new approaches to maths education for young children. Indeed, scientists are now calling for educational research exploring the explicit use of fingers in early approaches to number (Kaufmann, 2008). But how best to include such concepts in teaching? The young students in the Gracia-Bafalluy and Noel study carried out games intended to enhance finger gnosis, in small groups of about five supervised by the same student researcher. That is about all we know of the teaching approach that was used, with any associated social interaction generally absent or very underplayed by those reporting the research. This passive approach was helpful in providing experimental control, but contrasts with the important role placed by educators on teacher–pupil interaction. We have seen that educators tend to think about learning in terms of social construction, in which their role is to scaffold the students' understanding to enable them to build on what they already understand. Illuminating this process of social construction requires analysis of the dialogue in the classroom. For example, when understanding the potential of using building blocks to develop children's maths Casey *et al.* (2008) carried out qualitative analysis of the discourse in the classroom when children were using the blocks, compared with a control condition. They also studied the effectiveness of using the blocks within a story-telling context. Block building in a story-telling context was the most effective in terms of quantitative measures, but the qualitative analysis revealed how this came about. It occurred through providing the teacher a means to motivate and direct pupils' efforts, to increase the salience of the constraints in the problem, and through providing a meaningful context by which to scaffold learning through the logic and features of the story. This type of method, involving the meaning-based interpretation of social evidence, provides insights about the way in which a new teaching strategy manifests itself in the classroom discourse. It can illustrate how, through analysis of teacher–pupil interaction, practising teachers can use a strategy to build on the existing knowledge and contexts of their pupils, and so develop a more effective pedagogical approach. Other new ideas about teaching number, such as those involving the explicit use of fingers, may require similar methods of investigation to determine how best to include them in pedagogy.

Sociocultural discourse analysis

There are many ways to analyse language, including ethnographic approaches seeking to explain broad social processes and sociolinguistic approaches that seek to explore the relationship between language and society. However, in education, there has been an increasing interest in sociocultural approaches that focus upon the *use* of language and the types of talk generated. Sociocultural theorists see language as a cultural tool, with educators particularly interested in the use of this tool for learning. The sociocultural tradition builds on ideas about the social construction of knowledge developed by Vygotsky (Vygotsky, 1978). Sociocultural analysis of discourse focuses on the content and function of language, and how shared understanding is developed, within a specific social context, over time. For example, Mercer *et al.* (2004) wanted to assess the effectiveness of an experimental ICT-based teaching programme designed to foster children's ability to talk and reason together, and improve the application of these skills when studying science. They hoped to show the children's abilities in the intervention group improving, relative to control groups who did not receive its supposed benefits. To do this, they carried out a detailed qualitative analysis of the children's talk when working together. Typical interactions in the control groups showed a lack of co-operation, little sharing of knowledge or building upon each others' suggestions. Here, children did not provide reasons for their proposals or seek joint agreement. The sociocultural approach can provide valuable understanding about how learning does, or does not, come about. But it is also heavily situated in context of the study, making the generalization and transfer of findings potentially problematic. It can, however, be combined with more quantitative experimental approaches. In the study by Casey *et al.* (2008) discussed above, the qualitative analysis of language was used to explain the quantitative increases in mathematical performance. In the study by Mercer *et al.* (2004), quantitative approaches were applied to the language itself, with researchers counting the number of instances of the key words 'because', 'if', 'I think', 'would' and 'could'. These words occurred in greater numbers after the intervention and the statistical significance of this result suggests it may transfer to other classrooms. However, the underlying meaning of any quantitative result rests in its explanation. In both studies, this was revealed, in depth, by the qualitative analysis.

There appears, then, considerable benefit in applying social science methods, such as sociocultural discourse analysis, to understand how insights from our natural scientific knowledge of the brain can best be included in pedagogy. However, whatever the quality of the social science methods used to develop, disseminate and promote educational change and the adoption of new teaching methods, these may be wasted efforts if the concepts underlying the approach itself are unsound. Indeed, competent pieces of social science research on the implementation of pseudo science can result in unscientific ideas gaining further respectability. Studies exist that look carefully at the relation between educational practice and supposedly brain-based concepts such as learning styles and Brain Gym (Akkoyunlu and Soylu, 2008; Moore and Hibbert, 2005).These studies, however, fail to scrutinize the science underlying such approaches, undermining the usefulness of their findings. Interdisciplinary dialogue appears crucial when moving from scientific concepts about brain function to classroom studies, in order to ensure the science is well scrutinized before exploring the role of such concepts in pedagogy.

Experiential methods of investigation

In some structured interviews aimed at collecting participants' experiences, the information provided and the questions presented can focus a respondent's attention on a set of very specific issues in a very specific manner. For example, when exploring learners' experiences with a teaching strategy, it seems reasonable to ask teachers when they use such a strategy in their lessons. Here, the researcher may decide that meanings are so aligned to a particular data gathering context that the coding can be based securely on these, with interpretations 'anchored in the external appropriate reality'(Swift, 2006). In this case, it might be assumed that the researcher and participants share some similar sense of what 'using a strategy' means. But in interviews that aspire to capture the respondent's authentic experience, any assumption that the researcher shares a common set of meanings with their participants is more questionable. Indeed, the 'appropriate reality' of each participant must be part of what is being investigated, if we are to understand *their* meaning in what they are saying. For example, in a study of how learners value a strategy in their learning, it cannot be assumed that a researcher can pre-guess how their participant will approach the issue, the way in which he/she will want to express their experiences or even what questions or prompts the researcher should use to illicit the most valuable responses. On studying a recording of the interview, there may be many important clues in the language, terms and intonation used, but to predefine clear codes by which to identify these appears premature – how can the researcher already know what they are looking for? That creates a classic chicken and egg situation: interpretation is required in order to generate appropriate codes, yet codes are required in order to make the interpretation. Of course, a similar problem can arise in the type of qualitative interpretation of social evidence discussed above, when analysing social discourse and observations of social behaviour, but the aim of collecting someone else's authentic experience makes the determination of meaning (i.e. their meaning, rather than the researcher's) more problematic.

Grounded theory analysis

One solution appears to be for appropriate codes to emerge as part of the analysis process itself. 'Grounded Theory' methods are becoming a popular approach for achieving the emergence of such coding (Charmaz, 2005). Here, early analyses are used to prompt 'active, immediate and short' codes that focus further data collection. This data collection prompts further, increasingly abstract, forms of coding that, in turn, can be used to analyse new data and reanalyse old data. In this systematic way, the coding becomes increasingly refined as abstract conceptual categories emerge, allied to the research question. Unlike experimental approaches, such approaches do not attempt to eliminate the role of researcher in interpretation, but rather make that role explicit and open to reflexive analysis. In qualitative analysis of social evidence, grounded theorists are asking 'What is happening?' and 'What are people doing', thus taking an 'outsider' perspective (i.e. the researcher's) in order to make their own meaning of a situation. When the experience of the participant is the focus of the research question (e.g. 'How does the learner perceive what is happening?'), the researcher is seeking an 'insider' perspective, i.e. their participant's meaning, and wishes to consider their semi-structured interviewing data as experiential evidence. Again, the data can be analysed using similar 'emergent' coding techniques, this time focused on characterizing participants' experiences. However, one important difference is a greater involvement of the participants themselves in the analysis, either through direct participation in the analysis and/or through consultation upon interpretations and findings. This is an important check to ensure that the researcher's interpretation is a valid reflection (albeit only a reflection) of the participant's own 'insider' perspective.

An interesting example of the value of experiential evidence arises from research on attention-deficit hyperactivity disorder (ADHD). This affects about one in twenty children directly and, since its symptoms can give rise to disruptive behaviour, it can often affect the classroom environment for other children. The neuroscience of ADHD is still not clear but, from the many imaging studies conducted, some agreement is emerging that sufferers exhibit neural differences in regions such as the anterior cingulate and prefrontal cortex. Although understanding of ADHD at a brain level is still the subject of debate, its treatment has increasingly involved the psychoactive drug methylphenidate, most commonly sold as Ritalin. Prescriptions for these stimulants have been rising substantially, from 222,000 in England in 1998 to 418,300 in 2004 (Kendall *et al.*, 2008), despite increasing concerns about the possible long-term effects of drugs such as methylphenidate on the developing brain (Anderson, 2005).

The strong association of such drugs with changes in brain activity, and their increasing usage in attempts to provide a solution, can help deter perceptions of ADHD as an alibi for bad behaviour. As pointed out by Eric Taylor, an expert in ADHD at the Institute of Psychiatry (UCL), 'children cannot just choose not to have ADHD' (Howard-Jones, 2007). On the other hand, it was discussed in Chapter 5 how identifying neural correlates of ADHD does not provide evidence of a biological cause or suggest that educators should think of ADHD as a medical problem beyond their domain of influence. As well, teachers' sense of agency, the role of children's agency and sense of agency may also play an important role in more effective educational approaches to children with ADHD. But what constructs do young sufferers of ADHD have about their behavioural problems? To investigate this, Gallichan and Curle (2008) spoke with twelve young people with ADHD (aged 10–17) in semi-structured interviews (Gallichan and Curle, 2008). In this type of interview, a schedule of issues pertinent to the research questions usually exists but the interviewer uses prompts and spontaneous chatter to provide a conversation-like experience rather than reading a list a questions. This helps avoid outcomes being too greatly determined by the researcher's preconceptions, and facilitates the interviewee's freedom to say what he/she would like to say about the subject in the way he/she would like to say it. However, in the study by Gallichan and Curle, broad topics relating to the research questions were identified at the outset and researchers followed respondents' interpretations of their experiences in a conversation directed by the researcher around these topics, but without being committed to completing a defined semi-structured interview schedule. Instead, following the work of Charmaz, they applied 'theoretical sampling', whereby data collection and analysis proceeded simultaneously, using themes arising from initial data sets to guide the definition of further interview topics and selection of participants (Charmaz, 2000, 2005). Interview tapes were transcribed verbatim, and analysis procedures helped identify concepts expressed in respondents' own words, from which the researchers carefully formed more theoretical and broader concepts that could, finally, be expressed in diagrammatic form. Additionally, to ensure that the authentic experience of respondents had not been lost along the way, participants were consulted about the findings and their views (which were favourable) reported. The model produced by this process suggested a reciprocal relationship between young ADHD sufferers and their social environment. Young people with ADHD felt they were square pegs trying to fit into rigid round holes, with subsequent impact on sense of control and self-esteem. Environments that were adaptable and flexible, and the provision of support from, and acceptance by, others can positively influence the experience of ADHD, and may help sufferers escape from the vicious cycle they feel they are caught in (see Fig. 6.2).

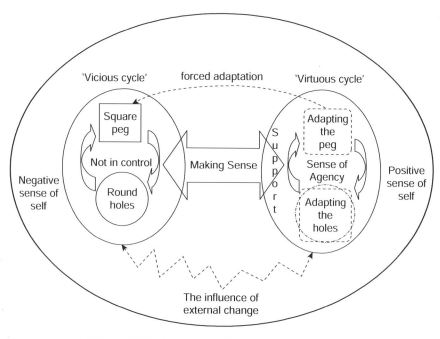

Figure 6.2 **A grounded theory model of the experience of ADHD:** fitting a round peg into a square hole.
Source: From Gallichan, D. J. and Curle, C. (2008) Fitting square pegs into round holes: The challenge of coping with attention-deficit hyperactivity disorder. *Clinical Child Psychology and Psychiatry,* 13, 343–363. Reprinted by permission from SAGE. Copyright © 2008.

It is worth noting that experiential perspectives about ADHD are valued differently in different parts of the world, providing an illustration of how research in neuroscience and education may culturally divide in the future. The study by Gallichan and Curle (2008) was carried out in the UK and provides a good sense of how experiential data can add to our understanding of important issues affecting education. This is in line with the views expressed by the National Service Framework for Children which emphasizes the value of listening and responding to young people's views when delivering health care (Department of Health, UK, 2004). In the US, however, the American Academy of Child and Adolescent Psychiatry has previously discouraged recording young people's views, on the basis that these 'lack insight' (AACAP, 1997).

Action research

In more general educational terms, empowering learners and teachers to contribute their own experiential perspectives can be an important contribution to understanding what the learning/teaching feels like. That can provide insights involving emotional response, free will, motivation and autonomy that might otherwise be overlooked. Experiential evidence arising from a teacher's 'insider' insights contributes to reflective teaching practice such as, for example, when teachers are seeking to improve implementation of new pedagogical ideas, and in developing the concepts upon which they are based. In projects involving neuroscience and education, reflection is most likely to be valuable when informed by both educational and scientific expertise, suggesting the need for group reflection and co-construction of concepts. An iterative process of development and change through reflection with others forms the basis of action research (Elliott, 1991). The methods reviewed until now can compare the before and after states associated with a predefined intervention or change in educational practice, but they have difficulty in capturing institutionally-based change at practitioner, department, school or school cluster level, which often evolves alongside changes in perceptions and meaning. Action research can make a valuable contribution here. If change is the moral imperative of educational research, then the methodological arsenal of neuroscience and education may need to include transformative research methods to study it. Indeed, this may be a particularly important concern for those working at the interface between neuroscience and education. We have seen that concepts involving the brain have a seductive allure, many are bound up with fundamental perceptions about how we learn and our potential for learning, and education has already shown itself vulnerable to a range of neuromyths. If we want neuroscience to contribute in scientifically valid and educationally relevant ways to learning, then special attention must be given to those institutionally based processes by which neuroscience enters the educational bloodstream. However, meaning itself, as constructed by participants, can be expected to change during the course of an action research intervention as can the methods used to implement ideas, as understanding grows. Any 'before' and 'after' judgements expressed in action research are often the subjective opinions of the participants, and a change in the perspectives of those producing the judgements is expected and encouraged as a valued outcome of this type of research. This places an important limitation upon the transferability of action research since, although it may develop practice that improves outcomes in a particular context, it cannot test the general educational value of a pedagogical approach or idea. Action research will be explored further through an example outlined in Chapter 8.

NEUROEDUCATIONAL STUDY DESIGN

It is clear that each of the methods above appears suitable for application in at least one of our three types of study. Experimental techniques appear well suited for developing scientific insights, interpretative techniques are often useful in understanding issues in the classroom – in bridging and practice-based studies, action research is particularly helpful for developing good practice. These methods are well established in the fields of enquiry they are derived from. However, we will now consider how the goals of neuroeducational research imbue these studies with additional challenges.

Scientific studies

There are currently a burgeoning number of neuroscientific studies that claim, sometimes implicitly through the making of links with everyday learning, to have relevance to education. Some even appear to have been undertaken with the aim, at least in part, of furthering the type of understanding that brings educational insight. Indeed, scientists are often required to justify their requests for funding in terms of the potential longer-term and broader benefits it may bring to society. But are neuroscientists, if they work in isolation from the educational community, even able to identify the most valuable research questions that can, and should, be tackled? It has already been noted that finding tractable research questions that are of scientific and educational value can be problematic. When, in 2001, the ESRC-TLRP commissioned scientists to produce a review of neuroscience they deemed of potential educational relevance, they consulted educators and scientists to each provide suggestions for possible research questions (Desforges, 2001). The lack of consensus was identified as a major reason for a temporary suspension of effort in this area. It is not, of course, the case that scientists have a natural disinterest in 'real world' problems. Rather, the chief difficulty is identifying where investigation would be both educationally and scientifically *meaningful*. Educational meaning is often defined by relating new knowledge to everyday learning contexts but, to be scientifically meaningful, the knowledge produced by a study must build carefully on what is already scientifically known. So the existing scientific knowledge base (as judged by scientists) must already be well-established enough to have meaning in the classroom (as judged by educators). Little surprise, then, that identifying such 'low hanging fruit' cannot be achieved by a questionnaire response from scientists and educators who are at present working in isolation from each other. Instead, some type of dialogue appears highly desirable at the very earliest stage of any scientific study that may wish later to claim educational relevance.

Although scientific studies should be executed by scientists, dialogue with educators is potentially valuable at other stages in the research process. There may be issues of ecological validity in experimental tasks, procedures and contexts that unnecessarily undermine the apparent educational value of the findings. These issues might be tackled in simple ways without compromising experimental validity – if identified early enough at the beginning of the project. For example, to allay fears regarding the ecological validity of an imaging experiment, participants can be asked to also carry out the same tasks in a less unusual environment, to understand how outcomes are being influenced by being inside a scanner. Educators also have considerable expertise in developing learning tasks, and so generating experimental tasks for such scientific studies may also be enhanced by educational consultation.

In writing up scientific studies at the interface of neuroscience and education, it would also appear advantageous to include a critical discussion about potential links between experimental findings and real world learning. At the moment, with many such studies being published in purely scientific journals, this type of critical discussion is rarely included, since it is of little merit within the scientific discipline concerned. Instead, a few lines of suggestive speculation are sometimes provided. Better than this, however, would be a considered appraisal of potential educational relevance, with clear indications of the limits upon such interpretation, if only to help prevent inappropriate conclusions being reached by readers without scientific expertise. Such a discussion, if planned from the outset, can also include other data collected alongside the experimental measurements. This can even be qualitative in nature, perhaps collecting 'insider insights' of participants about their strategies or their attitudes during the experiment. Scientific studies often refer to such data in passing as 'informal observation' or 'informal interview'. But, in scientific studies that, either in the short or long term, may wish to claim educational relevance, it would be far preferable to have this type of data formally collected and reported upon alongside experimental findings.

Bridging studies

It seems unlikely that results from a laboratory can immediately be rolled out as part of an educational programme. Brain scans cannot translate directly into lesson plans. To begin with, bridging studies are needed to help examine laboratory results for their potential educational value. These can be carefully designed interventions intended to test scientific principles derived from laboratory studies in real world learning environments. However, unlike in the laboratory, the many day-to-day features of such environments cannot always be controlled, as all educators are aware. Interventions which go some way to controlling extraneous variables (often called quasi-experimental) can include measurements and statistical analysis as with laboratory experimentation. Here, there needs to be a compromise of experimental control with ecological validity, since the more one manipulates the environment to gain control of extraneous variables, the less realistic it becomes. There is, therefore, also the need for more naturalistic approaches such as classroom observation. Such observations are usually qualitative and often not amenable to statistical analysis, which means one can evaluate but not test in the sense of, for example, demonstrating statistically significant increases in achievement. Mixed methods can combine both approaches but, again, rarely without some compromise in terms of maintaining a naturalistic experience and/or experimental control, and without judicious consideration of how findings from quantitative and qualitative data sets can be interrelated. All of this means that, in the bid to maintain experimental validity and educational relevance, bridging studies require some serious decisions regarding compromise, and these are best reached through a level of interdisciplinary collaboration that involves thinking together, rather than just consultation. This level of collaboration is likely to benefit all stages of such an enquiry, from identifying the research question to interpreting findings. The outcomes of bridging studies may afford insights into the scientific concepts on which they were based, and they may also provide findings for developing practice-based studies that are more meaningful than those derived in the laboratory. However, a bridging study can inform a practice-based study more effectively if the educational contexts and practices involved with the bridging study are reported in detail, and in ways meaningful to educators.

The level of collaboration and multiperspective thinking required by bridging studies is far from straightforward, but the goals of the field are unlikely to be met without it. Worse than that, the absence of such an approach seems likely to produce more examples of educational thinking that inappropriately draw on neuroscience, as well as scientists promoting ideas in education that inadequately draw on educational expertise. One example of the latter comes from the distinguished scientist Stanislav Dehaene whose success in understanding the cognitive neuroscience of mathematics has been outstanding. Commendable in its intentions, the work was taken closer to educational application by producing educational software for children with dyscalculia. Within the field of educational technology, it is generally accepted that the voice of the user needs to be included at the design stage (Facer, 2004). However, contrary to notions of user-centred design, experiential perspectives appear not to have been considered in the development of the software until the evaluation phase, when those who had been asked to use the software frequently labelled it as 'boring' (Wilson *et al.*, 2006). This lack of intrinsic interest among users also makes the effectiveness of the carefully devised scientific principles of the software difficult to evaluate.

Practice-based studies

One of the major challenges for practice-based neuroeducational studies derives from their need to draw on solid scientific expertise. The pedagogical concepts, language and understanding produced by these types of study will inevitably require valid interpretation of the science. We saw in Chapter 2 how overinterpretation or misinterpretation of scientific ideas can easily give rise to attractive neuromyths that, once established, are difficult to dislodge from educational thinking. An important way to avoid this is to ensure that scientific expertise feeds directly into practice-based studies. This may require a relatively smaller time commitment from scientific experts than the types of study already reviewed. Here, scientific experts may be required only on a consultative basis, to advise on the appropriateness of the initial direction, sit in and contribute to discussions, and review documents and reports arising from the project. However, recruiting this expertise into practice-based studies can still be problematic, not least because it contributes little to the professional goals of most scientists, whose careers usually depend more on the publication of experimental research than on providing educational consultancy. In bridging studies, the influence of scientific professional goals helps motivate and promulgate the research. Here, practice-based neuroeducational studies can prompt interesting scientific questions suitable for experimental study but, since they cannot yield publishable scientific findings in themselves, are unlikely to be of direct professional interest to scientists. And yet, even so, a key ingredient for their success is the appropriate scientific understanding and communication of concepts involving mind and brain. Practice-based studies may raise interesting questions to stimulate further scientific and bridging studies but, again, this is more likely if they include dialogue with scientific experts. This dialogue, as part of the study, may even prompt the collection of informal observations and measurements during practice-based sessions that can help inform the identification and development of such questions.

Summary

In this chapter, we considered how the construction of knowledge at the interface of neuroscience and education involves interrelating findings from three types of study, each potentially drawing on three fundamental types of evidence. There is no simple one-to-one correspondence between these three types of study and the three types of evidence they draw on. The methodology by which evidence can be collected and analysed to meet the goals of neuroeducational research has been reviewed in this chapter in respect of a small exemplar range of methods and techniques. This review is summarized in Fig. 6.3.

Whatever type of study is involved, we have seen that one important challenge for neuroeducational research is the level of interdisciplinarity. The intensity of collaboration may be influenced by the particular research topic and the present levels of scientific and educational understanding it enjoys. The depth and mix of collaboration required also appears to vary across study types, but some expert understanding of concepts from neuroscience and education will always be needed.

The goals of neuroeducational research require that the concepts, findings and direction associated with different types of study should be open to influence by one another. This has implications for methodology in neuroeducational research, which involves more than the unusual sequencing within the same investigation of conventional methods 'borrowed' from different perspectives (e.g. fMRI followed by observational classroom study). The process of interrelating studies is supported by adaptation of the methods and techniques they use, so researchers need to be mindful of neuroeducational goals from the outset. The interrelation of studies is helpful during the project, in order to orientate the direction of ongoing research, as well as in developing the ultimate multiperspective conclusions of an investigation. That means, for example, scientists who wish their findings to be credited with potential educational relevance should

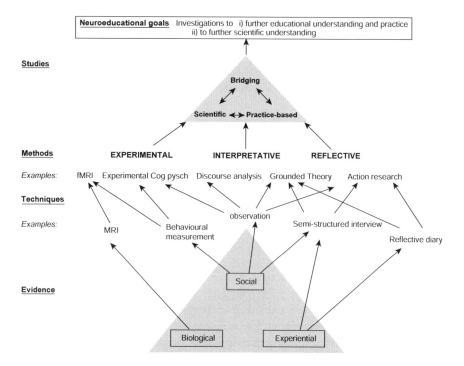

Figure 6.3 The complementary goals of neuroeducational research can be supported by three types of study (scientific, bridging, practice-based) that draw on three types of evidence (experiential, social and biological) via a diverse range of methods and techniques (only examples shown). These methods and techniques may be adapted to facilitate the interrelationship of findings and concepts across studies demanded by the higher goals.

act on this aspiration at the planning stage. Such action is currently unusual, but the speed with which neuroeducational research develops as a coherent field of enterprise may depend upon the extent to which each type of study is designed to facilitate their interrelation.

It appears, then, that the inclusion of biological evidence in educational investigation has some interesting, if not radical, implications for current approaches to research methodology. Neuroeducational research, as defined by two complementary goals, is likely to develop methodological foundations that will serve to uniquely characterize it, and which draw on understanding from both the natural and social sciences.

At present, few investigations, including those beyond neuroeducational research, combine and adapt methods and techniques in order to make links across natural and social science perspectives. Some of the reasons for this may be cultural ones, such as the present lack of established standards of rigour that acceptably integrate standards from both perspectives. (This is despite some methodological adaptations being 'add-ons' that cannot threaten any traditional notions of validity). Another reason, of course, may simply be the extra time, energy and effort required. However, as we have seen, the advantages are many. Without such cross-disciplinary practical enterprise, many areas of science will remain unhelpfully divorced from the realities they aspire to understand, and those realities will not receive the full benefit of their knowledge

Chapter 7

Neuroeducational ethics

This chapter will consider the ethical dimensions of issues involving neuroscience and education. It will focus on three areas. The issues around interdisciplinary research will be discussed first. Here, formal guidelines exist within associated disciplines, so this makes it a convenient starting point for comparing ethical perspectives. The second area is the scrutiny and communication of findings and concepts. This topic has dominated so many debates about the role of the brain in education and exercised so much concern, that it deserves special consideration. Finally, whatever neuroeducational research determines as possible, and however well its ethical processes and communications are policed, neuroscience will, directly or indirectly, provide challenging issues for educational policymakers. For this reason, the third area reviews issues of policy involving novel ethical considerations likely to arise in the future.

Research

Education and the sciences of mind and brain have developed their own culture around ethics, and their ethical guidelines for carrying out research have some distinct differences in terms of emphasis. A common-sense approach for projects that span two fields of endeavour might be to ensure procedures are subject to safeguards recommended by both fields. Yet the ethical guidelines from different disciplines are not always amenable to simple combination. For example, even if we claim we are merely borrowing neuroscientific techniques to answer educational questions, we cannot simply transfer the normal neuroscientific procedures along with the technology. One reason for this is that ethical review considers the risk–benefit ratio, and there may be some difficulties in equating educational risks with those in other disciplines. Neuroscience and education experts tend to consider different types of risk and benefit. Educational research often includes social consequence as a research focus in itself, and so it is natural that researchers here are wary of their own involvement contributing to unwanted social phenomena such as bullying or friendship difficulties due, for example, to procedures that highlight individual difference. Educators, therefore, have some basis for claiming greater awareness of some types of risk, such as negative social consequences. On the other hand, physical safety is rarely an issue in educational research, and yet it is frequently the major focus for researchers making physiological measurements. Thus, the ethical guidelines of education and the sciences of brain and mind express many of the same principles, such as the desirability of anonymity and the need to balance risk and benefit, but the arguments may be characterized by different levels of emphasis in different areas of concern. The justifiable sensitivity of educational researchers to social risk, and the need to ensure physical safety during neuroscientific experimental procedures, makes neuroeducational research an interesting context for ethical scrutiny which is not yet covered by any one set of guidelines. In order to explore these differences in ethical perspective more carefully and consider what implications these may have, there now follows a review of some specific issues regarding ethical procedures.

Physical risk

Most neuroimaging techniques can present some level of physical risk, however small. For example, MRI is a safe process for the majority of people, but it can be dangerous if the participant has metal within or on their persons. Screening procedures are essential in order to ensure that implants, piercings, etc. are detected before the participant enters the scanning room. Failure to follow safety guidelines and the use of outdated information regarding implants have been the sources of most MRI injuries and the very few fatalities that have occurred (Shellock and Crues, 2004). Based on the small number of epidemiological studies undertaken, it is currently assumed that no physical injuries result from exposure to the strong static and pulsed gradient magnetic fields used by fMRI, or the radiofrequency fields involved. However, it has been suggested that more research in this area might be undertaken.

In contrast to fMRI, which can be described as entirely non-invasive, participants in PET scans have radioisotopes introduced into their body but the dose of radiation is small, only three to four times the UK background level. Also, the radioactivity used has a short half-life and therefore does not stay in the body long. Nevertheless, there are physical risks involved with intravenous administration of radiotracers.

Indirect physical risk is referred to in the UK educational ethical guidelines. Here, researchers are reminded to 'avoid choices that in themselves have undesirable effects', such as offering 'cigarettes to young offenders or sweets to schoolchildren' (BERA, 2004). It is interesting to compare this type of consideration with those of cognitive neuroscientists. There are no known effects of MRI scanning on the human embryo, yet participants who are pregnant are often screened out of experiments as a precaution. Given the well-documented effects of smoking on health, and sugar on teeth, it could be argued scientists' levels of concern for the well-being of their participants is no less than educational researchers'. In terms of physical risk, then, the ethical perspectives of neuroscience and education promote similar levels of attentiveness to the safety and physical well-being of research participants.

Psychological risk

Participants in fMRI experiments must lie in a small-bore tube, sometimes for over an hour, wearing ear protection due to the high noise levels, with the head restrained inside a secondary head coil and experiencing a very restricted visual field. For some participants, this is a claustrophobic environment that may cause them fear, anxiety and distress. Participants may not be fully aware of the scanning procedures and environment when first consenting to participate and they may feel awkward about expressing their anxiety or desire to withdraw. Of course, present ethical guidelines emphasize that participants should feel able to withdraw at any time, and without explanation. Yet participants may realize that researchers have wasted time, effort and money if they withdraw after scanning has started, and feel pressure (albeit self-made pressure) to continue. Part of the solution may be the use of simulation. This can help participants become more fully informed about fMRI procedures. Simulating fMRI procedures using a mock scanner (of same dimensions and noise, etc.) can help anticipate any problems individuals may have with the scanner environment, and can also reduce psychological risk by helping acclimatize participants.

fMRI examinations of neural activity are often accompanied by anatomical scans that provide structural details of participants' brains. Although experiments may not be designed to detect structural anomalies, it is possible that researchers may sometimes identify them, or think they may have. Researchers are rarely trained in medical diagnosis. They may have some understanding of neuro-anatomy and function, but this can be limited to the focus of their research. If something unusual is spotted, participants are usually encouraged to make an appointment to see their own doctor. In a review of 151 MRI studies involving adults displaying no other neurological symptoms, it was found that an average of 6.6 per cent of participants had required medical referral (Illes *et al.*, 2004). The decision to suggest to a participant that they may benefit from medical referral can be difficult. The researcher must decide whether, often without radiological training, they should inform the participant (or their GP) that they have detected a possible anomaly, undoubtedly causing alarm. This action could, in retrospect, be seen as either needless or possibly even life-saving. Alternatively, they may decide the issue is not worthy of attention and hope their participant enjoys continuing good health. When viewed by expert radiologists, the identification of abnormalities is quite common but the need for referral is less so. The final discovery of a serious medical condition, such as a brain tumour, is unusual but it can occur. In a retrospective analysis of 1,000 brain scans by Katzman *et al.* (1999), 18 per cent demonstrated incidental abnormal findings, with 2.9 per cent suggesting a need for medical referral, and a final count of two participants confirmed with primary brain tumours (Katzman *et al.*, 1999).

A recent multidisciplinary appraisal of the issues in the US proposes that researchers should not disclose abnormal findings unlikely to affect a participant's health (Wolf *et al.*, 2007). Participants should, prior to the research being undertaken, be asked if they wish to be informed regarding (i) non-fatal but serious abnormalities (even if no intervention is possible) and/or (ii) life-threatening and grave abnormalities. Researchers must abide by these wishes. In practice, however, the effective implementation of such guidance in identifying serious conditions may still rely on the ability of researchers (who are not trained radiologists) spotting something that should be regarded as suspicious, before radiologists and clinicians become involved.

Social and educational risk

It is perhaps in the realm of social risk that views of educational researchers may depart from those of their colleagues in the natural sciences. Social scientists tend be acutely aware of the power difference that can exist between researchers and their participants, and how this can create ethical concerns and influence outcomes. Increasingly, educators have sought ways in which to empower the research participant, often with the explicit aim of ensuring that their voice is heard in the process and in the reporting.

Thus, when UK educational researchers seek informed consent, they ensure participants understand 'the *process* in which they are to be engaged, including why their participation is necessary ...' (italics are author's). This differs even from UK psychological guidelines that require participants to understand only the 'nature, purpose, and anticipated consequences' of their involvement (BPS, 2006) (or, for that matter, US educational guidelines that speak only of informing participants of the aims of the research (AERA, 2000)). But, if young adults are participating in a neuroimaging study, to what extent can information about the process of the research be effectively provided? Do they need to know about the preprocessing of image data (e.g. that their image data will be combined with those of others), do they need to know that a method of contrasts is being used (that data from two conditions will be subtracted), what hypotheses are being tested – and whether outcomes will be statistically tested in terms of the participant group and/or in terms of the general population? In recent educational research, participants are increasingly provided with information about the process in order to empower their voice as a valid source of data within that process. But what level of understanding would be required for participants to contribute their own reflections about neurological processes? It could be argued that participation in neuroeducational research can lead to a disempowerment of the learner's voice, due partly to the complexity of the research processes in which he/she is involved and partly to the traditional scientific paradigms and styles of reporting that usually omit such considerations. Neuroeducational researchers drawing on biological perspectives should feel no less committed than other educational researchers in empowering their participants to understand and contribute to the research process, but they may have to struggle harder to achieve this than colleagues using more conventional research methods.

There may, indeed, be a stronger case for the involvement of participants in educational research if it involves neuroscience. In his discussion of neuroethics, Leshner argues that one reason neuroscience creates special ethical issues is because the '... decision to alter brain structure or activity in any way involves potentially great cost-benefit tradeoffs that can go far beyond the specific intent of the intervention' (Leshner, 2005). Leshner goes on to discuss drug addicts and those with 'disordered brains' yet his argument might be equally applied to educational interventions, since we now have examples of even brief training programmes producing changes in brain structure and activity (see Chapter 1) (Draganski *et al.*, 2004). There may, of course, be no need for undue panic, since on this basis educators have been influencing the brain for decades using their own, well-developed ethical frameworks without any consideration of neuroethics. In further emphasizing the ethically problematic nature of neuroscience, Leshner points out that 'modifying the brain in any way has the potential to alter one's essential being'. Again, 'Education' could easily be substituted for 'the brain' in this sentence, and perhaps educational research has a longer history of considering the ethical dimensions of 'transformative' interventions. The potential significance of Leshner's point for neuroeducational initiatives, however, should not be dismissed lightly. This is because interventions with a strong neural basis could easily give rise to less freely-willed involvement of participants than other types of educational intervention, if only because neuroscience appears less capable of reflecting on concepts such as free will. For example, as a leading expert on the adolescent brain, Paus believes that 'the time is right for evidence-based, large-scale studies of interventions aimed at facilitating youth development. Neuroimaging-based approaches hold considerable promise, providing both the evidence as well as novel insights about the role of the environment in shaping the adolescent brain' (Paus, 2008). However, does such a belief reflect an awareness of the considerable ethical issues that would be involved with such studies, with their emphasis on neuroscientific evidence? How, for example, would participants negotiate which parts of their adolescent brain they would like 'shaped'? Neuroimaging studies of interventions aimed at remediation of reading difficulty have already been carried out, but remediation of character (one of the five 'c's of positive youth development (Lerner, 2005) discussed by Paus in his article) would take ethical dilemmas to a new level.

The insistence of participant involvement in the educational research process within current UK guidelines goes further. It states that researchers must recognize participants' rights to be 'identified with any publication of their original works or other inputs'. Presumably, this means that an individual's brain image or graph of brain activity should bear that participant's name, if they so wish. It is difficult to understand how such a detail can undermine the scientific value of findings, but it would mark a significant departure from the norms of scientific reporting.

Conflict between ethical perspectives may also arise when carrying out bridging studies. As discussed in the previous chapter, these need to maintain good levels of scientific and educational validity. Usually, studies of behaviour are tightly controlled in order to support scientific validity, and may consist of comparing two or more types of condition. In a study of learning in the classroom, this might mean comparing students' learning with and without an intervention. Within-participant designs, in which each participant experiences all conditions, are notoriously difficult when studying processes involving learning, due to transfer of what is learnt from the first condition to the second. Bridging studies may, therefore, benefit from between-group research designs in which learning outcomes are compared between an experimental group who has experienced an intervention and a control group who has not. These are similar to the Randomized Controlled Trials (RCTs) that constitute an established method of medical science for evaluating interventions. However, in education, since they involve randomly assigning learners to different groups, such designs are often disruptive of normal school routines and are difficult to organize for the researcher. This makes it more difficult to justify proceeding with such research unless there are good grounds for already believing the intervention should work. The ethical problem then, of course, is why the control group should be denied the assumed benefits of the intervention (Taylor and Gorrard, 2004). In medicine, this dilemma is no less great, yet RCTs appear culturally more acceptable than in education, where such designs are less common. Indeed, UK educational research guidelines clearly state that steps should be taken to 'minimize the effects of designs that advantage one group of participants over another, e.g. in an experimental or quasi-experimental study in which the treatment is viewed as a desirable intervention and which by definition is not available to the control or comparison group respectively'. Effects could be minimized by ensuring that the control group receives the intervention at a later date although, given school constraints on curriculum time, this may still disadvantage this set of students if they have to repeat a topic. Yet, when a developmental disorder and psychoactive drugs are involved, as in a study of the benefits of methylphenidate for children diagnosed with ADHD, RCT designs are considered appropriate and schools actively participate in them (Jensen *et al.*, 1999). Differences in potential risks and benefits of educational and pharmaceutical interventions may explain how the intensity of the debate can vary, but not how two contrasting sets of attitudes have come to prevail in these two fields of enquiry. It has been pointed out that the basic ethical dilemmas are similar, whether trialling methylphenidate or an educational intervention (Coch, 2007). Thus, despite sharing similar underlying principles of respect for the human condition, there appear to be cultural differences between the different ethical perspectives that may be used to guide neuroeducational research, suggesting there is a need to develop an acceptable ethical framework that specifically applies to such work.

The involvement of children in research

Neuroimaging procedures have been used in paediatric clinical contexts for many years. The need to understand more about normal development, not least as a source of insight into abnormal development, is now producing studies more closely related to mainstream educational aims. The development of neuroeducational research as an established field of enquiry will undoubtedly lead to greater numbers of imaging studies involving children. However, the procedures for children's participation in neuroimaging experiments are far from established. Guidelines for MRI scanning in paediatric clinical settings are emerging but the procedures here are likely to differ from those used by neuroeducational researchers. Paediatric clinical procedures can include features such as sedation (in order to reduce movement). This becomes less acceptable in experimental research whose outcomes are less promising in terms of immediate benefit to the individual, and they are wholly inappropriate in educational research. Another area of concern is safety screening (i.e. for the presence of metal). The standard screening procedures currently available are for adults, and a need has been identified for guidelines and procedures to be developed for children and their parents (Downie and Marshall, 2007). Even when an appropriate level of language has been used in these procedures, the disclosure by children of personal information (tattoos, piercings, pregnancy, etc.) can involve researchers in highly sensitive situations. Indeed, the role of parent and child throughout the research process, in terms of their presence, their contribution in meetings and their involvement in decision-making, requires careful consideration. Also, although the magnetic fields used in MRI are assumed to be safe with adults, less is known of the effects of such fields on the developing brain, and this suggests the need for additional caution. Incidental findings can also be a cause of particular distress for children and their parents, and these are not unusual, although usually without medical implication. In a retrospective review of 225 conventional paediatric MRI scans, referral rates were higher than those previously reported in the general population. Incidental abnormalities were detected in 21 per cent of instances (with seventeen requiring clinical referral and one urgent referral). Based on these results, the reviewers suggest there is an ethical case for MRI research involving children to always involve a trained radiologist (Kim *et al.*, 2002). Abnormal findings most usually require no referral but may, nevertheless, provide anxiety, particularly in school age children and teenagers, who may simply be concerned that something in their brain deviates from what others perceive as 'normal' (Downie *et al.*, 2007).

UK educational research guidelines point to Articles 3 and 12 of the UN convention on the Rights of the Child. Article 3 requires that, in all actions concerning children, the best interests of the child must be the primary consideration (BERA, 2004). That means any additional risk created by participation in research is unacceptable. Even so, however, the issues are still not straightforward. For example, this could provide an argument against participation in fMRI aimed at long-term benefits to the general population, simply on the basis of psychological risk of stress caused by incidental findings. On the other hand, such an argument might be defeated on the basis that such incidental findings might also protect the child's health. Article 12 requires that children who are capable of forming their own views should be granted the right to express their views freely in all matters affecting them, commensurate with their age and maturity. This has fed into the growing appreciation of the need for children to be more fully involved in decision-making in matters affecting them at school (Lundy, 2007) and this may include the research activity in which they participate. Consultation with children about research outcomes and their implications may become an important part of the neuroeducational research process, despite the additional challenge of ensuring that children's participation is informed.

Animal research

In-vivo imaging techniques now form the basis of most research relating to brain function and human learning. However, at cellular and chemical levels, much of what we know about the brain basis of learning derives from experiments with animals that usually involve their destruction. Feelings can run high about this type of experimentation. In 2004, it was actions and protests by a minority that caused the scrapping of plans for the Cambridge Primate Centre, which was to have been a major centre of UK research into human brain disease (Coghlan, 2004). The degree of controversy generated by animal experimentation is influenced by many different factors, including the type of animal involved. Around 55–70 per cent of people support the use of small rodents, but the involvement of dogs, cats and nonhuman primates reduces this figure to 32–55 per cent (Hagelin *et al.*, 2003). The type of research being undertaken also influences the acceptability of using animals. For example, acceptance appears to be stronger for using animals in medical research than in psychological research, even though the involvement and overall aims may be similar (Baluch and Kaur, 1995). How then might the involvement of animals in neuroeducational research be viewed? A survey by NEnet of the views of 188 trainee secondary school teachers showed divided opinions, with 38 per cent considering that animal experimentation should sometimes be carried out in order to address educational research questions, but with 48 per cent disagreeing with this, including 16 per cent who disagreed strongly.

Using information derived from animal research (including research carried out for other, e.g. medical, reasons) can promote its value and add to the case for using such methods. In that sense, simply using the results of such research to inform educational innovation could be viewed as an ethical decision in itself. In our survey of trainee teachers, 20 per cent felt that understanding about the brain derived from animal experimentation should not be used to inform educational understanding.

Scrutiny and communication of findings and concepts

We saw in Chapter 2 how the educational interest in neuroscience has helped spawn a number of neuromyths and unhelpful ideas that, at least, waste money and time and, at worst, also result in poor teaching and learning. In the face of such history, the scrutiny of educational ideas involving the brain should be of major ethical concern. But, how should such ideas be scrutinized and who should be scrutinizing them? We have seen that the language and concepts of neuroscience and education are very different. Some basic terms such as 'learning' may mean different things when used in an educational or neuroscientific context. It cannot be assumed that separate scrutiny by educational and scientific experts working in isolation from each other will always be sufficient. It is bound to be the case that the more innovative and valuable ideas will rest on how judiciously concepts from both disciplines have been integrated. Neither type of expert may feel comfortable making that judgement if they lack understanding of the other field. Until sufficient professionals exist with expertise in both areas, successful scrutiny may rest on *dialogue* between expert reviewers in dedicated interdisciplinary forums.

The ethical guidelines for researchers in education and for those in the sciences of mind and brain both emphasize the importance of accurate and honest reporting. However, guidelines for educational researchers usually make special mention of the quality of the communication and that it should be, for example, in 'clear, straightforward, and appropriate language to relevant research populations, institutional representatives, and other stakeholders' (AERA, 2000). Good communication has been identified by teachers as a key factor in the successful educational application of concepts from neuroscience (Pickering and Howard-Jones, 2007). Teachers, who are usually short on time, need clear and concise information in non-specialist terms that can be conveniently accessed. This is a serious challenge for any research community, especially one competing with an established host of unscientific ideas promoted by commercial interests. In a survey of teachers' opinions about collaboration between neuroscience and education, one teacher put the problem bluntly:

> ... the neuroscientists ... some of them have got a fantastic wealth of knowledge, but it's difficult for them to translate that knowledge ... they're not seen as communicators always, whereas the snake oil sellers often are gifted communicators and they're the ones that the teachers pay to come and talk to them on their INSET [in-service training] days ...
>
> (Pickering and Howard-Jones, 2007, p. 112)

Quality of communication, including communication of complex concepts to non-specialists, must clearly be an ethical priority for researchers in this interdisciplinary area. Here, however, there is undoubtedly a fine line to walk between producing understandable prose with minimal technical language and over-simplifying a message until it becomes misleading. Appropriate communication of findings in academic and practitioner journals, but also in the wider community, can require anticipation of how ideas will become interpreted. For example, researchers have an ethical duty to ensure images of brain differences between different groups of children do not contribute to stigmatization, lending unjustified weight to ideas of biological determinism and 'broken brains', and influencing the attitudes of children, parents and teachers in unhelpful ways.

Agency is another area of deliberation preoccupying the new field of neuroethics, and of relevance in communicating ideas in neuroeductional research. Understanding about the processes of control and self-regulation in the brain is constantly feeding discussions about the extent to which neuroscience challenges concepts of free will and voluntary decision making. The currently impoverished state of neuroscientific understanding in areas such as free will has already been touched upon in this book, but the beginning of a movement to use such evidence in legal judgements has begun (Morse, 2006). In the US, neuroscientific evidence of brain maturation was provided by both sides in the case of Roper v. Simmons. Here, the question of whether 16–17-year-olds found guilty of capital murder were sufficiently culpable to be executed was being considered. Morse reviewed the issues involved and concluded, prior to the outcome of the case, that the neuroscientific evidence alone could not decide such a question. In Roper v. Simmons, the court decided against the death penalty. However, as might have been predicted from Morse's review, the reasons provided by the Supreme Court in its judgement did not refer to any of the neuroscientific evidence that had been presented by both sides. It remains to be seen when, or if, new findings will be used to rekindle similar arguments in the future.

In educational domains, the inclusion of biological concepts can also threaten notions of agency. Here, however, it may already be influencing outcomes, if only through its potential for unfortunate and unjustified influence on teachers' and learners' attitudes. One example involves tentative insights about teenage behaviour based on emerging understanding of adolescent brain development. These have quickly become represented in public domains as deterministic, with headlines such as 'Stroppy teenagers can blame their brain' (Horton, 2006). Patience is a virtue, and probably ideas that help generate patience and tolerance of teenage behaviour might be helpful too. But at what point do such ideas relieve adolescents of responsibility for negative social behaviour? Unscientific communications that contribute to a diminished sense of agency among adolescent learners could be unhelpful for their development. Overly simplistic communications in the popular press may be unavoidable, but can be considered unethical if they arise from sources considered as expert.

Agency also became an issue in the public debate in the UK around dyslexia stirred up by the television documentary 'The Dyslexia Myth' (Mills, 2005). Here, effectiveness of interventions that resembled the type of 'normal' remediation classes for poor readers was presented as evidence that dyslexia was a myth.

The programme created a huge amount of controversy and discussion on blogs and web-sites, much of it quite emotional. However, in an article in *The Psychologist*, Nicholson pointed out that that the argument appeared to be that a 'true' disorder would not be remediated by such interventions, as if a 'true' disorder would need an intervention based on something other than good educational practice (Nicolson, 2005). Clearly this conflicts with what we know about the plasticity of the brain, but such arguments can significantly influence teachers' sense of agency in supporting children with developmental disorders. They also reflect the ease with which development disorders, which are increasingly being studied from biological perspectives, can take on a biologically determined character in the minds of non-specialists that makes them appear less amenable to educational remediation. The documentary was criticized for promoting an 'all-or-none' theorizing among the public and the sense that an individual case was sufficient evidence to reach general conclusions about a disorder. Nicholson suggested that the incorporation of modern views on brain function into existing approaches is part of the solution for avoiding such misunderstandings and, certainly, such an unhelpful oversimplification of the facts would be unethical if produced by a neuroeducational researcher.

When the facts are not simple, managing discussions among non-specialists can appear daunting but, excluding public discussion, can no longer be considered a serious option in ethical issues of public concern. Increased involvement of biological perspectives in educational thinking and practice are likely to generate many such discussions. There may be several areas of knowledge around which the public feels uncomfortable, and may even prefer to know nothing about, such as the relationship between genes and educational attainment. However, as Leshner (2005) points out, both complexity and public discomfort are arguments for working at public discussion, not for excluding it. Without an effective science-public partnership, the motives and values inherent in neuroeducational initiatives may become suspect, undermining the considerable benefits that may arise from this new, and therefore vulnerable, area of enterprise.

Whatever difficulties arise in attempting to communicate and discuss neuroscience in straightforward terms, there exists a clear argument that scientists should be involved in these efforts. In Chapter 2, we saw how neuromyths often begin with some set of scientific concepts that are then misinterpreted or overinterpreted by non-specialists. There is no-one better placed to police such erroneous interpretation than the scientists most closely associated with the concepts themselves. That places a clear moral duty on neuroscientists to engage in dialogue with education (Howard-Jones, 2009). That duty, however, is quite different from expecting them to don an educational 'hat' and be ready to make judgements about the educational suitability of supposedly brain-based ideas. That may be an unreasonable expectation that is, itself, ethically dubious. Indeed, Sheridan *et al.* warn that research combining neuroscience and education can easily suffer from what they call the 'hat problem', i.e. that people often get into ethical trouble when they wear too many hats, or do too much switching between them (Sheridan *et al.*, 2006). They point to the example of the academic geneticist who accepts public funds for basic research and then creates a private biotechnology company that operates in secret and profits illegitimately from the research. The ethical problem arises because business and science have different goals, as do neuroscience and education. A neuroscientist may have met his/her scientific goals in providing new understanding of a particular brain system, but when donning an educators' hat to promote or deny its educational merit, they may fail to embody the values and standards of the hat they are now wearing. Based on such considerations, Sheridan *et al.* make an ethical argument for the creation of a new type of professional – the 'neuroeducator'. Neuroeducators, they suggest, will assume a number of roles but all focused on issues interfacing neuroscience and education, thus minimizing hat swapping by a range of different types of experts that each possess only partial knowledge of the area. Neuroeducators could anticipate and monitor how neurocognitive advances may influence education, helping to make recommendations on developing educational knowledge, practice and policy that includes such insights. Although not directly solving any of the ethical issues discussed here, Sheridan *et al.* lay out a strong case for the effectiveness of individual expertise in concepts bridging neuroscience and education, and this may be a more effective way to develop this area than continuing to rely on mixed-discipline teams. However, they also accept that the creation of the 'neuroeducator' may bring its own ethical challenges. Such professionals will naturally be drawn to the possibilities of involving neuroscience in educational solutions. With closer ties to education, they will be in a strong position to implement interventions in schools and their natural bias may result in a premature introduction of ideas. The development of clear ethical guidelines for neuroeducational research will still be essential and possibly more so if education is to benefit from the professional 'neuroeducator'.

Policy

Even when research is carried out with careful consideration to ethics, and its findings scrutinized and communicated ethically, it will only tell us what *might* be done. It may indicate likely outcomes and perhaps some sense of their probability. Researchers will rarely go further and provide opinions of what *should* be generally done – this is left to policymakers who often foster and draw upon debate and consultation to help them make decisions. But who should be included in this dialogue and how? It might be argued that the public is not well educated enough to involve themselves in discussions about neuroscience, and such involvement may lead to outcomes that are uninformed. As we have seen, there may also be areas around which the public feel uncomfortable and less willing to engage, but avoiding public discussion risks distrust, further anxiety and conflict. As argued by Leshner in regard to neuroethics, it is far better to bring members of the public in early so that researchers can be made aware of public hopes and concerns, and ensure their research does not leave behind broader human values. In fostering a healthy science-public partnership, communication by the field itself, as discussed above, will be crucial. Such a partnership will enable government to tackle a range of policy issues that may arise in the future, some of which will be now be reviewed.

The potential policy issues are legion and might include decisions about curriculum (whether to focus more on developing basic cognitive function, whether to include understanding about the brain as an aid to developing study skills), scheduling (in the light of our emerging understanding of circadian rhythms and adolescent development) and futuristic possibilities involving brain-computer interfaces. However, in the new field of neuroethics, Farah suggests that issues which are new and imminent are more worthy of our attention than those with which we are already familiar or only likely to arise in the distant future (Farah, 2002). These are the criteria that will be applied here although, within neuroeducational research, the word 'new' will be interpreted as novel within the educational arena. This is because ethical issues already examined within, say, a medical context may need reconsideration in terms of the unique set of priorities, practices and concerns that help characterize educational contexts. The following issues of potential political interest survive the criteria of being new and imminent:

Cognitive enhancers

In the US, students are increasingly using prescription drugs in order to provide cognitive enhancement and thereby support their studies. Usage varies widely from one university to the next, with an average figure of 6.9 per cent of students indulging in non-medical use of prescription stimulants (McCabe et al., 2005). In another study, however, that surveyed 1,811 students at a large Southeastern US university, 34 per cent reported the illegal use of ADHD stimulants (e.g. methylphenidate), and these mostly to improve their cognitive function during periods of fatigue and stress (DeSantis et al., 2008).

The production of new and stronger drugs for cognitive enhancement appears set to increase, mostly as a result of efforts to combat the effects of Alzheimer's disease. One such drug is donepezil (marketed as Aricept) that increases levels of acetylcholine (ACh). ACh is thought to modulate the rate at which neural connections adjust themselves when learning, with increases in ACh able to bring about increases in learning rate. Donepezil reduces cholinesterase that mops up ACh, thereby increasing levels of ACh and improving cognitive function, including memory, among those suffering from Alzheimers (Roman and Rogers, 2004). The potential value of this drug for others was demonstrated in a study that administered donepezil to healthy young adults for only 30 days, and revealed significant improvements in episodic memory performance (Gron et al., 2005).

Scientists have been speaking out in positive terms about the 'new enhancement landscape' for healthy adults (see Chapter 3) (Gazzaniga, 2005). In a recent article in *Nature*, one group of scientists suggested that the growing demand for cognitive enhancement should be responded to, and that the response should begin by 'rejecting the idea that enhancement is a dirty word' (Greely *et al.*, 2008). However, a modest UK consultation showed more ambivalence (Horn, 2008), with concerns that included:

- possible side and long-term effects including personality change;
- the devaluation of 'normal' achievement and the intrinsic value of effort and motivation in learning;
- inequality if such drugs are expensive;
- pressure to use such drugs and the exacerbation of an already over-competitive culture.

In our NEnet survey of trainee teachers, most (73 per cent) felt that grades achieved with the help of cognitive enhancers should not be valued as highly as grades achieved without them, with 60 per cent anticipating they would contribute to the educational effects of the poverty gap, but with 63 per cent against them being made freely available. Most (54 per cent) also felt that random drug testing should be introduced if the use of such drugs became popular.

The apparently divergent views of scientists and educators suggests public consensus on cognitive enhancers may be some time arriving. Policymakers will expect answers to arise out of public and professional debate, but the readiness with which they arrive, and the usefulness and value of these answers, may rest heavily on how that debate is managed and conducted. Even when discussions are formally organized, educators cannot assume they will have a voice in them. When the governments' Foresight Programme appointed stakeholders and experts to discuss how cognitive enhancers (or 'cogs') might affect the UK, education was not represented. The 2005 consultative report predicted that cogs would start appearing in the UK around 2011 and, by 2017, might become 'an acceptable part of the knowledge professional's tool kit' (Jones *et al.*, 2005). Perhaps unsurprisingly, given the background of those compiling it, the report failed to consider what this would mean for education.

Brain-based screening

Event-related potentials (ERPs) refer to a set of distinct electrical signals emitted by the brain and detectable using a non-invasive technique involving the attachment of electrodes to the scalp. Some ERP waveforms of newborn infants have been identified that can differentiate between children who will later, at eight years old, be poor readers or be dyslexic (Molfese, 2000). Measurement of ERPs has been shown as an effective method of predicting dyslexia in new-borns with and without a family history of dyslexia (Guttorm *et al.*, 2005) and such techniques could form the basis of very early screening, so that children at risk of dyslexia are able to benefit as quickly as possible from suitable intervention (see also discussion by Friedrich of neural markers and specific language impairment (Friedrich, 2008)). Such techniques and possibilities are not limited to literacy. Another type of ERP has been identified that is sensitive to children's response to numerical distance (Szucs *et al.*, 2007) that may be a helpful neural marker for magnitude processing in infancy. This signal may provide an early indicator of later educational risk in respect of mathematics.

The use of neural markers to provide very early detection of educational risk for dyslexia is an area identified by Goswami where a neuroscience approach may provide particular promise for education (Goswami, 2008) However, when asked whether all infants should be screened for risk of dyslexia at the first opportunity, in order to allow early intervention, most (52 per cent) of the trainee teachers NEnet surveyed thought not, with 53 per cent considering that infant screening would give rise to undesirable 'labelling' of children.

Genetic profiling

The area where genetic knowledge is first likely to impact, and appears likely to do so in the next one to two decades, is in the area of learning difficulties. Gene-based diagnoses of potential learning difficulties will be able to predict general learning difficulty as well as difficulties within specific areas such as maths (Plomin, 2008). Such very early predictions, combined with emerging educational understanding of effective interventions, will provide the soonest possible implementation of appropriate help. Genetic knowledge will provide opportunities for new levels of personalized learning and these should ameliorate or even prevent the manifestation of some learning difficulties.

Ultimately, genetic knowledge should allow educational programmes to be better tailored to suit all individual genetic profiles. It has been suggested that, in the future, 'Educogeneticists' will be able to provide informed recommendations to schools and families about how a child's education may be planned in order to optimize academic outcomes (Grigorenko, 2007). Genetics may, therefore, have considerable educational potential beyond the early identification and amelioration of learning difficulties. This wider application, however, will only add further controversy to a plethora of ethical issues and questions about using genetic knowledge in education. What may result when genetic testing proceeds without full understanding of the educational intervention required? Who makes the decisions about testing and interventions, and by what processes? What precautions are needed to prevent this new educational opportunity feeding demand for genetic engineering and eugenics?

Among the cohort of trainee teachers we surveyed, 57 per cent thought the use of genetic information in education should be prevented, with a clear majority of 70 per cent considering it unlikely that the use of genetic information in education could be controlled sufficiently to make it desirable.

Summary

In the ethics regarding research procedures, neuroscience and education share similar levels of sensitivity regarding physical safety. The use of neurophysiological measurement in educational research raises some new issues regarding psychological risk, specifically in the area of incidental findings. Here, helpful guidelines are emerging, although the psychological stress from being alerted to potentially abnormal findings is an issue when considering risk-benefit ratios in neuroeducational research.

Social risks, to which educators are especially sensitized, are likely to be a frequent focus of ethical discussion around neuroeducational research procedures. These concerns would include the extent to which participants are empowered to be involved and have their views represented, and issues around the use of control groups. The tendency for change in brain function and structure to be seen as more fundamental than behavioural change (when, in fact, these two are interrelated) may, rightly or wrongly, exacerbate such concerns. The involvement of children in research makes it particularly important that steps should be taken to avoid/minimize all these types of risk, and presents additional challenges for those wishing to develop ethically sound protocols (e.g. in terms of facilitating fully informed consent and ensuring voice).

Given the ease with which unhelpful neuromyths have become popular and influential in schools, the quality with which findings are scrutinized and communicated to specialists and non-specialist audiences is likely to be a key ethical concern for the successful development of neuroeducational research. There is a need for researchers to thoughtfully anticipate and discourage misconceptions by non-specialists (e.g., such as those involving agency).

Increased understanding and advances at the interface between neuroscience and education will rapidly give rise to a host of policymaking decisions with salient ethical dimensions (including cognitive enhancers, infant screening using neural markers, genetic profiling). Opinion may be divided on these issues between educators and scientists, and among educators themselves. Policymakers will need to draw heavily on public consultation and debate, and the contribution of neuroeducational researchers to these debates will be crucial. More broadly, neuroeducational researchers have an important role to play in strengthening the science–public relationship, not least by ensuring their research proceeds in a manner sensitive to public hopes and concerns, and reflective of broader human values.

Chapter 8

Neuroeducational research case study A: Creativity

To illustrate how neuroeducational research can be pursued in practice, the next two chapters will provide overviews of research involving NEnet. The first of these focuses on creativity in drama education and was something of a journey for the author, with insights about methods and techniques, and their potential interrelation, often arising during the undertaking of the research itself. Always, however, the work was guided by the two goals of neuroeducational research described previously. In the present context, these translate as:

1   To further educational understanding and practice regarding the fostering of creativity in drama education, through the inclusion of insight derived from the sciences of brain and mind.
2   To further scientific understanding of the complex interrelationship between mind, brain and creative behaviour, through the engagement of natural science with the context of education.

Creativity is a higher-level thinking ability that draws on a potentially complex set of cognitive processes. For that reason, it is a challenging, possibly controversial, area of study for cognitive neuroscience (Szucs and Goswami, 2007). Progress has been made, however, in constructing the tasks and techniques to achieve this (Bechtereva *et al.*, 2007; Bowden and Jung-Beeman, 2007; Fink *et al.*, 2007). At the same time, from an educational perspective, there is an increasing interest in creativity in the curriculum and a surprising lack of guidance available for trainee drama teachers about how to develop it in their pupils. With such considerations in mind, tentative discussions began between the author and trainers of drama teachers about the psychology and neuropsychology of creativity and what, if anything, this might tell us about fostering it.

In 2003, these discussions helped identify a research question that could be addressed using scientific means and inform educational thinking with its implications. We had become interested in strategies involving randomness, such as when students are required to incorporate material and stimuli into their work that, in terms of their overt meanings and associations, are unrelated to each other and/or their current topic. Such strategies are not new but resemble the types of pragmatic strategy developed by many distinguished artists (e.g. Ernst, 1948) who have succeeded in 'elevating the appeal to chance and accident into a first principle of creation' (Hunter on Jackson Pollock (Hunter, 1958)). Many of the techniques used by these artists include an element of randomness reflecting their 'disdain for thesis' (Motherwell, 1981). Examples include using found objects that may bear no relation to each other or any predetermined theme, such as Kurt Schwitters' work generated from the contents of his wife's waste paper bin. Neither is it difficult to find such strategies being used already in classrooms, with established teaching techniques asking students to incorporate elements into their solution that are unrelated to each other and/or the problem (Gordon and Poze, 1980). However, as we reflected on how similar strategies were being used in the classroom, we wondered whether these were engaging students in the types of mental process that they should be rehearsing as budding creative artists. Behavioural evidence can suggest this may be the case, with independent panels of judges rating outcomes as more creative when such strategies have been employed. For example, when volunteer trainee drama students were asked to create twenty-second stories from sets of three words, a panel of judges rated them as more creative when the students had to incorporate three unrelated, rather than related, words. However, was this because the 'random' strategy had stimulated cognitive processes associated with creativity, or simply because the judges appreciated stories more when they contained three unrelated words? Understanding the effect of such strategies at a brain level can help with this question. An imaging study cannot, of course, prove that someone is thinking more creatively. Cognition, as discussed in Chapter 5, cannot be directly observed or measured. But if the strategy increases engagement with creative mental processes, we should expect activity in brain regions associated with those processes to change also.

The educational question of whether these strategies encouraged rehearsal of creative processes crystallized into a testable scientific hypothesis, and one that would be educationally informative. The basic hypothesis was this: when participants incorporated unrelated, compared with related, words in the generation of a creative story, activity in those brain regions associated with creative effort in the task would change. (Based on our understanding of the role of these regions – see below – we hypothesized an increase.) Although testing this hypothesis would not *prove* additional creative engagement, it would provide valuable evidence to support such a claim. Also, the location of the changes within the brain might provide clues about how the strategies worked at a cognitive level, helping to inform how they should be used in the classroom.

Study 1: Scientific experimental study of a creativity-fostering strategy

The testability of the hypothesis relied upon a number of scientific considerations. One factor likely to determine our success in testing it was the current state of scientific knowledge in the area. Was it sufficient to provide an anatomical hypothesis? In this particular case, this translated to 'can one form a reasoned expectation of where in the brain the correlates of creative effort in story telling will be found?' In life, knowing where something might be found, whether it's the car keys or one's coat, allows the search area to be reduced and makes success more likely. A similar rule holds in neuroimaging: if you need to search the whole brain, the statistical threshold for accepting the significance of an activity should be raised, and that means small (but potentially interesting) activities may get ignored. An anatomical analysis that predefines the search regions thus makes smaller activities within those regions potentially more significant. Having an anatomical hypothesis in relation to a cognitive task is also important because it means you have a theoretical brain–mind model for the task that can help make sense of your findings. This is a model that your findings can build on, and contribute to. Otherwise, if you take a purely exploratory approach with no expectation of what cognitive processes and brain activities are likely to be involved, any activation you do find may be challenging to explain or contextualize within existing scientific understanding.

The creation of stories is a language task, and language processes are considered, in most people, to be strongly lateralized to the left hemisphere. However, divergent semantic language processing may be one of several exceptions. This is important here because creative processes can be considered as characterized by making meaningful connections between concepts that are normally unassociated, i.e. divergent semantic processing. For example, event-related potentials (ERPs) have been measured when participants generated uses for stimulus nouns (Abdullaev and Posner, 1997). In this study, it was found that that ERPs were lateralized to the left hemisphere when uses and stimulus nouns were related, but were bilateral (i.e. left and right) when uses were generated that were less commonly linked to the nouns. Thus, right-hemisphere representations appear more suitable than left-hemisphere representations for the semantic processing of distant associates. It is the right inferior frontal gyrus that is most commonly implicated by imaging studies of those language processes associated with the right hemisphere (Bookheimer, 2002) but this region is thought to be involved with making decisions about making inferences and producing a complete representation of meaning and intent. However, in the fMRI study of Seger *et al.*, when participants generated unusual verbs for nouns (which is likely to involve divergent semantic processing), as opposed to the first verb that came into their head, there was increased activity in the right middle and superior frontal gyri, and right medial frontal gyrus (Seger *et al.*, 2000). Thus, it may be that prefrontal parts of the right hemisphere support the processing of distant associations and, as proposed by Seger *et al.*, creative thinking in language-based contexts. These results also concur with a PET study by Bekhtereva *et al.* (2000). In short, we now had some idea of where our correlates of creative effort might be found.

As well as helping to decide where to look, Bekhtereva's research also helped inspire our experimental protocol. In Bekhtereva's research, participants were required to generate a story from a set of sixteen unrelated words presented simultaneously. When participants used unrelated compared with related words, their analysis revealed additional activity for unrelated words in prefrontal regions of the right hemisphere, in the superior frontal, mediofrontal and inferior frontal gyri. In our study, we decided to use fMRI, with its improved spatial resolution, to investigate the neural correlates of creativity in a story generation task by comparing brain activity when participants were producing creative and uncreative stories from sets of three words. The activity revealed by this analysis would identify those regions of the brain associated with creative effort. According to our cognitive hypothesis, we were testing whether activity in these regions would be further increased by the strategy intended to foster creativity (i.e. using unrelated rather than related words). Thus, following Bekhtereva, we also compared the effect upon activities when using related and unrelated words but we employed a factorial design, which allowed comparison of creative and uncreative objectives (to identify regions that became more active with creative effort), and also related and unrelated word sets (to identify which regions associated with creative effort were further activated by the unrelatedness of the words). It was the interaction between objective and relatedness that would be of greatest interest. Our anatomical hypothesis suggested this interaction effect would include additional activity in the regions of the right frontal hemisphere identified by Seger *et al.* (2000), based on Carol Seger's suggestion that these regions are critically associated with divergent semantic processing. The stories that were generated in the experiment would also be judged by an independent panel, to ensure that the strategy was increasing the *perceived* creative value of the stories being produced (using the Consensual Assessment Technique (Amabile, 1996)).

More information about this study can be found in *Cognitive Brain Research* but, given the scope and audience of such journals, some details reflecting the interests and issues of educators were underplayed or even excluded (Howard-Jones *et al.*, 2005). These details, however, will be reported more fully here because they illustrate how imaging studies with educational aims may differ from those with purely neuroscientific ones.

One major difference between cognitive neuroscientific perspectives and those found in educational research is a greater concern for ecological validity. Potentially, of course, an appraisal of ecological validity highlights major drawbacks for those wishing to use fMRI to explore educational issues. The environment of the scanner is very different to that of the classroom, and in ways that might raise serious issues when it comes to interrelating outcomes from these two environments. In the case of creativity, a variety of environmental factors are thought to influence these outcomes, including stress and mood. It appeared entirely possible at the outset of the study that the physical and visual restrictions, and the presence of considerable noise, might unduly influence and possibly reduce the creativity of participants.

To investigate this issue of ecological validity, a mock scanner was constructed with identical dimensions to the real scanner we intended to use. It played recordings of MRI noise and provided similar visual constraints. Participants were asked to generate stories in each of the four conditions to be used in the fMRI experiment. They were asked to do this in the environment of the mock scanner and also when sitting at a desk in a quiet room. Perhaps surprisingly, the different environments did not appear to influence the creativity ratings of the stories produced (see Fig. 8.1). The effect of the four conditions when sitting at a desk followed a similar pattern as that observed when creating under simulated scanning conditions. Further checks compared ratings of stories recalled after authentic scanning with those recalled after simulation. In all environments (scanner, simulated scanner and at a quiet desk), conditions were tightly controlled and so this approach does not remove all of issues of ecological validity when transferring laboratory findings to the classroom (which is not, of course, a quiet room). It does, however, go some way to demonstrating that creative performance in the scanner environment was not being unduly influenced by its more salient and 'unnatural' features.

Concerns about ecological validity also influenced the choice of task. Originally, we thought about simpler tasks involving word generation, which would be much easier to control. But these bore little resemblance to typical classroom activities. Using a story generation task improved ecological validity but at the expense of some scientific control. A major issue was that stories could not be reported verbally during scanning, due to noise. Verbal reporting would also recruit speech articulation regions of the brain and produce head movement, with both effects confounding image analysis. We could ask participants to generate the stories in their heads, but how would we know the participants were really doing this? In an attempt to tackle this problem, participants were prompted (using some of the same word sets they had been presented with) to recall a selection of their stories immediately after they had left the scanner.

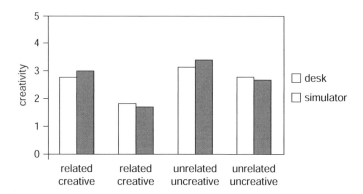

Figure 8.1 Responses of eight participants to different objectives (creative, uncreative) and relatedness of words to be included (related, unrelated) in a story telling task when seated at a quiet desk and when experiencing simulated fMRI scanning conditions.

These stories were judged by our independent panel along with those recorded during simulation, when stories could be recorded as they were produced. In the retrospective story telling, participants were not reminded which condition the words had occurred in, but the creative ratings followed the same pattern as observed when participants were producing the stores spontaneously. This provided some reassurance that participants were quietly generating stories in the scanner according to the instructions they were given.

Another unusual feature of the experimental procedure was the use of qualitative techniques. These included semistructured interviews to collect participants' reflections on their experiences, thus informing our understanding from an 'insider' perspective. These interviews supported our textual analysis of the stories participants generated, helping us to understand more about the literary devices that were being employed and shedding further light on the cognitive processes that might be involved. By identifying the ways in which participants made links between remotely associated concepts (between those provided, but also between concepts they had generated themselves), it was possible to demonstrate that our creative story generation task involved considerable amounts of divergent semantic processing, supporting the theoretical basis of the hypothesis. For example, when attempting to be creative, stories contained carefully selected divergent connections between contextual elements that operated on more than one level. The following story is from a participant trying to be creative with unrelated words. Here, the cow has been connected to the star through a space-related nursery rhyme. This also allowed the introduction of the word 'zip' (original stimulus words in bold, rated creative score out of five in parentheses):

> This **cow** got so fed up with people doubting that cows could jump over the moon that it decided to jump over a star. To do this, it wore a special rocket suit. The cow **zip**ped up the space suit, lit the blue touch paper and flew up over the **star**. (4.0)

In another story, when participants were trying to be creative with related words, the participant introduced their own unrelated context of being marooned on a desert island. Through this device, additional connections could be made between the original three words that were related through a football theme:

> Marooned on a desert island with nothing to do I **kick**ed around watermelons. I became so good at it that, when I was finally picked up by a passing boat, I was encouraged to join the local **football** team – I scored lots of **goal**s and was soon recognized for the amazing talent that I'd become. (3.6)

In contrast, when being uncreative, participants tended to stay focused upon a single and unelaborate connection between the words, thus minimizing the introduction of any additional contextual material. Often, as in this story from the uncreative-related condition, the participants achieved this by simply restructuring the same connection in a somewhat repetitive way:

> The children were told that they must **brush** their **teeth** when they are young in order to make them **shine** and that they wouldn't have any friends if their teeth weren't shiny. So every single night, the children brushed their teeth to make them shine. (2.4)

In the unrelated-uncreative condition, as in the following example, some additional contextual retrieval and divergent association was necessary, but at least one of the words was often linked to the narrative in a superficial manner:

> I looked at the sky on a really dark day not so long ago – it was really black and one particular **cloud** looked as though there was lightening going to come out of it. The **strike** just happened then and it hit the bunch of **grapes** I was eating at the same time – not me. (2.6)

It appeared creativity was influenced more by objective (i.e. by whether participants were trying to be creative or not) in the related conditions than in the unrelated conditions. This reflected what the participants themselves told us, about how they found being uncreative with unrelated words quite difficult. Indeed, according to our model above, some remote association must be found between the unrelated words and our participants were clearly aware of this.

Ethically, in order to provide additional reassurance with respect to physical safety, participants were screened soon after volunteering to identify potential issues, e.g. the presence of metal in the body. This early action allowed time, if needed, for the participant to refer to their medical records or for other checks to be made, while participants began preliminary experiments using only the simulator. All participants were then screened again just prior to being scanned, to double check information and pick up any new issues that might have arisen during the interim period. Apart from exploring issues of ecological validity, the simulator proved itself useful in supporting ethical procedures. It provided participants with an opportunity to become more informed about the experience of being scanned, helping them to make an informed decision about whether to participate in the real thing. It also provided some acclimatization, helping to reduce anxiety later.

From a scientific perspective, the findings of this scientific research supported the suggestion that some prefrontal regions of the right hemisphere can be involved with the divergent semantic processing associated with creativity – as suggested by Carol Seger (see Chapter 2 and Fig. 2.1). Current scientific understanding prompts an explanation for this involvement that includes the need for additional episodic retrieval, monitoring and higher cognitive control. Of most interest, however, was the effect of the strategy on these correlates of creative effort. As expected, the use of unrelated, as opposed to related, words increased the rated creativity of outcomes. Image analysis of this interaction between relatedness and objective showed that requiring participants to incorporate semantically unrelated material produced additional activity in one of these prefrontal regions. Specifically, activity associated with effortful creativity in the right medial gyrus increased when participants used unrelated, as opposed to related, words (see Fig 8.2). This is the additional activity linked to the observed increase in creative ratings of stories due to using the strategy. Qualitative analysis of the stories highlighted the making of additional associations between the stimulus words that complemented, or at least did not contradict, the initial connection found between them. Such elaboration might require additional episodic memory retrieval, but the location of the activity did not correspond well with this explanation. Instead, it appeared more suggestive of increased high level conscious control.

In a study by other researchers, intentional false responding was found to share neural substrates with response conflict and cognitive control, and a cluster of activity similar to ours (centres 11 mm apart) was identified when participants falsified responses to autobiographical questions (Ganis *et al.*, 2003). As with the falsification of information, effortful creativity requires the inhibition of responses that are unconvincing (be it in terms of likelihood or novelty)

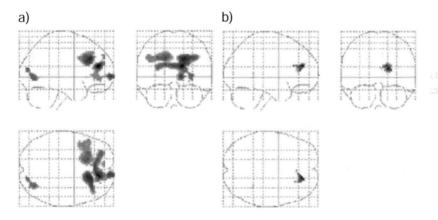

Figure 8.2 a) Activity in bilateral prefrontal regions associated with creative effort in a story-telling – suggesting involvement of right hemisphere regions, despite the linguistic nature of the task. b) Where the activity identified in the previous diagram is increased in response to the strategy of incorporating unrelated material, i.e. in the right medial gyrus.
Source: From Howard-Jones, P. A., Blakemore, S. J., Samuel, E., Summers, I. R. and Claxton, G. (2005) Semantic divergence and creative story generation: An fMRI investigation. *Cognitive Brain Research*, 25, 240–250. Reprinted by permission from Elsevier. Copyright © 2005.

or self-conflicting. Additional effort to creatively combine words and contexts from different semantic fields may result in combinations that are greater in number and diversity, consequently demanding increased inhibition of inappropriate outcomes.

From an educational perspective, the behavioural results concurred with outcomes observed in practice when using such a strategy. More interestingly, the fMRI data shows the strategy can increase brain activity in those regions associated with creative effort, providing some evidence (but short of proving) that it is not simply a 'cognitive short-cut' to something that appears more creative but actually requires no additional creative cognitive processing. The location of the additional activity suggests that, although such strategies themselves appear a little 'wild', the extra cognition they can encourage includes additional high-level evaluation and filtering of ideas, rather than just boosting low-level associative/generative thinking. Increased blood flow does not always mean additional mental performance but, in this case, with improved outcomes and increased blood flow according to a predetermined anatomical hypothesis and cognitive model, such a link can be tentatively made. This also makes it more likely that such strategies are helpful in the longer term (and, indeed, increased activity in regions associated with a task has been linked to structural change (Draganski *et al.*, 2004), see Chapter 1 and Fig. 1.1), although more research is required looking specifically at this issue.

Study 2: Practice-based study of the experiences of using the strategy, using performance research methods

The fMRI study had provided more understanding of the effectiveness of the strategy, but chiefly from an 'outsider' perspective and in a very constrained context. A subsequent two-day theatre workshop was arranged to investigate 'insider' insights about this type of strategy, as well as the experimental processes we had used to investigate them. The team consisted of three professional actors, a theatrical director (Michael Walling, of the Border Crossings Theatre Company), a drama consultant and the author, all of whom participated actively in the workshop. This workshop also provided an opportunity to explore how understanding the strategy at a brain–mind level could inform insights in more 'real world' contexts about their application. It would be filmed so that excerpts could provide meaningful starting points for later discussion with educators that would be more directly aimed at developing educational 'praxis' – that part of teachers' knowledge that guides their actions. In a general sense, performance methodology can be considered as 'a deep kinesthetic attunement that allows us to attend to experiential phenomena in an embodied, rather than purely intellectualized way' (Pineau, 1994). However, this broad construction can be broken down further into a range of ways in which performance can be strategically used. Our piece of research would investigate creativity fostering strategies related to those investigated in the scanner, but in dramatic contexts that also included neural and psychological concepts. In these senses, then, it was using performance methodology in two quite different ways: as a method of educational inquiry but also as a means to re-enact and incite some of the cultural issues involved with the sciences of brain and mind (Alexander, 2005). The second aspect was a valuable introduction to understanding the existing field of cultural values with which any innovative educational ideas involving the brain and creativity might interact. This was helpful in the later discussions around teachers' praxis, not least in allowing early identification of common misconceptions.

One thing was clear from the outset: to clearly communicate/explore any single research finding about the brain, it needs to be communicated as part of a broader set of concepts, particularly those that make it meaningful. For example, there was a need to explore the meaning of 'creativity' in dramatic contexts and how we think about the role of our brains in our behaviour. One investigation of our relationship with our own brain involved adapting a common drama exercise, in which a listener intermittently challenges a story-teller by saying 'that's a lie'. This challenge must be immediately accepted and prompts the teller to shift the narrative of their story in a different direction. This exercise was adapted such that one performer told a story, while another played analyst and challenged them by objectifying their perceptions with scientific concepts and jargon, suggesting their neurobiology may have altered self-perceptions. For example, 'Was your emotional reaction due to low levels of serotonin?' or 'Was your excitement caused by stimulants?' would immediately cause perceptions to be revised and the narrative to continue in a new direction. In this way, a scene developed which gave an interesting portrayal of how our self-perceptions may be mediated by our constructions about our brain function. After having watched the character's identity shift and disintegrate in the face of scientific explanation, the audience reflected on resonances with events arising from their own experience and the idea of our identity responding to what experts choose to objectify. At what point, we wondered, do we decide that some aspect of our behaviour is indisputably us? Who is in control?

Many of the improvisations generated in the workshop focused around this theme of 'control', exploring our sense of agency in creativity, including when strategies (such as the one investigated in scanner) are imposed upon us by others aiming to enhance it. A case study by Lythgoe was used as the basis for one improvisation, in which the patient had suffered a disruption in control networks causing long-term obsessive compulsive creativity (Lythgoe *et al.*, 2005). T had been a 51-year-old builder with no previous interest in the arts, who suffered a subarachnoid hemorrage – a bleeding in the space around the front of the brain – resulting in frontal dysfunction. In the weeks following his injury, T became a prolific artist. He first began filling notebooks with poetry, then began drawing sketches and in the following months produced large-scale drawings on the walls of his house, sometimes filling whole rooms. His artistry continues to this day and has become more developed. T cannot stop generating material, often only sleeping two to three hours a night between days filled with sculpting and painting. He shows verbal disinhibition, albeit creatively, by constantly talking in rhyming couplets – effectively a loss of control over inhibiting and expressing ideas entering consciousness. In an improvisation of the patient's condition, the actor maintained a poetic 'flow of consciousness', as observed by Lythgoe. The actor described the experience as liberating, hard work, but also slightly risky, with little sense of control. The 'think aloud' nature of the exercise left the actor feeling slightly exposed and vulnerable. The cognitively and emotionally demanding nature of creativity would be returned to in later discussions with teachers, and this exercise provided an initial basis for educational discussions about such issues, including in relation to 'random' strategies. Being the subject of a creativity-fostering strategy is not, of course, comparable to suffering a disorder, but the exercise did help us think about how such strategies can shift the focus of control away from the student. In some senses, by ameliorating any sense of fixation that might exist, this can be liberating but it could also be constraining and controlling. Supposing, for example, that a student wished to create directly around their own chosen elements, to maintain focus upon elements close to their own identity? A random strategy imposed by a teacher could be seen as subverting this freely willed creative direction.

Some of the improvisations were aimed at directly investigating the use of random strategies in dramatic improvisation, while another reconstructed (using the simulator) the fMRI experiment detailed previously. This provided some further critical examination of the experimental protocol from an entirely experiential perspective, and even provided some further insight into the results. For example, a specific question had arisen when the experimental study was being reviewed for publication. This was about the additional brain activities produced in the visual cortex when participants were being uncreative, compared with being creative. This was a little surprising since visualization, which can activate the visual cortex, tends to be commonly associated with being creative (not being uncreative). One possible explanation for these activations might be that participants were avoiding the task by looking around the scanner environment. However, actors who participated in a reconstruction of this condition reflected on how they had visually fixated on a single unchanging and stereotypical scene and unadventurously redescribed it, in order to reduce the creativity of their outcome, echoing some of the reflections produced by participants after the experiment. One actor, for example, maintained a low level of creativity by describing themselves in a room and giving an extended description of a (somewhat conventional) door. He maintained his attention upon this door through visualizing it in all its dull detail. When being creative, however, he did not fixate upon the door in his visualization but walked through it, elaborating on his story and moving on in the narrative. It appears that strategies involving visualization can be helpful when attempting to be uncreative, as well as creative.

Method + practice of teaching — as a academic Subject or theoretical Concept

Study 3: Practice-based study to develop co-constructed concepts with practitioners about the fostering of creativity in the classroom

Some scientific insights had been achieved, together with a better understanding of the broader issues arising when we reflect on the brain, creativity and the strategies intended to foster it. To understand what all this might mean for pedagogy would require a deeper involvement of educational practitioners, and so the next phase of research was back at the department of Drama Education where discussions had originally begun. The objective now was to 'co-construct' pedagogical concepts enriched by scientific insights about the brain and the mind, with a group of trainee teachers led by a team with both educational and scientific expertise in the area. The research team consisted of two very experienced trainers of drama teachers and the author. The methods used to communicate concepts and the details of the content covered in sessions was negotiated between members of the research team and informed by the responses of the trainees as the project progressed. In terms of content, note was made of what trainees found useful in terms of understanding their own and their pupils' experiences and learning. In terms of developing communication methods, the research team took particular interest in the appropriateness, relevance and validity of the ideas expressed by trainees during sessions.

Sixteen trainee teachers, in the second year of their training, voluntarily took part in what was advertised as a short programme of seminars and activity-based workshops exploring concepts about creativity (Howard-Jones *et al.*, 2008). An action research spiral was followed by the researchers (see Fig. 8.3) consisting of initial discussions between members of the research team and with the trainee teachers, followed by three cycles of research meeting, seminar, workshop and student discussion. This cycle ended in a final meeting of the team to reflect upon the project as a whole. Workshops, seminars and trainee discussions were videoed. After each of these events, an analysis of the video data was used as a basis for discussions during subsequent research team meetings that deliberated upon progress and revised future plans. An audio recording was made of these research team meetings and this was transcribed to help track the issues raised and decisions made.

Initial discussion with trainees about how to foster their pupils' creativity

Before introducing any new concepts, we had an initial discussion with the trainees that provided some sense of baseline regarding existing ideas about creativity. Trainees felt comfortable with definitions of creative thinking as producing outcomes with originality and a sense of value (NACCE, 1999). They expressed strong personal convictions about the importance of creativity; a capability that enriched many parts of their lives and that was especially appreciated in

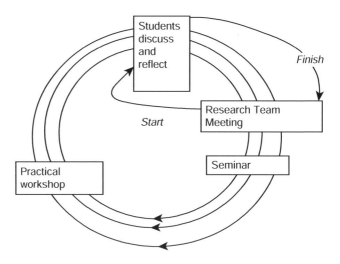

Figure 8.3 The action research spiral followed by the researchers in Study 3. After an initial meeting of the research team and an initial discussion with the student participants (trainee teachers), there were three cycles of research meeting, seminar, workshop and discussion with participants, ending with a final meeting of the research team to reflect upon the project as a whole.
Source: Howard-Jones, P. A., Winfield, M. and Crimmins, G. (2008) Co-constructing an understanding of creativity in the fostering of drama education that draws on neuropsychological concepts. *Educational Research*, 50, 187–201. Reprinted by permission from Taylor and Francis Ltd. Copyright © 2005.

drama education. Many had chosen to become drama teachers because, as pupils themselves, they had discovered drama was a subject area that embraced creativity. However, creativity was generally seen as a spontaneous process mostly beyond influence and that should simply be allowed to flourish:

> Kids they just – they draw so many things from so many places and they can bring it all together and they can – and there's your creativity – you can't teach it.

Trainees generally considered creativity appeared in the absence of poor teaching rather than resulting from good teaching, with a 'hands off' notion of fostering creativity. This was evident in the frequent use of phrases such as 'you're allowing them to be creative'.

First cycle

It had become clear in the performance research that introducing a piece of scientific research, extracted from its own scientific contexts, can undermine its intended meaning. Therefore, rather than simply provide detail of the fMRI study just undertaken, it would be necessary for this, and other findings from psychology and neuroscience, to be presented as part of a broader scientific understanding of creativity. With cognition as a key part of the conceptual bridge between neuroscience and education, the team agreed that the initial seminar should begin with introducing a simple model of creative cognition. The model we used was originally developed to support the teaching of design and it describes creative cognition as involving two modes of thinking: generative (G) and analytical (A) (Howard-Jones, 2002). (Note that the existence of two such distinct modes of thinking is not a new one (Kris, 1952; Werner, 1948; Wundt, 1896)). The model emphasizes the difference between thought processes we use to critically evaluate an outcome and those we use to generate it in the first place, the latter requiring access to concepts that are more remotely associated with the matter at hand. When engaged in analytical thinking, an individual is expected to be focused and to constrain their attention upon the analysis. However, when accessing remote associates, there is benefit from being less focused and allowing attention to drift towards concepts that have not, previously, been directly associated with the brief. Analytical thinking can also be useful elsewhere in the creative process, such as when researching a topic or context before generating any ideas. Creativity may be characterized by an ability to move from one mode of thought to the other without difficulty. Production of even a single creative idea can require alternation between a focused analytical state when exploring what is known about an issue, a generative state when finding associations beyond the context of the issue itself, and a return to the analytical state to assess the value of what had been generated. However, in the production of a short piece of drama, more complex trajectories between these two modes of thinking can be assumed. It was pointed out the conditions for supporting analytical and generative thinking can be quite different. Trainees were reminded how our analytic abilities can be supported by being encouraged to remain focused, being offered some monetary reward for our performance, or by the mild stress of knowing we may be evaluated and assessed. Generative ability, on the other hand, can benefit from changes in context (Howard-Jones and Murray, 2003), tasks that require divergent semantic association (Howard-Jones et al., 2005), intrinsic motivations such as fascination and curiosity (Cooper and Jayatilaka, 2006) and relaxation (Forgays and Forgays, 1992). Trainees were then introduced to 'random strategies' as one demonstrable way of how the creativity of pupils might be directly influenced by a teacher.

In the discussion that followed this initial seminar, there was great enthusiasm for enriching pedagogy with what we know about the brain and mind. Much of the dialogue focused on the fMRI study. The power of brain-imaging to engage interest is well known and research has shown that it stimulates a sense of objective evidence and a 'physicalization' of concepts of the mind (Cohn, 2004). There are attendant dangers in this interest, such as encouraging notions of static brain states with activity restricted to a few small regions. However, judging by the response of the trainees, it can also help 'concretize' psychological concepts that might otherwise remain too abstract to be of interest to non-specialists. Trainees were keen to find real-world analogies with the fMRI experimental task and resonances with their own experience. A trainee reported how she had recently asked every pupil in her class to construct a story around any two of four items: a map, a set of car keys, a ballet show and a bottle. Two of these items, the map and car keys, seemed more obviously related and she noticed the effect on the pupils' creativity:

> ... the majority of people in the class chose the map and the keys and there were just different variations of car crashes and that was pretty much all they came up with, and the bottle and the ballet shoe – that really worked a lot more creatively.

These observations were, at first, simple behavioural cause-effect links, without great reference to any underlying cognitive process and echoing some of the ideas raised in the initial discussion. For example, the trainees again seemed to refer to creativity as a spontaneous process, but now as one which required the right level of constraint – not so constrained that it cannot flourish, but requiring enough guidance to provide reassurance. Such ideas have been expressed in studies of creativity in dance education, as a balance between control and freedom (Chappell, 2006). It appeared that the trainees' ideas about creativity were becoming more sophisticated, as they suggested that their own creativity sometimes depended on the right level of constraint being provided by their tutor.

As the trainees began to focus more upon underlying cognition, one voiced a realization that such reflection might transform their perceptions and their strategy:

> ... as soon as you build an understanding of how people work, and why they work like that then you don't necessarily see someone's behaviour in the same way ...

A practical workshop followed, aimed at providing trainees with experiences that could later, with support, be linked to some of the scientific concepts of mind and brain they had been introduced to. The research team was aware of the likely importance of developing trainees' ability to identify transitions between G and A modes of thinking. So, after the workshop, trainees were asked to produce a line graph indicating where they might have been along the G/A continuum at various points in the workshop. Outcomes were very varied but the process prompted trainees to begin reflecting upon their own creative cognitive processes.

> In the last task, you were able to be very ... like ... um generative in the process of creating. And then ... because we were in a group and we knew

we had to perform ... we had to bring it back and be like ... analytical ... so my last line is going up and down ... we did go back and look at what we were doing ... (laughter) ... but obviously not enough!

Reflecting on the workshop, trainees discussed the ease with which thinking can tend to the obvious, and how it feels when the obvious option is made less available. For example, trainees commented that the items they had selected themselves appeared to them already connected, and they had often begun making a story with them at once. When trainees were required to improvise by linking together unrelated objects selected by the research team, the task became more challenging and difficult, possibly reflecting the additional frontal medial activity observed in the fMRI study of semantic divergence:

I felt really limited by the fact that you'd given us objects and the fact that we couldn't choose our own ... I felt really like I'd hit a wall and was going to have to really think about how I was going to move on ...

Not all the exercises had produced the levels of creativity expected. In the first exercise, the trainees suggested they had needed a warm-up as a way of clearing away some of the unwanted foci of the day to make a space for new ideas. The trainees were excited by the importance of relaxation and the generative state, and they also discussed how planning one's actions can sometimes diminish generation of ideas. This gave rise to the idea that planning, in which one sets out the stages by which one will achieve a goal, can encourage an analytical mind set that discourages the generation of new direction and ideas. The trainees appeared comfortable classifying *tasks* as being creative or uncreative and seemed to avoid considering their role in creativity more broadly, i.e. whether they supported the type of thinking required in a particular context. For example, one trainee had begun believing that planning always diminished creativity and the inclusion of randomness always increased it:

I've got it into my head now that to be uncreative you plan and stuff – so now I think that the last improvisation we did was completely uncreative because I planned it? Because we discussed it as a group and I don't know now I'm all confused ... I think that the last task was more random ... you gave us lots of randomness ...

The team gave examples of how different levels of planning can be good or bad for creativity depending on contextual issues, such as the individuals involved and the types of cognition one might wish to encourage at a particular stage in a creative process. The generative part of creativity had been the main focus of discussion but the team felt it was important to remind them that analysis is also needed at appropriate times.

Second cycle

In the next research team meeting, we discussed how trainees had a tendency to make short cuts from teaching strategies to outcomes without consideration of underlying cognitive processes and context. There was a danger that our efforts were producing a new neuromyth: 'neuroscience tells us randomness is creativity'. We needed to diminish the temptation to classify teaching strategies themselves as always producing creative or uncreative outcomes. Instead, we wanted to encourage trainees to think more about the appropriateness of teaching strategies in terms of particular contexts, in terms of the cognitive processes they encouraged and whether these might be helpful in progress towards creative targets. It was possible that some of the students would feel daunted by this task. The team identified the abstract nature of cognitive concepts as part of the challenge. We wanted to make our cognitive model of creativity more concrete for the trainees. We had noticed how they had been fascinated by mention of the neuroscientific case study of T (as had the participants in the performance research), so it was decided to detail two such studies in the next seminar, to illustrate extreme examples of the two modes of thinking. This was felt appropriate in the context of training teachers, but the use of such case studies with children would clearly raise some ethical issues. Trainees would, therefore, be discouraged from using a similar approach with children. The team felt that classroom discussions about disorders of the mind might easily lead to misconceptions that could confuse and distress some pupils if the (trainee) teachers leading the discussions were not versed in the necessary expertise.

In the next seminar, the trainees were introduced to the cingulate cortex – an island of cortex below the external surface of the brain. The front (anterior) part of this region shares a controlling function with the frontal lobes and is associated with executive attention – the cognitive mechanism by which we control the focus of our attention (Gehring and Knight, 2000). Hyperactivity in this region has been associated with obsessive-compulsive disorder (OCD) and the associated preoccupation of sufferers with correcting perceived mistakes (Fitzgerald et al., 2005). The trainees were played an interview with a sufferer of OCD, who described her ritualistic repetitive routines. It was discussed how this type of rehearsal resembled the analytical and evaluative rehearsal processes used to hone a piece of creative work, but taken to an obsessive and very uncreative extreme. It was as if sufferers of OCD are caught in an analytical mode of thinking. In contrast, the team then presented the case of compulsive creativity discussed earlier (Lythgoe et al., 2005). Trainees discussed how T appeared to be caught in a generative mode of thinking. Trainees listened to an interview with T who explained what his world was like and they read a poem Brain Explorer – it's for you that he had written for the author of his case study. The voices of those suffering from very generative or analytical mental states helped characterize these modes of thinking more clearly for the trainees and support them in monitoring their own modes of thinking.

In the improvisational exercises that followed, trainees were occasionally interrupted and asked to hold up G or A cards to indicate their current mode of thinking. The first exercise was 'talk for a minute', in which they had to speak without pause or hesitation on a topic chosen for them. That was followed by a 'delayed copying' exercise in which students had to continuously reproduce not the movement just made by the leader, but the movement previous to it. Trainees almost always held up the generative card when interrupted during the first exercise and the analytical card during the second. When talking-for-a-minute, trainees generated ideas with little time to reflect and reject unsatisfactory elements. When copying movements, trainees focused on a very specific routine, analysed what they saw and rehearsed this mentally before reproducing it. A more complex task followed called 'story in the round', in which trainees sat in a circle and, when asked, had to continue the story their neighbour had been telling. This produced a spread of A's and G's, which trainees explained in terms of individual differences in approach, but also according to where they were in their own creative process when asked to report. Trainees often held up a 'G' when generating links between their ideas and the story their neighbour was telling, or produced an 'A' when evaluating possible stories or those they were hearing. 'Tag improvisation', in which trainees had to step into an improvisation and take over from another performer, also provided an example of this complexity.

Trainees were then asked to produce a piece of movement using the textures and sounds they had encountered during an imaginary journey into a magic wardrobe. Researchers observed and identified points of transition (e.g. in terms of posture, strategy, focus), asking whether trainees were aware that a transition had occurred and whether they could explain why it had happened. Although some trainees had been initially unaware that transitions were even happening, they quickly began to recognize them. They often chose to explain them in terms of a need to move from one mode of thinking to the other. Transitions to rehearsal were often justified as a need to evaluate and hone what had been generated, and so an attempt to run through the work in progress was usually seen as a return to a more analytical thinking mode. This was something of a turning point in the project. Subsequent discussion developed a new richness and depth in terms of the trainees thinking about their experiences in the workshop and in their teaching.

Trainees began talking in reflective and often emotionally expressive terms about generating and analysing material. Generative processes were described in both positive and negative terms, as highly pleasurable but also slightly frightening. One trainee also described how analytical rehearsal, as in OCD, can become an unhelpful response to anxiety, i.e. the apprehension of having to generate ideas.

> When I'm creating work I feel like I have to keep going back, and like you said 'what would happen if I didn't go back?' I don't know, but that's what I'm too afraid to find out, I couldn't just keep on creating ...

The generative process was described as 'scary', 'like a void' but also as a 'delight', with the workshop reminding trainees how much they enjoyed being generative. Again, the spontaneous nature of creativity that had been mentioned in the earliest session arose, but this time spontaneity was assigned to a particular part of creativity: the ability to generate. The trainees had observed how young children can be highly generative in their thinking, although often less developed in their ability to critically rehearse their ideas. Adults, on the other hand, often find it difficult to maintain such effortless generation of ideas, needing instead to pause, analyse and refine meaning:

> ... when you told us to talk for a minute, I think the poem (by T) is what we find so hard to do. Like in the poem where there's no links, you said to us don't worry about the links, but automatically everybody tried to make a story even when you'd told us that we didn't need to ...

Metacognitive awareness, to the extent of regulating as well as monitoring cognitive processes, became evident:

> I started off by being analytical, thinking 'what am I expected to get out of it – what am I supposed to be doing with this visualisation?' And then I just thought no, right, cut that off, just leave it, let it go, and just made myself switch off that ...

Interjection by the research team during salient moments of transition not only raised awareness of cognition but also appeared to encourage self-regulation:

> ... I knew I was trying to change it and I knew you'd go 'Why?' ... but then I'd go 'oh I'm being too analytical let's just change it let's just go with something different and not keep knocking our head against this brick wall'...

Third cycle

At the next research meeting, the team selected two pieces of footage from previous workshops that would be suitable for analysis with the trainees at the next seminar. At this final seminar, the team first showed footage of a failed exercise from the first workshop that had produced little of creative value, and some excerpts from the discussion with trainees that had followed it. In reflecting upon the outcomes of the exercise, trainees watched themselves improvising on film and afterwards discussed the considerable repetition within and between individuals, the regular occurrences of blocking during the improvised dialogue and a tendency towards fixating upon cues from the team. They also noted the feelings of discomfort they had expressed afterwards. In understanding why the exercise had not succeeded in generating ideas, discussion centred around feelings of anxiety about not knowing what was required and the lack of introductory relaxation exercises. Additionally, the tasks that had preceded the exercises had been very analytical in their goal, including analysis of the term 'uncreative' and writing an 'uncreative' story which most students achieved by the self-imposition of constrained boundaries and use of frequent repetition. This may have impacted on generative tendencies in the subsequent exercise, a type of transfer that has been observed in a quasi-experimental study of creativity (Howard-Jones *et al.*, 2002). It was discussed whether seeing a member of the team carry out the task first would have helped. This gave rise to a discussion about mirror neurons which, it has been speculated, may provide a basis for the embodiment of cognition and even the unconscious communication of mental states (Rizzolatti *et al.*, 2002).

Some hypothetical options after such failure were considered. What should those leading the workshop have done? The trainees were asked: Should we have stopped and evaluated what had gone wrong? Should we have gone into some relaxation exercises? Should we have just ploughed on to the next exercise? It was agreed that an evaluative exercise would probably have further entrenched everyone in an analytical mode of thinking. Recalling the effects of relaxation on free association (Forgays and Forgays, 1992), there appeared a clear case for relaxation exercises. Continuing directly on to the next exercise (which is what actually happened) was the more uncertain course which, as it turned out, was productive. The trainees were then asked to consider why this subsequent exercise (object improvisation) had been more successful. Three issues emerged from the discussion. First, it was a familiar exercise and the trainees immediately felt more relaxed. Second, the task required links to be made between objects that the trainees had not selected themselves. Third, the trainees felt they had time within the exercise to produce ideas which, as discussed above, may be needed in order to select appropriate links between elements that are disparate. So, the trainees were asked, if this was your class and you found one group were staying focused on the brief, asking a lot of questions about boundaries and unable to generate ideas beyond the obvious, what would you do? Alternatively, if another group rushed straight into the improvisation and were generating a lot of incoherent ideas that were not being developed appropriately, what would you do? In this way, the trainees were encouraged to start thinking about their effect, as teachers, on the creative cognitive processes of their pupils.

This session on analysis provided a warm-up for the trainees to 'hot-seat' about reflections on their own practice. Volunteers took turns to sit in front of the group and recall specific instances for discussion and analysis by the group, which now often included reference to their own pupils' modes of thinking. For example, it was discussed how questions about procedure and process often reflected an insecure adherence to analytical processes, and how the confidence to create was often accompanied by a diminishment in questioning the teacher. Lower ability groups often suffer from this lack of confidence, and another trainee drew attention to how a teacher's response to questioning can also be used to orientate pupils' modes of thinking. This trainee described how she used 'teacher in role' and then prompted pupils' interpretations. Questions from the class about whether their idea was correct were deflected by the response 'it's whatever you think it is', leaving the arena open for other pupils while legitimizing all suggestions as valid self-generated ideas. At first it was the louder children who were interrogating her for the right answer but then, when it was clear that none existed, the quieter children came forward with their ideas. There was discussion about how the personal interpretation of the actions and ideas of others can also be a creative act. This gave rise to interesting ideas for further fMRI investigations that might investigate the creative act of being an audience. These studies could measure the brain activity when participants were reading the creative stories of others. To what extent would we expect brain regions involved with reading creative (compared to uncreative) stories to resemble those activated by generating creative (compared to uncreative) stories?

The use of 'teacher-in-role' prompted many other accounts of how pupils can be directed towards a particular mind state through imitation, again producing references to the concept of mirror neurons. For example, 'they'd got to the point where you know ... they hadn't got much and what they had got was very limited and it was very clichéd ... they couldn't seem to generate ideas ... (but) they worked so much better when we showed that we were willing to generate ideas too'. There was a sense in which acting and generating in front of the children communicated both the types of mental processes required and their legitimacy:

> I can't do it wrong if I do what she's done ... so it's ok I can take part in this now ... I can allow myself to be generative, even though people have told me I'm wrong before, this can't be wrong now ...

Trainees spoke of there being transitions within a lesson, describing some lessons as 'like a sandwich' of thinking modes. They also discussed how transitions between dominant modes of thinking could sometimes be helpfully positioned at the boundary between lessons. Trainees also referred to instances when changing context and suspending evaluation had succeeded in dissipating fixated mind sets. As in the discussion of 'teacher-in-role' above, working with others was also seen as a valuable way of encouraging children to make links, including those links between interpretations of their own and others' ideas:

> ... but also working with other people and seeing what they do and taking your own interpretation of what they do – because they don't explain what they're doing and what they're saying – that in turn helps you generate ideas ... like with the Rorschach tests with the ink splots – what do you think you see? – you take your own interpretation and that helps you create your own mental links which puts you on further in the generative process'

Although the team had been at pains to point out that this was not the case, there was still a residual tendency for some trainees to talk in terms of a simple anatomical mapping of cognitive processes, including those associated with generative and analytical modes of thinking:

> You're using almost two different parts of the brain there to do it, so like separating them into generative now and analytical at a different time ... so trying to switch ...

Finally, the teacher trainees and their trainers were asked what they had got out of this experience of reflecting upon their practice in terms of psychological and neuropsychological concepts. First, there was a sense of having an improved theoretical understanding that supported existing practice, especially in terms of the role of 'warm-ups'. Second, the trainees expressed a sense of being more empowered to intervene and support children's creative cognitive processes:

> ... so that when you go into the classroom you can identify the different states, you know that you can then manipulate or change it, and what's the point of that change. You as a teacher can then change their way of thinking and make a more productive learning environment for your pupils.

Trainees referred to a number of issues influencing creativity that they felt provided insights into their own practice, and overall there appeared a new sense of responsibility for fostering abilities they had initially considered as entirely spontaneous and not amenable to teacher intervention:

> ... not all children/pupils/adults find it that easy to be creative, and then when we go into schools you can't just expect them to just improvise, just 'cos we can do it. It's up to us as teachers then to differentiate ...

Issues regarding the difficulty in combining the language and perspective of natural science with educational thinking remained salient even in this final discussion, as some trainees struggled to find the appropriate terms by which to express their thoughts:

Trainee:	I think its reawakened (1) my curiosity and (2) some previous revelations about environment and the effects that it has on people and what they're capable of doing and how, and this is the only way I can think of saying it, how you can psychologically manipulate (laughter) – there's probably a better way to say it!
Suggestion from other:	Effect change?
Trainee:	That's the one ... (laughter) but you can look at and influence the environment and (thereby) people's way of thinking and how to change that and get the best out of people by doing that ...

Co-constructed concepts

The concepts identified by the project were those that the trainee teachers appeared to find most useful in understanding their own practice and that reflected current evidence. There was a focus on the usefulness of a cognitive model in understanding the social evidence of creativity we observe in the classroom, and also on the role of metacognition as identified by experiential accounts:

- Creativity appears to require movement between two different modes of thinking: generative and analytical.
- Cognitive fixation occurs when we become unable to move beyond an idea or set of ideas. It can be thought of as being stuck in analytical mode. However, in normal circumstances, we can monitor and, to some extent, regulate which mode we are using. In this sense, creative thinking appears amenable to metacognition.

Other experiential aspects of the concepts included the emotional experience of creativity and issues of teacher agency:

- Rehearsing the same idea can feel reassuring, whereas generative thinking can feel like a step in the dark, especially when there are few constraints or guidelines. Avoiding anxiety and fixation requires the teacher to provide an appropriate degree of constraint: not so constrained that creativity can't flourish, but sufficient to provide some level of reassurance.
- Although every creative act contains elements of spontaneity, teachers can play a critical role in fostering creative thinking processes through use of environment and strategy.

The concepts included attempts to dispel neuromyths and common misconceptions:

- No single part of our brain is responsible for creativity. Some regions linked to producing divergent associations, of the type needed for creativity, appear usually located in the right hemisphere. However, creativity is a complex thought process that calls on many different brain regions in both hemispheres. Left-brain/right-brain theories of learning are not based on credible science and are unhelpful in understanding creativity, especially when used to categorize individuals.

They drew on biological evidence in considering strategies and their implementation:

- Generative thinking can be supported by strategies that require the making of unusual connections, such as being required to incorporate unrelated stimulus into an outcome. A recent neuroimaging study supports the notion that incorporating unrelated material into a creative outcome enhances the rehearsal of creative thinking processes. This study, together with reported experience, also suggests that such strategies can be challenging and extra time should be provided to ensure quality outcomes.

But there was a strong emphasis on context:

- Teachers can help their students during a creative process by identifying when their thinking needs to be more generative or more analytical and enabling this transition through influencing the environment and/or through the application of particular strategies. However, the decision to apply such influence at any moment in a creative process must take into account the learner(s), their progress and the wider context.

This selection of concepts is reproduced here to provide some sense of the type of communicable messages for teachers that were ultimately derived, blending insights from the various perspectives involved. A fuller account of the concepts generated by the project can be found in the project report (Howard-Jones, 2008).

In this co-construction of concepts with educators, it was found that imaging and other neuroscientific research (e.g. case studies) were very effective for engaging non-scientists in thinking about the mind and the brain, although, with this power to engage, also arose the attendant dangers of encouraging myths such as simplistic phrenology. The trainee teachers passed through a number of stages in developing their own praxis that reflected not only the dangers but also the opportunities in this process:

- an initial high degree of enthusiasm about the brain;
- a flourishing of behavioural and prescriptive neuromyths;
- a daunting realization that things were more complex and more attention to underlying cognition was required;
- an increase in meta-cognition, with neuroscience helping to 'biologize', 'concretize' and deepen concepts. Trainees' efforts to understand their own personal experiences of learning/creativity in terms of underlying cognitive processes appeared an important step in developing related insights into their teaching practice;
- emergence of concepts, language and reflective capability that allows deeper reflection, sensitivity and insights around personal practice in specific contexts, in terms of mind and brain.

Summary

This chapter reported on a series of studies aimed at constructing pedagogical knowledge and neuroscientific understanding relating to creativity. These two goals transported researchers from a scientific fMRI study of brain function to two practice-based studies drawing more on social and experiential evidence. This was necessary because, although scientific studies measuring neurobiological function can provide insights about mental processes that are educationally interesting, they do not provide findings with fit-for-purpose educational meaning. The negotiation of meaningful educational understanding will always require the inclusion of experiential evidence, as well as social evidence drawn from more naturalistic contexts (e.g. the classroom) than found in laboratory experiments. The two practice-based studies also drew on a greater range of concepts about mind and brain than those involved with the fMRI study. Understanding the significance of findings from a scientific study will always require a broader scientific perspective than that provided by the study itself.

A fundamental challenge was the meaning of creativity. This was expressed in the scientific study in terms of concepts such as semantic divergence, but it became entwined with identity, emotion and free will during the performance research and, as constructed by trainee teachers during the action research, developed from being an entirely spontaneous set of processes to a thinking ability that could be fostered by thoughtful teaching. Far from disrupting the development of pedagogy, however, this multi-perspective and fluid approach to meaning can support the co-construction of useful and valid educational concepts for theorizing about, and reflecting upon, classroom practice. In this way, neuroscientific understanding and insights from other perspectives can be thoughtfully integrated together, avoiding, for example, the simplistic 'brain-based' approach that characterizes many commercial educational products.

Furthermore, each type of study was informed by the other, and this was because of, rather than despite, being derived from an entirely different way of looking at things. As well as a source of primary insights, the fMRI study was a useful stimulus that prompted purposeful questions about our relationship with our own biology that could be explored in the performance research. The performance research, in turn, provided experiential insights into experimental conditions used in the fMRI study. The action research drew on fMRI findings, and concepts and video footage from the performance research, but also prompted new research questions of educational interest that might be amenable to imaging studies (such as whether similar regions of the brain are involved with the interpretation and generation of creative work).

The methods used in the different studies were also influenced by simultaneously pursuing the two goals of neuroeducational research, as discussed in the previous chapter. The task chosen for the fMRI study reflected issues of ecological validity, as did preliminary procedures experimentally investigating the effects of the scanner environment on the behaviour of interest. Qualitative techniques were used to unravel the types of cognitive strategies participants were using in the complex task. Also procedures related to ethical considerations (e.g. acclimatization and enhancement of informed consent) reflected increased attention to the comfort and well-being of participants in the face of an increased risk/benefit ratio for participating individuals relative to clinical work.

It is not, of course, suggested that neuroeducational projects should always include a theatre company (or fMRI for that matter). Methods and techniques must be chosen to match aims, objectives and contexts. The curriculum area being studied made the application of performance research methods particularly appropriate here. However, the need to generate meaning from diverse sources of evidence is a key challenge for neuroeducational researchers, and that may often require imaginative approaches that appear radical in the range of techniques and methods they involve. Interrelating findings from methods such as fMRI and performance research is not straightforward and requires many caveats and cautions. However, such challenges are an inevitable and natural consequence of the desire to enrich our understanding of complex educational contexts with neurobiological insights (and vice-versa) – a bringing together of two very different worlds. The development of processes by which meaning can be co-constructed across the diverse fields of neuroscience and education will clearly be of great value here. As well as producing useful and valid concepts, such processes can produce the language needed to communicate them to others. This approach also allows neuromyths to be exposed and scrutinized along the way and some important limitations on interpretation to be made clear, including what neuroscience cannot tell us.

Chapter 9

Neuroeducational research case study B: Learning games

Attempts to design games that provide educational value to their players have had mixed success, causing some commentators to judge such enterprises as doom-laden (Zimmerman and Fortugno, 2005). There have been several efforts to identify the elements contributing to the excitement of computer games, in the hope of incorporating these in educational software, but these efforts have not got far. Various candidates for the magic ingredients have been put forward. Malone identified components of fantasy, challenge and curiosity (Malone, 1981). Johnson, S. (2004) has drawn attention to how most computer games now require no initial knowledge or manual, with children learning right from the moment they switch on (Johnson, S., 2004). However, such explanations are insufficient for the many simple (and somewhat repetitive) games that can provide higher levels of engagement than a well-planned lesson. The popularity of 'Snakes and Ladders', 'Tetris' and online Bingo suggests uncertainty and risk may be an important factor that engages attention and provides excitement across age groups.

Psychologists have known about the attractiveness of uncertain reward[1] for some time. Experimentation (e.g. Atkinson, 1957) has shown moderate risk taking (with 50 per cent success probability) heightens motivation – a result that has been explained by theories of attribution (Weiner, 1985) and intrinsic motivation (e.g. Csikszentmihalyi and Csikszentmihalyi, 1988). However, more recently, our understanding of neuropsychological reward has shed new light on our attraction to uncertainty. Here, 'wanting' and 'liking' are considered as two dissociable components, with the wanting of a reward being coded by the levels of dopamine released in mid-brain regions (Berridge and Robinson, 2003), a process also implicated in how we orientate our attention (Adcock, 2006). The predictability of an outcome influences the amount of dopamine released. In primates, a peak occurs when the likelihood of receiving reward is about half way between totally unexpected and completely predictable, i.e. 50 per cent likely (Fiorillo *et al.*, 2003). Dopamine levels in this region of the human brain have been linked to our approach motivation[2] for a variety of pleasures, including sex, food, gambling (Elliot *et al.*, 2000) and computer gaming (Koepp *et al.*, 1998). The link between the predictability of an outcome and mid-brain dopamine activity is helpful in understanding why humans are so attracted to games of chance (Shizgal and Arvanitogiannis, 2003). Dopamine in this region has been studied non-invasively in humans during gaming using fMRI. These studies have shown that activity is predicted less by reward in 'real' concrete terms and more to do with winning what is available in the game. In laboratory studies, activity has been shown to increase with the size of a potential payout (Knutson *et al.*, 2001) but, rather than being proportional to monetary gain, activation peaks at the same level for the best available outcome in different games (Nieuwenhuis *et al.*, 2005). The relationship between reward and motivation is thus mediated by context.

In more real-life environments such as school, we can expect social factors to play a major role. This is illustrated by how our natural attraction to uncertainty falls off when the task is perceived as educational. Students generally prefer low levels of academic uncertainty and choose problems well below moderate (<50 per cent) challenge (Clifford, 1988; Harter, 1978). Interestingly, however, when the same tasks are presented as games, students will take greater risks (Clifford and Chou, 1991). This may suggest that individuals can be deterred from tackling academic tasks with higher levels of uncertainty due to the implications of failure for social status and esteem. Being drawn towards tasks where our ability requires only perfection through further practice is not a bad thing. Such rehearsal is important in consolidating knowledge. However, it could be argued that such tasks provide lower signals in the reward system – i.e. lower approach motivation. This reduced level of uncertainty also reduces instances when outcomes are considerably better or worse than might be expected, i.e. emotional contexts that can support memory formation and learning.

The above arguments offer a theoretical basis for including a suitably integrated gaming component to enhance engagement with a learning context, i.e. as means to provide a source of uncertainty that is less associated with issues of social status, increasing approach motivation and providing a more emotionally stimulating experience. NEnet undertook several studies to investigate this idea and its implications for practice. The investigation was again guided by the two interrelated educational/scientific goals for neuroeducational research which, in terms of the chosen topic area, were:

- to further educational understanding and practice regarding learning games, through the inclusion of insight derived from the sciences of brain and mind;
- to further scientific understanding of the complex interrelationship between mind, brain and behaviour associated with learning games, through the engagement of natural science with the context of education.

A seemingly fundamental concern was whether such an effect could be observed in a classroom. Such a theory might only have value for schools if the addition of chance-based uncertainty to a learning task could be shown to increase its attractiveness to school-aged children. This could not be assumed. The idea of losing marks due to chance contradicts the established philosophy of 'reward consistency' as a motivating principle in schools. According to this viewpoint, chance-based uncertainty might provoke frustration and disappointment of the type that undermined the learner's interest. A bridging study was needed that could determine whether the alleged attractiveness of chance-based uncertainty survives in a learning context where it disrupts the relationship between academic performance and assessed outcome. To provide a result that could be generalized, a quasi-experimental study was called for, using a task that was educationally meaningful and could be carried out in a school environment.

Study 1: Quasi-experimental bridging study of children's preference for gaming uncertainty in a learning task

This initial study involved fifty 11–12-year-olds in an inner-city primary school in Cyprus (Howard-Jones and Demetriou, in press – now published online). We asked the children to practise their mental maths by playing a purpose-built computer quiz game in which they answered true/false to thirty mathematical statements (e.g. $13 \times 42 = 564$) with the aim of maximizing their score. However, before seeing each statement, they had to decide whether it would be asked by Mr Certain or Mr Uncertain. Both would provide the same set of questions but, if a participant answered correctly, he/she would receive one point from Mr Certain and either zero or two points from Mr Uncertain, depending on the toss of an animated coin. Answering a question incorrectly resulted in zero points for that question, whoever presented it. We emphasized that an equal chance existed of receiving two or zero points from Mr Uncertain for a correct answer. In an attempt to control extraneous variables, the children worked individually and quietly, two together in the same room to minimize any sense of isolation. The computer game was designed to record the order in which questions were presented and the responses of the children.

In addition to attempting a (partially) controlled experiment, this was also an opportunity to collect some experiential notes. What were the children's ideas about their preferences? How would their ideas about their choices relate to our ideas? So, after all students had experienced the game, five girls and five boys were randomly selected from the sample to participate in semi-structured interviews. These participants were encouraged to discuss their emotional responses and their rationale for choosing Mr Uncertain or Mr Certain. Prompts included a request to identify moments of strong feeling and being asked to reflect upon why they may have experienced these feelings.

Over the fifty participants, the mean percentage of occasions that Mr Uncertain was chosen was 61 per cent (s.d. = 6.9) and analysis over all questions confirmed a statistically significant preference ($\chi^2(1) = 77.98$, $p < 0.0001$). (Boys were

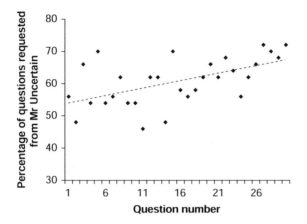

Figure 9.1 The percentage of the sample requesting questions from Mr Uncertain is
shown here as a function of question number (i.e. in terms of when it was
presented). The graph shows how the preference for Mr Uncertain increased
over the duration of the quiz.
Source: From Howard-Jones, P. A. and Demetriou, S. Instructional Science, advance
online publication, Thursday, September 11, 2008 (doi:10.1007/s11251-008-9073-6).
Reprinted by permission from Springer Science+Business Media. Copyright © 2008.

responsible for 67 per cent of occasions when Mr Uncertain was chosen, girls only
53 per cent). Overall, thirty of the fifty participants chose Mr Uncertain more
times than Mr Certain, which also demonstrated a statistically significant preference by participant (($\chi^2(1) = 4.26$, $p = 0.04$). The percentage of the sample
choosing Mr Uncertain is shown as a function of the question number in
Fig. 9.1, providing an indication of how preference for Mr Uncertain varied over
the duration of the quiz. Linear regression analysis determined question number
was a highly significant predictor of preference for Mr Uncertain ($F(1,28) =
12.25$, $p = 0.002$) accounting for 30 per cent of the variance.

This provided a sense of the general attractiveness of gaming uncertainty,
and how this increased as learners experienced it. The preference for gaming
uncertainty shown by the children, and the tendency for this to increase with
repetition of the task, concur with current neuropsychological concepts predicting physiological multiplication of incentive value with repeated exposure
(Tindell *et al.*, 2005). The interviews provided a glimpse of the emotional
experience provided by Mr Uncertain. Emotional responses to Mr Uncertain
appeared more intense compared to Mr Certain, and these responses were
characterized by a range of contrasting emotions. Sometime Mr Uncertain
created frustration (quotes are translated from Greek): 'With Mr Uncertain ...
I was feeling very frustrated when the coin was tossed and I was getting no
points'.

However, as illustrated in the exchange below, this frustration was not necessarily describing an aversive feature of the game:

Researcher: Were there instances that made you feel frustrated?
Participant: Yes.
Researcher: When?
Participant: When I was getting zero points with Mr Uncertain. I knew my answer was correct but he was giving me no points sometimes.
Researcher: Did that frustration make you want to quit the game?
Participant: No … no … It made me want to try my luck with Mr Uncertain even more.

Overall, consistent with the experimental result, the attraction to Mr Uncertain did not appear dissipated by the disrupting effect he had on scores, even though this was sometimes frustrating. Participants also described Mr Uncertain as being more exciting and one, when asked to explain further, discussed how this compensated for the stress he sometimes induced: 'Hm … Because you don't know what will happen and you want to win. You are stressed but if you win then you forget about that!'

Generally, participants tended to explain their preference for Mr Uncertain in emotional terms such as 'like' and 'exciting', but one interesting quote from a participant trying to explain his preference for Mr Uncertain did so in terms of analogy:

> When I play football with my friends and kick the ball to score, I hope I'll manage to trick the defenders and the goal keeper and get the ball in the net. Whenever I kick I'm never sure that I will score. But I feel very happy when I score. If there isn't a goal keeper then everything is easier and I don't feel so excited when I score. I know that if I kick the ball at a specific point then it'll be a goal but if I miss then it won't.

This explanation appeared to resonate with our underlying theory. i.e. that a learner can find a task more emotionally appealing when an element of uncertainty is introduced that is not defined by their own ability.

This first study demonstrated children's preference for gaming uncertainty in a context that might be described loosely as educational, at least in respect of the quiz assessing and providing feedback on their performance. Caution was needed, however, especially since this preference appears at odds with notions of fairness and just reward that are currently promoted and valued in schools (e.g. Ofsted, 2001). The study has been carried out on an individual basis, and so we knew little about how gaming uncertainty would influence the ethos of the classroom. It was possible that the dangers of violating reward consistency might become more apparent in a more social environment. How, for example, would gaming uncertainty influence the discourse around learning? A valuable next step was to understand how gaming uncertainty features in the dialogue between students. This would begin building a basis for understanding the teacher's role in contributing to and mediating such discourse in order to support learning.

A practice-based study was needed that could reveal more about the ways in which playful subversion of reward consistency influences learners' constructions, particularly around success, failure and fairness.

Study 2: Practice-based study of classroom discourse around learning with gaming uncertainty

The practice-based nature of this study required the implementation of a learning game that exploited gaming uncertainty to pursue a clear set of learning outcomes (Howard-Jones and Demetriou, in press – now published online). We developed a purpose-built learning game called 'Wipe Out'. It was a quiz game testing factual knowledge relevant to Attainment Target 2 (Life Processes and Living Things) drawn from the UK National Curriculum for Science for Key Stage 3 (QCA, 2000). Two animated dice were rolled and the combined score could be won if the subsequent multiple choice question was answered correctly. If this was achieved, there was the choice of rolling again or passing the dice to the opponent. Continuing to roll was always a little risky because, if a single 1 was rolled, all points for that turn were lost. Worse still, rolling a pair of 1's resulted in a 'wipe out' and all points currently accumulated for the game were lost. Students competed against an artificial opponent (i.e. the computer) in pairs. The first to reach 100 (either the team of two players or the artificial opponent) won the game. When the students or the computer answered a question incorrectly, or rolled a 1, the sound of an audience sighing was heard. A 'wipe out' was accompanied by an explosion. On occasions when the team of players won, they were congratulated with a sound effect of loud applause. On occasions when the artificial opponent won the game, they received a loud 'raspberry' noise.

Questions were randomly selected from a sample of 26 and, if answered incorrectly by the students, the correct answer would be highlighted in red for three seconds. Students could also learn from watching the artificial opponent answer questions which, being a very knowledgeable opponent, it always did correctly. By attending carefully, students could improve their subject knowledge and chances of winning. Although the computer never answered a question incorrectly, it faced the same odds when throwing the dice as the students. In this respect, both the students and the artificial opponent were vulnerable to misfortune. So, although participants could help themselves by improving their subject knowledge, the outcome of the game was always influenced strongly by chance. A screen shot from the quiz is shown in Fig. 9.2.

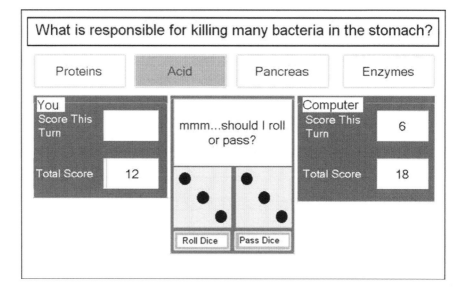

Figure 9.2 Screen shot from 'Wipe Out'. The computer has (as always) chosen the correct answer but now appears to be vacillating over whether to roll the dice
again or pass them to the player.
Source: Howard-Jones, P. A. and Demetriou, S. Instructional Science, advance online
publication, Thursday, September 11, 2008 (doi:10.1007/s11251-008-9073-6). Reprinted
by permission from Springer Science+Business Media. Copyright © 2008.

The game was played by ten pairs of 13–14-year-old students in a science
class (ages 13–14 years) in an urban comprehensive school in the South West
of England. This group was the lowest ability of six sets of similar size. Paper-
based pre- and post-tests confirmed that a good level of factual knowledge had
been accumulated as a result of playing the game, at least in the short term.
Of greater interest, however, was the dialogue between students. Four pairs were
selected as being of mid-range ability (two female: F1 and F2, and two male:
M1 and M2). These four pairs were sat at computers behind which there was an
unconcealed video camera arranged to record responses and dialogue during the
game. A microphone from the video camera was placed between the pair, and an
additional audio recorder (as back up) was connected to hands-free behind-the-
ear microphones worn by the children. The amount of recording paraphernalia
might have been intimidating, but the level of engagement provided by the game
appeared to overcome inhibitions.

The audio recordings were transcribed and thematically analysed using predefined categories that included elements of fairness, learning talk, gaming talk,
and emotional response to specific events and to the game in general.

It was found that dialogue between students often included explicit reference to issues of fairness, but these were never about losing points on the throw of a dice. Instead, concerns about unfairness revolved around the artificial opponent knowing the answers and suspicions that the opponent was getting all the easy questions:

M2L: This isn't really a fair game
M2R: Yeah it's not because the computer knows the answers.
M2R: ... why is he, why is the computer getting all the easy ones?

The F1 pair also expressed fairness concerns about their opponent's level of knowledge and also when they themselves answered a question incorrectly. Again, however, they never expressed concerns about fairness when losing points on the dice:

F1L: You should've went for that one.
F1R: So unfair.
F1L: (Sighs) ahhh.
F1R: But it's not fair that he knows all the answers.
F1L: So greedy.
F1R: Urr hope you *(referring to opponent)* get a ... zero.

As in the last example, the vulnerability of the artificial opponent to the throw of the dice was seen as a means of rebalancing the difference in knowledge level between players and the artificial opponent. Gaming uncertainty was often a source of hope:

M2L: I want the computer to get a wipe out.
M2R: Get a one.
M2L: Because then we can actually get some points.

The three pairs (M1, M2 and F1) each wished such ill fortune upon their opponent several times, the M1 pair as many as twelve times. There was also celebration when these wishes came true, resulting in a taunt from the F1 pair.

F1R: Hahaha – double one – what a loser.

Despite students' indifference to related issues of fairness, the outcome of throwing the dice clearly had its emotional impact. When players lost their points to the dice, they expressed considerable dismay and, at the beginning, a sense of surprise:

M1L: ... you're joking ... 73 points (and) I got wiped out.
M1R: This gonna be impossible ...

In the light of such events, however, getting a question wrong was not seen as disastrous:

M1L: That was out wasn't it ... yeah ... I want them to get double ones now cos then that'd be ... alright ... I've got to get this ... annelid?

M1R: You never got it wrong mmm ... oh that wasn't a ... thought (that) was it ...

M1L: That wasn't a wipe out – we didn't lose anything.

All pairs indulged in large amounts of gaming and learning talk and these sometimes occurred closely together within the same exchange:

M1L: That's 10 points – I'm not passing that off.

M1R: Yes yes yes ... a 2 part ... ar no.

M1L: No way ... got a 2 part body 4 pairs of legs.

M1R: But no wings?

M1L: ... got to be because 4×2 is 8 and spiders have 8 legs and spiders arachnid. I rock.

M1R: Come on ... yes.

M1L: We're gonna win, we're gonna win ... what is responsible for killing many bacteria.

M1R: Acid.

M1R and
M1L together: Yeah ... come on!

As in the previous example, there were several examples of team spirit in the face of threat from the opponent, with shared decision making and mutual exhortation to each other to remember certain facts:

F2R: Yeah ... remember that in case we get it again ... and remember that.

F2L: Ah.

F2R: ... Bones is that?

F2L: Yeah ... what shall we do? Pass or shall we roll?

F2R: Pass, cos if we (roll) we'll lose all our points.

From the outset, there seemed a sincere determination to beat the artificial opponent expressed by all players:

M2R: This game farts when it wins.

M2L: It shouldn't be able to win. Oh yeah definitely I'm going to play this game and I'm going to make sure we win ... Does protein (reading) ...

Failure was generally attributed to bad luck and talked about in gaming terms:

M2L: Agh – we got obliterated. Completely annoying, we haven't had any
         good rolls.
M2R: No.

But success was celebrated vigorously (often with singing and dancing) as a
triumph of ability:

F1R: We're just too good – I can't believe we're doing good.

Which seemed also to increase the determination to win again:

M2L: Roll, pass pass … yay … 105.
M2R: 105.
M2L: We beat him.
M2R: 105 … we beat him, we beat him, yeah.
M2L: I'll roll first get a roll … pass … he never passes it … wait … errr …
         I couldn't think of it.
M2R: Agh
M2L: We're going to have another bad game aren't we?
M2R: Bad now, I'm a bad loser.

The students appeared highly engaged throughout the session, playing continuously with very short breaks between games. At the end of the session, when
researchers asked the students about their experiences, the words 'fun' and
'annoying' were commonly used to describe the game. This seemed to suggest
a compulsive element to participants' motivation to engage with it, illustrated
in this spontaneous exchange between two students who had been playing for
30 minutes and just won a game.

F1R: Shall we play again?
F1L: So annoying …
F1R: Don't mind … shall we?
F1L: Yeah, roll the dice …

In short, this practice-based study revealed a close intermingling of game talk
and learning talk during the game. Fairness was discussed with respect to differences in player-opponent ability but not with respect to losses due to chance
(i.e. gaming uncertainty). Such losses made a significant emotional impact but
did not appear to deter students. Indeed, the gaming element appeared to
offer hope and emotional support, as a means to overcome the intellectual
advantage of the artificial opponent. The game appeared to provide high levels

of engagement, but was also described as both fun and annoying, again echoing a mild dissociation of appetite (wanting) and consumption (liking).

The study provided some initial ideas about how gaming uncertainty can subvert the conventional learning discourse, culturing the types of constructions and exchanges about learning tasks that are more often observed in sport. Inclusion of gaming uncertainty was contrary to prevailing educational notions of reward consistency, but our results suggested children find this less problematic than might be expected. Furthermore, results suggested gaming uncertainty might encourage additional resilience to failure, as well as increased motivation to succeed.

This was encouraging, but there also arose the question of whether gaming uncertainty was simply providing a 'sugar coating' for the sometimes bitter pill of learning, or whether the medicine itself now tasted different. It appeared possible that any heightened emotional response due to gaming uncertainty might be restricted to the gaming components, and that learning processes could remain unaffected. In games such as Wipe Out, learning and gaming components are experienced in close sequence to each other, but still remain essentially separated in time. Can gaming-related emotional responses spill over into events related to formal learning outcomes? If not, then gaming may not support memory formation and may even be more of a distraction than a support. High learning scores, the emotionality of participants' responses to quiz questions and the close intermingling of gaming and learning talk in Study 2 suggested that gaming emotions do spill over into learning. Wipe Out's element of gaming uncertainty might well influence affective response during answering of questions and receiving of feedback – but we had no firm evidence of this. Given that declarative memory formation can be enhanced by emotional context (e.g. Brierley *et al.*, 2007), this was a potentially important issue for the application of our theory in learning game design. To investigate it further, the researchers went back to the laboratory. There, we implemented an experiment to compare the skin conductivity, referred to here as electrodermal activity (EDA), of adults tackling quiz questions, with and without gaming uncertainty.

Study 3: Scientific experimental study of the influence of gaming uncertainty on physiological response of adults

In terms of linking this study to observations in the classroom, we would prefer to have had children participating in the EDA experiment. However, the connection of electrodes to children involves significant ethical issues and requires more laboratory resources than we had access to (e.g. waiting rooms for parents, preferably with CCTV monitoring of experimental procedures). Such studies, if carried out in school, are also time consuming and impact more substantially on curriculum time. Therefore, we made a pragmatic decision to carry out the study with adult volunteers.

In this experiment, sixteen adults individually experienced two conditions of gaming uncertainty (Howard-Jones and Demetriou, in press – now published online). The 'gaming' condition exposed participants to gaming uncertainty using Wipe Out as above (it was found that the science content was sufficiently challenging for adults). The 'no gaming' condition used the same quiz, but the dice always threw a double three (so no penalties for throwing a one) and turns alternated automatically and continuously between player and computer. In both versions, there was a pause after the rolling of the dice, i.e. just before the question was presented. During this pause, the word 'REST' appeared on the screen. This allowed the affective response to the throw of the dice to dissipate before measuring the response to answering the question. The mouse used by the participants was modified to produce a logic pulse to the EDA recording equipment when pressed, to help synchronize our measurements of EDA with the players' quiz responses during the game.

Data was analysed in terms of EDA peaks following correct and incorrect responses, with and without gaming (see Fig. 9.3). Within-subjects analysis showed main effects of gaming uncertainty ($F(1,16) = 11.12$, $p = 0.004$) and correctness of answer ($F(1,16) = 23.84$, $p < 0.001$). That is, the gaming condition increased the emotional response of the participants, as measured by EDA, when they were answering questions. Fig. 9.4 shows a typical example of this effect.

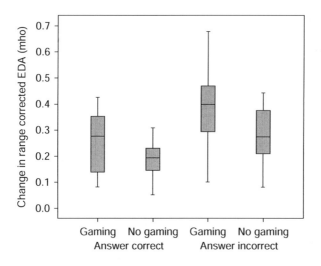

Figure 9.3 Box plots of participants' average changes in range-corrected EDA in siemens (mho) during response to correctly and incorrectly answered questions for the two conditions of gaming uncertainty (gaming and no gaming).
Source: Howard-Jones, P. A. and Demetriou, S. Instructional Science, advance online publication, Thursday, September 11, 2008 (doi:10.1007/s11251-008-9073-6). Reprinted by permission from Springer Science+Business Media. Copyright © 2008.

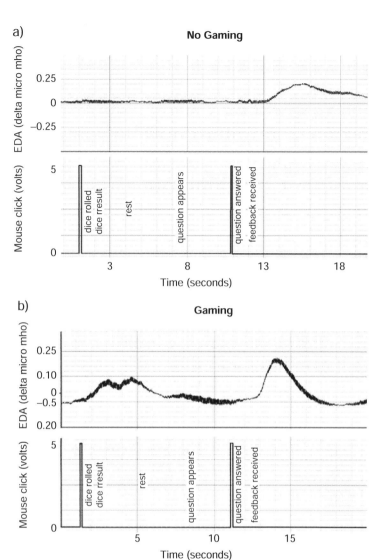

Figure 9.4 a) The affective response of a participant in the 'no gaming' condition. Here, the participant first watched a dice roll which was 'fixed' to provide a double three. There is no detectable response to this very predictable event. A question was then presented to which the participant responded incorrectly. The impact of answering the question and receiving the feedback did produce an increase in EDA, slightly delayed by 2–3 seconds due to the physiological processes involved. b) The response of the same participant when answering a question incorrectly in the 'gaming' condition. Here, the rolling of the dice, with its unpredictable outcome, did generate an EDA response but, more interestingly, also appeared to increase the intensity of response to answering and receiving feedback for the subsequent question.

Source: Howard-Jones, P. A. and Demetriou, S. Instructional Science, advance online publication, Thursday, September 11, 2008 (doi:10.1007/s11251-008-9073-6). Reprinted by permission from Springer Science+Business Media. Copyright © 2008.

This result implied that the affective response to learning itself can be influenced by elements of gaming uncertainty, even when these are combined in a fairly superficial and sequential manner. This finding could be linked to observations in the practice-based study, where the excited exclamations and gestures of game talk were not restricted just to the dice throwing but also seemed present in the answering of the quiz questions.

Taken together, these three studies supported the potential value of games involving chance-based uncertainty in the classroom. Two further interrelated strands of research are now underway in this area, aimed at further developing both educational and scientific understanding.

Study 4: Scientific experimental study relating prediction error to memory performance during game play

To develop effective learning games based on the above concepts, it would be helpful to understand the interaction between gaming and learning on smaller time scales, e.g. determine how different chance-based events influence approach motivation during the progress of a game. One would think that the magnitude of the reward available and its probability would have some influence and, as discussed above, other researchers have shown dopamine levels in the reward system are indeed related to payout. However, this relationship appears context dependent, with peak dopamine levels corresponding to the maximum payout *in that context*. In a game, contextual detail is constantly shifting, with the value of the dice potentially perceived as high or low depending on current progress (e.g. 4 can be high if you've been throwing 1's and 2's). This would explain why, in the study above, there was no simple correlation between EDA when answering questions and the points available for a correct answer (i.e. preceding dice score).

We were interested to know whether there was any way of estimating the dopamine level at a particular point in a game. If there was, it might be possible to link dopamine more directly to learning outcomes, based on the assumption that it orientates attention. Recent work by Nathaniel Daw and his colleagues suggested such a thing was possible. These researchers had been studying behaviour in a foraging task. They provided their participants with a four-armed bandit task, in which the value of each bandit's pay-out of points was drifting noisily in time. Participants were asked to continuously sample four bandits, in order to maximize their total point score. This resembles a type of serious game that has confronted our ancestors, and many other animals, for millions of years. The amount of food you may find somewhere is never wholly predictable in the wild, but usually some food sources are generally better than others. However, which one is the best source also changes with time, so you have to actively sample to know which is currently best. This is the classic explore/exploit dilemma faced by our ancestors: our reward system will orientate us towards exploiting what we know, but sometimes we need to explore in order to update that knowledge. It is a problem that is difficult to solve with mathematics and logic, but our brains (and those of many other species) appear well adapted to cope with it.

Daw *et al.* (2006) showed that behaviour in this task can be modelled on our understanding of the reward system. One internal signal generated by such a model is positive prediction error (PPE). In simple terms this is 'happy surprise' – the extent to which an outcome is greater than expected. In reality it is a more sophisticated concept than this since, as discussed above, games involve constantly changing contexts. What we might predict depends on the continuously changing context of recent history. The PPE signal is thought to be coded by dopamine in the reward system. Among other findings, Daw *et al.* (2006) showed that the internal signals of the model that best fitted bandit selection did correlate, as might be expected, with dopamine-related activity in the reward system of his participants, as they received the outcomes of their decisions.

According to our theory, since PPE appears correlated with dopaminergic activity, high levels of PPE should enhance attention and, potentially therefore, enhance learning performance. To test this idea, we combined Daw's foraging game with our quiz design, such that participants could win the points they found in the bandit if they correctly answered the subsequent question (Howard-Jones *et al.*, 2009). We were interested to know whether PPE could indicate the likelihood of two types of learning event following an incorrectly answered question: would the PPE for those points just lost help encode the correct answer for its next presentation, and would the PPE of the points that might be gained on this next presentation help recall it? The evidence for the first phenomenon was not conclusive, probably due to our estimation of the reward signals being confounded by having just received negative feedback about a quiz question. This feedback may have countered positive attention effects since, for example, if a surprisingly large number of points for the question had produced a large PPE, the participant would also be told they had lost these points before trying to encode the correct answer in readiness for its next presentation. There was, however, a strongly significant relationship between PPE and the ability of participants to recall the correct answer. PPE, as a type of 'ready to learn' signal, may be a helpful concept in understanding how the potential for learning varies during the progress of a learning game involving chance events.

However, back in our practice-based study, we had also observed that much of the discourse revolved around the competitive nature of the game. The present neuroscientific literature offers few insights into the changes in dopaminergic activity when a player is observing a competitor's experiences, rather than their own. To understand more about this response, we have been extending Daw's neurocomputational modelling techniques in our own fMRI study. In our study, participants are foraging competitively against an artificial opponent. As well as providing insights into competitive learning games, this study promises to reveal more about the interrelationship of mind, brain and behaviour in competitive situations. This is a neuroeducational study of the scientific type, modifying established neurocomputational techniques to construct new fundamental scientific understanding, but a scientific study which has been deliberately focused on an area of educational interest.

Other work in progress includes attempts to understand the teacher's role in learning games. We have studied how gaming uncertainty can influence the discourse between collaborating learners, but how should the teacher mediate and direct this discourse? NEnet is currently involved in an action research project to develop good practice in implementing learning games in the classroom. To ensure that the emphasis is on the teacher, we are presently using games that are not computer-based. Instead, teachers are using a 'wheel of fortune' which allows chance-based events to be introduced into learning in a variety of engaging ways. This is a practice-based study employing an action-research spiral, similar to that encountered in the previous chapter. It is helping to co-construct, with practitioners, a language and set of concepts suitable for transferring the ideas underpinning good practice to other teachers, while at the same time developing the practice itself. (We term the practice of teaching through games 'pedagaming', to emphasize its distinctiveness from traditional pedagogy, and the central role of the teacher in such learning). Although the studies discussed above have focused on factual recall, we believe gaming uncertainty can mediate learning processes through increased attention, so there is no reason why such methods cannot be applied to deeper types of learning. The learning focus of the pedagaming project has also moved beyond simple factual recall and concerns itself more with conceptual learning, as in the application of principles to novel problems.

Summary

Our investigation of learning games has involved disparate types of methods and techniques, although all studies pursued the twin goals of neuroeducational research and all revealed their relevance to each other. Each study benefited from the insights provided by the other, and each showed the potential to influence the design and direction of the other type. The first study was quasi-experimental and demonstrated how the attraction of gaming uncertainty could be observed in the classroom, but it also provided the opportunity to collect some evidence of how students might experience learning when combined with gaming uncertainty. It was this experiential evidence that yielded the first clues about how such uncertainty might influence the discourse around learning and highlighted the need for a study focusing on this issue. Neuropsychological appreciation of the potential dissociation of wanting and liking helped provide insight into some of emotions experienced by students in the classroom in Study 2, demonstrating how the sciences of brain and mind can contribute to interpretative research processes. In Study 3, the modifications to the software, the use of adult participants, and the isolated nature of interacting with the game were all compromises made to support experimental measurement and control in a successful attempt to show how gaming can increase the intensity of the emotional experience of learning. However, despite these compromises, the basic direction of the experiment was inspired by the classroom study and used an almost identical type of task. This made it easier to interrelate findings and draw comparisons between the physiological signals observed in Study 3 and the emotional content of the discourse observed in Study 2. Study 2 was practice-based, but the high profile of competitive talk in the discourse has stimulated the team to pursue the neurocognitive processes involved with competition. It has prompted an ongoing neurocomputational study that is experimental but, as a result of the practice-based studies, is centred on an issue of educational interest. As you might now anticipate, semi-structured interviewing techniques are being used in this study to debrief participants after being scanned, in order to gain their 'insider' insights about the decision strategies they use. Additionally, in the experimental study (Study 4) of the relationship between positive prediction error and memory performance, the educational focus of the research again persuaded us to use the same type of quiz-based memory task developed previously. If this had been a purely psychological or behavioural study, a more abstract laboratory-like task might have been employed in order to diminish experimental variance (or 'noise' in the results) due, for example, to variations in question content. As in the case of creativity, significant differences arose in the use of language by educators and neuroscientists, such as with the terms 'motivation' and 'reward'. These differences had to be carefully examined as the work proceeded, and their existence supports the need for a further practice-based study (ongoing) to co-construct concepts with teachers and carefully develop the language with which to communicate praxis.

It should be emphasized that the quality and rigour of neuroeducational studies should, wherever possible, be policed according to the traditions and conventions from which they individually derive. Changes made to help interrelate studies should provide added value and not undermine the validity of its core constructs. So, scientific studies must always demonstrate adherence to high standards of experimental rigour, and practice-based studies must always aspire to authenticity. This rule of privileging convention will, of course, be more difficult to apply in the case of bridging studies, since these usually require researchers to make some compromise due to the desirability of both authenticity and control. Here, researchers will need to explore the rationale for their decisions carefully and explicitly, providing a strong case for the balance they strike. Ultimately, therefore, each type of study will be characterized by its own set of demands in terms of maintaining rigour.

In this and previous chapters, we have seen that an integrated 'bricollage' methodological approach to generating neuroeducational findings derives naturally from the need to include insights about learning across perspectives. This approach ensures the educational relevance and scientific validity of outcomes. Despite differences in the perspectives that use them, a variety of techniques and methods have been able to inform each other, constructing an understanding of learning processes that includes biological, social and experiential evidence. Indeed, these differences underlie the potential of the three types of neuroeducational study (scientific, bridging and practice-based) to complement each other.

Part III

The future

Chapter 10

Neuroscience, education and the future

Crystal ball gazing can be dangerous, raising false hopes and fears that only serve to distract from more important and pressing issues. However, we have seen that educational ideas about the brain already lag behind modern scientific understanding, and an eye to the future may help prevent education slipping further into the scientific past. We need to start contemplating what is ahead now, since change within educational institutions requires (and deserves) time-consuming discussion and consultation, while the rate at which our understanding of the mind and brain is advancing appears to be accelerating. As the future unfolds, it will be all too easy for the gap between scientific knowledge and educational benefit to widen.

Educational innovation involving valid neuroscientific concepts is a relatively new phenomenon and we have seen that the challenges involved are considerable. However, it should also be anticipated that progress in this area will accelerate with the growth of scientific understanding. This chapter identifies some of the educational changes that may occur in the next one to two decades, as a result of this growth. It deals chiefly with those changes that are a probable outcome of neuroscience and education working together, but also reminds us that some changes associated with neuroscience may occur even without such positive collaboration. After considering what these may mean for the professional development of teachers, it briefly reviews what developments may occur in the more distant future. Finally, it reviews the types of educational developments that, often despite popular belief, are never likely to be accomplished with the help of neuroscience. These include notions of a brain-based natural science of education.

Probable educational advances involving neuroscience

Since this chapter deals with changes, the author is differentiating between the types of scientific insight that support existing practice, and those insights, sometimes counter-intuitive, that challenge it. The following are examples of areas where insights regarding brain function tend to resonate with existing educational attitudes and concepts, and these findings are significant in their potential to strengthen and consolidate present practice.

Brain plasticity

Many studies from neuroscience emphasize the extent to which the structure and function of the brain can respond to environmental influences, including education. Such studies tend to emphasize the general importance of educational influence on neurocognitive development, and will always find favour among those who feel passionately about the value and promise of education. For example, Immordino-Yang presented two complementary case studies of boys who had undergone the surgical removal of an entire brain hemisphere (Immordino-Yang, 2007). Both were able to develop language and social skills far beyond expectations, by developing individual processing strategies that exploited the functionality associated with the remaining hemisphere.

The role of phonological processing skills in understanding reading processes and reading difficulties

Imaging studies have linked dyslexia to reduced functioning in regions of the brain associated with phonological processing, and have demonstrated that both the reading difficulties and this reduced functioning are amenable to remediation using approaches that emphasize sound–spelling relationships (Shaywitz *et al.*, 2004).[1] Ongoing research continues to emphasize the importance of modern 'phonics' approaches in the classroom.

Creativity

Research shows the inclusion of remotely associated concepts increases activity in brain regions linked to creative effort, supporting the use of such strategies as a means to foster creativity (see Chapter 8).

Visualization

Brain imaging shows visualizing an object recruits most of the brain regions activated by actually seeing it (Kosslyn, 2005), supporting the use of visualization as a learning tool.

Neuroscientific studies in the areas discussed above may play a vital role in consolidating existing educational attitudes and approaches, and they deserve further attention from researchers, including neuroeducational researchers. However, perhaps the more salient influence of neuroscience in education will arise from more counter-intuitive findings. That is, it may be the findings about brain function that are more surprising in their content and implications that stimulate the more dramatic changes. By definition, of course, it is difficult to predict surprises. Yet results in some areas of neuroscience already challenge the types of assumptions teachers work with and may soon give rise to new directions. These areas will, therefore, now be given special emphasis.

Early numeracy

Our new understanding of an infant's ability to approximate, which is ancient and language-independent, challenges our thinking about how formal mathematical skills initially develop. This mathematical ability, that appears so early in our development, is likely to have a critical role in helping learners to formally grasp exact differences and procedures. As we come to understand more about this 'bootstrapping' process, so we will be able to better support it, improving children's early experiences with number that underlie later learning. Such approaches may be helpful in tackling dyscalculia, but also in supporting the development of mainstream mathematical ability. Innovation also appears likely in areas involving children's use of fingers and number lines (see Chapters 1 and 6).

Adolescence

It may be natural to consider that a teenager is essentially a young adult, with a fully formed brain but lacking the social experiences of his/her elders. However, we have seen that scientific investigation is revealing a very different picture, with frontal and parietal regions still undergoing radical structural changes until the late teens, relative to other regions of the brain which appear more fully developed. Synaptic pruning (the cutting back of neural connections) and myelination (improving the efficiency of neural connections) also continue throughout adolescence in frontal regions. Such change suggests the teenage brain may be less ready than an adult brain to carry out a range of specific processes, including directing attention, planning future tasks, inhibiting inappropriate behaviour, multitasking, and a range of socially-orientated tasks.

Although more studies are needed, some psychological research backs this up, even showing a 'pubertal dip' or discontinuities through development in some areas of performance. Recent research has shown that the 'social brain' network is also activated differently in teenagers compared with adults when thinking about intentions (Catherine et al., 2008), and brain regions responsible for the control of impulses appear less well functionally connected in adolescents' than in adults' brains (Steven et al., 2007). Additionally, in Chapter 1, it was discussed how teenagers appear to activate different regions of the brain from adults when learning algebraic equations, with this difference associated with a more robust process of long-term storage than that used by adults (Luna, 2004; Qin et al., 2004). Adolescents, then, are not simply older children or younger adults, and cognitive development cannot be expected to proceed in a continuous linear manner. Apart from explaining some of the difficulties teenagers experience, such changes also suggest how and why adolescence can be a potentially sensitive period for learning, within and beyond academic contexts. For example, teenagers often tend to perceive risks as smaller and more controllable than adults, and they are generally more vulnerable than adults or children to a range of activities which are inappropriately risky, such as gambling and drug taking. Appropriate decision making appears to require a balanced engagement between harm-avoidance and reward orientation that is regulated by processes within the prefrontal cortex, where teenage development may lag (Ernst *et al.*, 2005). Imaging studies comparing adults and adolescents show reduced activity in these prefrontal regions when making risk-based decisions (Bjork *et al.*, 2007; Eshel, *et al.*, 2007), and this reduced activity correlates with greater risk-taking performance. Such studies provide new insights into how adolescent risk taking may be linked to neuro-maturational events and these insights may influence educational perspectives on teenage behaviour, helping to understand a potentially problematic, and sometimes even dangerous, period of children's development.

It seems likely that these and future findings from neuroscience may generate new educational approaches in future years (e.g. strategies that take a more informed account of the temporary lagging of brain function in some regions).

Motivation

Motivation will always be of great interest in education, where the under-achievement and disengagement of boys with their academic pursuits is currently of great concern. In Chapter 9 we saw how a number of findings from neuroscience are stimulating some fresh educational thinking about motivation, including the types of intense engagement provided by computer gaming. The concepts around motivation emerging from neuroscience are very different from those in education and, although providing extra challenges in terms of neuroeducational research and communication, this difference also promises an entirely fresh perspective on a very old problem. It seems particularly encouraging that insights are arising about gender differences in the development of the reward system (e.g. Hoeft *et al.*, 2008). Ideas such as the introduction of chance-based uncertainty into learning may conflict with current traditionally held principles of reward consistency, suggesting some interesting debates in the future. Our increasing understanding of the brain's reward system has the potential to prompt a significant departure from present educational thinking (see Chapter 9).

Early screening for some developmental disorders

Event-related potentials (ERPs) refer to a set of distinct electrical signals emitted by the brain and detectable using a non-invasive technique involving the attachment of electrodes to the scalp. It was mentioned in Chapter 1 that some ERP waveforms of newborn infants can differentiate between children who will later be poor readers or dyslexic. This provides the possibility of very early screening, so that children at risk of dyslexia can benefit from the earliest possible intervention, and similar applications of ERP are being considered for early detection of specific language impairment (Friedrich, 2008). Such techniques and possibilities are not limited to literacy. Another type of ERP has been identified that is sensitive to children's response to numerical distance (Szucs *et al.*, 2007) that may be a helpful neural marker for magnitude processing in infancy. This signal may provide an early indicator of later educational risk in respect of mathematics. The use of neural markers to provide very early detection of educational risk appears a very real possibility in the not-too-distant future (although see discussion of ethical issues in Chapter 7).

Cognition and the brain in the curriculum: Curriculum aims and content

There is now good evidence to show that brain function can be trained, in the sense that repeated practice on exercises that focus on a cognitive function can produce improvement in that cognitive function. Cognitive training also appears able to reduce risk of Alzheimers (Wilson *et al.*, 2002). A five-year study has shown that training can provide sustained improvements in a range of cognitive functions among older people (Ball *et al.*, 2002), although there is less evidence confirming impact of cognitive training on everyday functioning that is not specifically targeted by the training. As research continues, however, such evidence is emerging (Mahncke *et al.*, 2006; Willis *et al.*, 2006). In the study by Willis *et al.* (2006) sustained improvements were shown in targeted function over five years, following an intervention that consisted of only ten sessions of about 60–75 minutes each. Positive effects were also observed in daily functioning involving the phone, laundry, cooking, etc. (Willis *et al.*, 2006), and we are understanding more about the impact of training cognitive function on other, non-targeted areas.

Perhaps more notable is the recent research on fluid intelligence, a measure seen as a good predictor of professional and academic achievement. This research has shown that fluid intelligence can be improved by rehearsing a working memory task – the so-called N-back task[2] (Jaeggi *et al.*, 2008). Unlike most other studies (which have been undertaken with older participants including those at risk of dementia), the average age of the participants in this study was 25, demonstrating the relevance of this type of cognitive training for the younger population.

In terms of developing cognitive function among children, it is the targeting of WM, together with the closely allied concept of attention, that has again produced the most interesting results. In a study involving children with ADHD, training of WM was found to successfully transfer to non-targeted areas of behaviour, producing improved complex reasoning skills and reduced parental ratings of ADHD symptoms (Klingberg *et al.*, 2005). Training of visual and auditory attention has been found to benefit literacy achievement for children with dyslexia (Chenault *et al.*, 2004), and a study using ERPs with children with specific language impairment (SLI) has shown that neural mechanisms of selective auditory attention and the associated language difficulties can be remediated through auditory attention training (Stevens *et al.*, 2008).

This scientific research converges with other forces that are encouraging educators to move their focus away from content towards thinking skills and, more specifically, the training of cognitive function. Advances in technology are likely to continue improving our access to information, with some commentators believing this will increase the need for specialization as it begins placing 'any human knowledge at the fingertips of any human' (Stewart, 2008). Such advances may, therefore, make it desirable for learners to be better equipped for manipulating information than for encoding and recalling it. The demand for specialization will also make it more difficult to predict and include the type of content that an individual may benefit from in the initial stages of their education.[3] These factors may combine with the developing dialogue between neuroscience and education to encourage greater general emphasis upon cognitive function within education. Cognitive function is a central construct of cognitive neuroscience, and some scientific enthusiasts of collaboration between neuroscience and education seek to redefine the aims of education[4] as an attempt to 'nurture' the brain and cognitive processes. Increasing interest in the training of cognitive function as a means to enhance learning potential is also reflected in current public interest in 'brain training' products, although it should be noted that no quality research exists that evaluates the claims made by the manufacturers of these products, or even the design principles upon which they are based. Despite this lack of evaluation, but in line with the concerns about infectiousness of neuromyths expressed in Chapter 2, this public enthusiasm with these commercial products has already begun to extend itself to some schools.[5]

There has also been a broader interest in the development of children's cognitive function, in ways that involve emotional aspects of behaviour. These include the development of 'Executive Function' (EF) – an umbrella term referring to the underlying processes responsible for children's ability to direct, maintain and focus their attention, manage impulses, self-regulate behaviour and emotion, plan ahead and demonstrate flexible approaches to problem solving.[6] EF skills are predictive of academic achievement (Bull *et al.*, 2008), and social and emotional development (Hughes, 1998). For this reason, attempts have been made to find ways of developing EF skills and some interventions in schools have reported positive results in terms of improved behaviour (Greenberg, 2006).

Unlike simple cognitive training, such programmes require learners to understand and reflect upon their behaviour in terms of a set of mental processes. In this sense, they are delivering an explicit, if sometimes ill-defined, psychological content into the curriculum of many schools. These programmes are becoming associated with protecting the mental health of children[7] as well as improving academic standards and behaviour. They have been explicitly linked to neuroscience by some experts (Greenberg, 2006), although (in the opinion of the author) such links would benefit from further scientific scrutiny and consensus. What does appear clear, however, is that education is becoming influenced by attempts to directly attend to the development of EF, in order to promote emotional well-being, mental health and academic achievement. It has been known for some time that the level of education can influence mental health in later life, but there are now growing voices for educators to become actively involved in fostering the mental health of their learners. A 2005 policy paper produced by the Sainsbury foundation (together with the National Health Service Confederation) predicts 'by 2015, mental wellbeing should be a major concern for schools, from dedicated classroom time to the overall approach of the school towards its pupils and staff' (SCMH, 2005) p. 13.

It can also be predicted that advances in neuroscientific understanding may broaden the aims of education further still, thereby influencing the curriculum and the ways in which it is delivered. For example, rising levels of obesity among children has drawn new attention to the importance of exercise in schools, but this may gain further emphasis as exercise becomes linked to learning via neural processes (Hillman *et al.*, 2008). Understanding how even short bouts of exercise improve subsequent learning (Winter *et al.*, 2007) makes it foreseeable that regular exercise breaks during the school day will become more popular as a means of raising academic standards and fostering mental and physical health. Although it is certainly not a good example of science, evidence for the likelihood of such developments arises from the popularity of Brain Gym. The principles of Brain Gym appear unscientific and bizarre (see Chapter 2), but its popularity in the face of unfavourable media exposure must surely derive, in part, from its associations with academic achievement and neuroscience. Such associations, in the case of Brain Gym, do not withstand scrutiny, especially in terms of neuroscience, but it is likely that the authentic value of exercise in learning will become well understood by educators in future years. It can be predicted that, within the next decade or so, neuroscience will have contributed to scientifically sound and educationally evaluated methods of incorporating frequent exercise breaks into the school day, and these will have become established in most schools.

Attempts to introduce exercise into the academic curriculum will need to ensure learner motivation, and this may depend on learners knowing something of its benefits for neurocognitive function. A learner's understanding of their own brain can have several benefits. It was mentioned in Chapter 1 that, providing learners with a basic knowledge of the brain can provide significant help in improving self-image and academic achievement (Blackwell *et al.*, 2007). Since an increasing number of benefits appear linked to understanding something about brain function and brain health, these topics seem likely to be included in future school curricula.

Neuroscience-related issues arriving without invitation

The potential changes so far discussed are expected to come about through initiatives involving educators, and their final form is likely to be mediated by educational understanding, sensitivities and opinions. Some influences involving neuroscience, however, may arrive without invitation. One such issue, reviewed in Chapter 7, is the use of cognitive enhancers. In the US, the use (or abuse) of prescription drugs by students for cognitive enhancement is widespread in some universities and colleges, and the development of new and stronger drugs will continue. It seems probable that the use of cognitive enhancers among the general UK population will increase as public sensitivity diminishes and the drugs become more socially acceptable. This will stimulate significant ethical debate among educators. Some educational institutions may, with parental permission, choose to introduce drug testing. Since there are few clear precedents for the issues involved with these drugs (it is debatable whether a comparison with the use of drugs in sport is helpful) there may, for some time, exist a diverse range of attitudes and practices among learners and educational institutions in respect of cognitive enhancers. This may impede the development of any necessary legislation.

The influence of neuroscience on educational professional development

We saw in Chapter 3 that educators' ideas about the brain often diverge from scientific notions, and in ways that can undermine good practice. When teachers consider learning processes, they tend to think about mental rather than neural processes, although in the future we can expect constructions about these mental processes to be increasingly informed by neurobiological understanding. If the training of teachers continues to ignore the brain and mind, this will encourage the proliferation of unhelpful neuromyths, allow the gap between educational and scientific understanding to further increase, and deprive teachers of the insights into their own practice that such science can provide. Hopefully, we will see important elements of modern psychology return to the initial teacher training curriculum, together with some neuroscience.

Developments that may occur in the future, but not the near future

Genetic profiling in mainstream education

Early gene-based assessment for risk from specific disorders may make an appearance in the next few years, but widespread use of genetic testing to predict learning profiles of mainstream students can be expected to meet more resistance.

Since biotechnology companies are now marketing genetic tests directly to the public, it is possible this issue will eventually arrive without educational invitation, as with cognitive enhancers. It may not be long before all parents have the opportunity to independently purchase a genetic profile of their child, and then ask what their school intends to do about it. However, whilst the educational application of smart pills requires only that a bottle is opened and a pill consumed, there remains much educational (or 'edugenetic') research necessary in order to utilize genetic knowledge in mainstream education. This knowledge gap and the ethical issues mentioned above will provide some barriers to progress. Due to the potential benefits to individual learners, public attitudes are likely to become increasingly positive and demands for edugenetic approaches will slowly grow, but it seems unlikely that schools will develop established approaches to genetically based differentiation of mainstream teaching and learning in the next one to two decades.

Brain-computer interfaces (BCIs) in mainstream education and 'brain reading'

The computer that knows your thoughts may seem like the stuff of science fiction, but something similar already exists. Brain-computer interfaces have developed the potential to provide valuable aid to some profoundly disabled individuals. For example, severely paralysed patients can control prosthetic limbs and computer cursors by thought alone. Non-invasive BCIs often adapt the type of technology used by ERP and EEG measurements, using a patient's electrical brain activity sensed by electrodes placed on the scalp. The EEG/ERP signal is analysed and interpreted automatically by a computer, which then produces an appropriate output. In this way, the user can generate some rudimentary signal to the outside world by producing the predefined type of thought that the computer is programmed to decode. For example, by imagining different body motions (e.g. left versus right hand), the user can generate different EEG signals to communicate answers to binary (yes/no) questions with high, but not perfect, accuracy (Neuper et al., 2006). However, significant challenges exist for those wishing to use this approach to communicate more complex messages. Limitations arise from the noisiness of the signal and its variability between individuals. However sophisticated the technology becomes, significant advances in BCIs will require greater neurobiological and psychological understanding of the signals themselves.

At present then, although the usefulness of non-invasive BCIs for the profoundly disabled may develop further in the next one to two decades, the likelihood of the wider population using them to communicate with everyday technology is a long way off. This will only happen when our understanding of brain function is unimaginably superior than at present.[8]

Similar limitations also apply to 'brain reading'. Some neuroimaging experiments demonstrate that the new technology can reveal socially sensitive and

relevant information, such as racial group identity and unconscious racial attitudes. For example, white subjects with more negative evaluations of black faces
showed increased amygdalic activity in response to unfamiliar black, compared
with white, faces. Some correlates of deception have also been identified (Nunez
et al., 2005) which may be helpful in counter-terrorism efforts in the future.
Such examples, however, tend to compare a very small set of conditions, differentiating between a correspondingly small set of possibilities regarding mental content (e.g. truth/lies). As Farah suggests (p. 1126) in relation to brain-reading,
'even a major leap in the signal-to-noise ratio of functional brain imaging would
leave us with gigabytes of more accurate physiological data whose psychological
meaning would be obscure' (Farah, 2002).

Improbable educational advances involving neuroscience

Chapter 4 exposed considerable differences between the views of educators and
scientists about how neuroscience is relevant to education, although consensus is emerging in both areas that the relevance exists. Perhaps unsurprisingly,
educators associate possible advances in neuroscience with those brain-based
concepts already commonly found in schools, which are often not well-founded
on science. Educational expectations, then, of how neuroscience may influence
education in the future may often be unreasonable, because they are influenced
by prevailing neuromyths. Neuroscience is not likely to be helpful in developing
or supporting such educational ideas as multiple intelligences theory, learning
styles or educational kinesiology.

A brain-based science of education

Although researchers at the interface of neuroscience and education have done
much to counter the neuromyths prevailing in schools, they must also be careful
not to create new ones. Some enthusiasts of bringing neuroscience and education together can, accidentally or intentionally, provide the impression that
including the brain in education can produce a natural science of education.
The titles of some prominent books on the subject (*Towards a New Learning
Science*, *Birth of a New Learning Science*) may even contribute to this impression (OECD, 2002b; OECD, 2007). Policymakers may find this an attractive
idea because neuroscience seems a more secure basis for learning theory, with its
images of brain activity appearing more concrete than abstract psychological concepts. And, of course, we know that neuroscience is seductive, with references to
the brain (even irrelevant ones) increasing the satisfaction of a reader (Weisberg
et al., 2008). However, this book has argued that, like social and experiential
evidence taken in isolation, biological evidence is, on its own, limited in terms of
what it can tell us. A science of teaching and learning which is chiefly *based* upon
the brain is unlikely to develop in the foreseeable future, because neuroscientific

perspectives struggle with many concepts (such as meaning and autonomy) that are central to educational aims and understanding. On the other hand, the greater *inclusion* of biological perspectives in educational thinking, alongside other perspectives, appears increasingly desirable and probable.

Introducing neuroeducational research

Although appearing under many different names (e.g. educational neuroscience, neuroeducational research, neuroscience and education) a field of research at the interface between neuroscience and education is establishing itself. This is despite a long-standing and unhelpful divide between the natural and social sciences within academia. Neuroeducational research throws down a gauntlet to science, because it demands a unique type of 'reality relevance'. Clinical areas of neuroscience already face challenges involving 'real world' cases, but neuroeducational research is possibly the first area where neuroscientists can observe the efficacy of their concepts in real world situations involving 'normal' brains.

Most importantly, however, the very existence of this field of enquiry provides a daunting challenge to those concerned with education. Historically, despite a common sense of its immense relevance, the world of education has ignored or carelessly misrepresented the brain. This could only be acceptable if including biological evidence in educational thinking was theoretically unhelpful and/or practically impossible. Yet, the emergence of this field is helping to provide evidence that neither of these things is true and that the relevance of neuroscience to educational practice is encroaching daily. Can education afford to ignore the brain any longer?

Summary

It is anticipated that the following educational developments involving neuroscience may arrive in the next one to two decades:

- New educational approaches will become established for the teaching and learning of mathematics in the early years, as a result of insights from cognitive neuroscience.
- Adolescents will become recognized as a more distinct group of learners, and educational approaches will be developed that are better tailored to meet their social, emotional and educational needs.
- A new understanding of motivation will be developed and new approaches to engaging learners will become established (e.g. in areas involving the use of games) informed by insights into the brain's reward system.
- Early screening will be available for a range of learning disorders, using neural markers and genetic testing.
- Attendance to the development of some targeted cognitive functions, including working memory, will feature across year groups in the school curriculum.

- The reflective understanding and development of executive function will feature in the school curriculum for young learners.
- Understanding of mental health issues will become a stronger feature of the curriculum, as the aims of education become broader. This will include a basic understanding of brain function, with the associated academic benefits that such an understanding may bring.
- Exercise breaks will become a feature of the curriculum, as the link between exercise and academic achievement becomes clearer, and the developed world struggles with increasing levels of obesity.
- The use of drugs to enhance cognitive function will become commonplace, remaining chiefly unchecked by legislation as the government remains unwilling to intervene in the absence of clear public consensus. The attitudes and practices among different groups of learners and educational institutions will diverge.
- Psychology, and some neuroscience, will become an accepted part of teachers' professional development and training.
- There will be no brain-based natural science of education that is meaningful in educational terms, but a new field of neuroeducational research will become established, together with the development of professionals trained in both education and relevant natural sciences (e.g. cognitive neuroscience, genetics). Through such endeavours, the sciences of mind and brain will become increasingly important contributors to educational understanding, practice and policymaking.

Appendix I

Some neuroanatomy

Understanding the educational significance of neuroscientific findings does not require a high level of specialist knowledge. However, acquiring a few anatomical terms and phrases can be useful and some of those you will encounter in this book are explained here.

The adult brain contains about 100 billion brain cells – or *neurons*. Each neuron, such as shown in Fig. A.1, consists of a *cell body*, from which are connected *dendrites* and an *axon*.

The *presynaptic terminals* at the end of the axon make contact with the dendrites of other neurons and allow connections, or *synapses*, to form between neurons. In this way, complex neural networks can be created. A simple network is shown in Fig. A.2.

Within such networks, signals can flow down the axons of one neuron and cross the synapse to other neurons, allowing neurons to communicate with each other. The signal passing down the axon is electric, and its progress is hastened by insulation around the axon known as *myelin*. However, the process that allows the signal to pass through from the synaptic terminals to the dendrites of the next neuron is chemical. This process involves transmission across the synaptic gap of special substances known as *neurotransmitters*.

Our brains, like those of other vertebrates, consist of three main parts, shown in Fig A.3. The hindbrain includes structures regulating body function such as sleep and blood flow, but also the cauliflower-like structure at the back of brain called the *cerebellum* – visible in Fig. A.3. The cerebellum is involved in some cognitive processes, including those involving timing such as language, music and movement. The midbrain includes structures that relay sensory and movement information. In humans, the forebrain has evolved to be largest part of the brain and this includes the cortex. The cortex is often described in terms of two cortical hemispheres, left and right, joined together by a mass of fibres known as the *corpus callosum*.

The cortex can be further divided into four *lobes*: the *frontal, parietal, occipital* and *temporal,* as in Fig. A.4. Each lobe has been associated with a different set of cognitive functions. The frontal lobe may, perhaps, be of particular interest to educators due to its involvement with many different aspects of reasoning as well as movement. The temporal lobe is associated with some aspects of memory, as well as auditory skills. The parietal lobes are heavily involved in integrating information from different sources and have also been associated with some types of mathematical skill. The occipital lobes are critical regions for visual processing. However, it is not advisable to consider any one part of the brain as solely involved with any one task. Any everyday task recruits a large and broadly distributed set of neural networks that communicate with each other in a complex fashion.

Beyond identifying an area of the brain by its lobe, scientists find it useful to name each valley or trough on the lobe's wrinkled surface. A valley is referred to by the latin name of *sulcus* (plural *sulci*) and a ridge is called a *gyrus* (plural *gyri*). Other types of label such as *dorsal* or *inferior* can help identify where in the lobe a sulcus of gyrus of interest is. These terms (see Fig. A.5) indicate general directions (rather than parts) in the brain.

Some sulci and gyri have special names such as the angular gyrus – which is a ridge in the parietal lobe close to the superior edge of the temporal lobe. The intraparietal sulcus (marked in Fig. A.6) is a valley between upper and lower (inferior and superior) parts of the parietal lobe. The orientation terms in Fig. A.5 are also involved in references to broader regions of cortex, as in Dorso-Lateral PreFrontal Cortex (DLPFC) which refers to the upper part of the anterior (as suggested by 'pre') frontal lobes in both hemispheres (i.e. bilateral) – see Fig. A.6. Another term which you may encounter is medial (not shown), which means at or near the middle of the brain where the two hemispheres meet.

The cortical surface (sometimes referred to as the neocortex) is more wrinkled in humans than any other species, a characteristic thought to reflect our greater reliance upon higher level thought processes. The evolutionary pressure to maximize cortical area has resulted in some of our cortex existing well below the outer surface. One notable example of this is the *cingulate cortex* (see Fig. A.3). The *anterior* (or forward) part of the cingulate cortex becomes active when we engage with a wide variety of tasks, and appears to have a significant role in the allocation of attention.

Fig. A.7 shows some important structures deeper within the forebrain that include the *hippocampus* – a part of the brain critical to consolidating new memories, and the *amygdala* which plays an important role in our emotional responses. These belong to a set of structures collectively called the limbic system, often considered to be the system responsible for our emotional function. However, aspects of brain function related to emotion are no longer attributed to a single system, but are related to pathways and processes throughout the brain. For example, levels of the neurotransmitter dopamine in the mesolimbic pathway are related to the feeling of wanting, and this pathway begins in a mid-brain region before connecting to several structures (including the hippocampus and amygdala) in the limbic system, and another region of the forebrain known as the striatum (Fig. A.7). Also shown in this diagram is the thalamus, which is the major sensory gateway to the cortex. This is located in the deeper region of the forebrain referred to as the diencephalon, just above the mid-brain.

Glossary

Acetylcholine (ACh) – a neurotransmitter involved with *synaptic plasticity*.

Attention deficit hyperactivity disorder (ADHD) – a developmental disorder involving inappropriate impulsivity, difficulties in maintaining attention, and sometimes hyperactivity.

Adenosine – a neurotransmitter with a role in promoting sleep.

Bilateral – both sides of the brain.

Critical period – see Sensitive period.

Declarative memory – our capacity to recall memories that can be discussed, including facts from textbooks, and *episodic* memories of what we have experienced. It does not include procedural memories such as how to ride a bicycle.

Dopamine – a neurotransmitter with different functions in different regions of the brain. In the mesolimbic pathway (an important part of the reward system – see Appendix 1), it is associated with anticipatory desire (or 'wanting').

Dyslexia – a developmental disorder involving difficulty in learning to read.

Dyscalculia – a developmental disorder involving difficulty in acquiring mathematical skills.

Ecological validity – the extent to which a study approximates to the real life situation it claims to investigate.

Electroencephalography (EEG) – a brain-imaging technique that uses a net of electrodes placed on the scalp to measure minute changes in electrical field due to neural activity.

Event-related potential (ERP) – a stereotyped EEG response that is known to occur in relation to a particular type of event.

Episodic memory – the ability to recall autobiographical events (times, places, etc.).

Functional magnetic resonance imaging (fMRI) – a brain-imaging technique that measures changes in blood oxygen levels in the brain.

Grapheme – the fundamental unit of a written language (e.g. alphabetic letters).

Glial cells (or glia) are cells in the brain that support neurons.

Grey matter – those parts of the central nervous system that consist of masses of neuronal cell bodies. This is in contrast to those parts containing only axons – see White matter.

Long-term potentiation (LTP) – a long-lasting improvement in communication efficiency between two neurons (i.e. better connectivity) brought about by being activated simultaneously.

Long-term depression (LTD) – a long-lasting decrease in communication efficiency between two neurons (i.e. poorer connectivity) brought about by being activated simultaneously.

Mirror neurons – neurons that increase their activation, both when carrying out an action, and when observing the same action being carried out by another.

Myelination – the process by which myelin, a white sheath of fat and protein, forms around the axons of neurons and improves their ability to transmit electrical information (see Appendix 1).

Neural atrophy – wasting away of neurons.

Neurotransmitter – a chemical that crosses the synapse (connection) between neurons enabling the transfer of information across it.

Neurogenesis – birth of neurons.

Nondeclarative memory – our capacity for memory abilities that are not of the declarative type (see above). These include skills and habits, conditioned emotional responses and habituation due to repetitive exposure to a stimulus.

Noradrenalin (or norepinephrine) – a neurotransmitter involved with the control of attention and impulsive response, also operating as a hormone in the body involved with fight-or-flight responses.

Obsessive-compulsive disorder (OCD) – a mental disorder involving intrusive and repetitive thoughts, and compulsive behaviour.

Phoneme – smallest distinctive speech sound.

Plasticity – the brain's ability to continuously change in response to environmental stimulus.

Positron emission tomography (PET) – a neuroimaging technique that involves the detection of radioactivity in the brain following after a positron emitting tracer has been introduced into the body.

Sensitive period – a period of time during which we display a heightened sensitivity to certain environmental stimuli and develop in particular ways due to this experience.

Synaptogenesis – formation of new synapses (or connections) between neurons.

Synaptic plasticity – the ability of synapses to modify the efficiency by which they communicate information.

Synaptic pruning – elimination of synapses (or connections) between neurons.

Synapse – a connection, or specialized junction, between neurons usually consisting of a small gap across which information is passed by chemical processes.

Transcranial magnetic stimulation (TCMS) The temporary disruption of brain processes by applying magnetic pulses near the scalp.

White matter – masses of axons that appear whitish due to myelin.

Working memory – the ability to recall and temporarily maintain information in consciousness.

Notes

Introduction

1 *Brain, Mind and Education*, Wiley.
2 Initiatives combining neuroscience and education are presently emerging under many names such as 'educational neuroscience' and 'Brain, mind and education' (see Tokuhama-Espinosa, 2008). The term 'neuroeducational research' will be used in this book because it best reflects the process of knowledge construction that is proposed (i.e. one that judiciously interrelates concepts from both fields through research based activity, whose goals include the furthering of educational and scientific understanding, and is uniquely characterized by its own methodology).

1 What has neuroscience got to do with education?

1 Neuroscientists tend to consider the nature/nurture debate in terms of biological predisposition (as coded in the genome) and the environment (a word that, when used in the scientific sense, covers a broad range of issues, from ingested nutrients and toxins to personal experiences such as those provided by education or the home).

2 Neuromyths

1 A reported electrical sensation in the spine and limbs produced by bending the neck forward.
2 However, general intelligence might also be distributed throughout the brain in terms of overall brain efficiency and, contrary to Gardner, some scientists point to the positive correlation between a measure of general intelligence 'g', brain size (see McDaniel, 2005; Toga and Thompson, 2005) and the level of brain activity (Geake and Hansen, 2005) to suggest that 'g' may be an important concept in understanding individual performance.
3 The myth that we only use 10 per cent of our brains may have arisen from the experiments of Karl Lashley who removed large parts of the cerebral cortex in rats and found they were still able to relearn some tasks (Lashley, 1929). The myth gained a boost when it was claimed Albert Einstein used it in a radio interview to encourage people to use their brains more (Beyerstein, 1999b). But, although not all neurons are firing at any one instant, even making a cup of coffee causes a 'a lightning storm of neuron activity occurs almost across the entire brain' (Boyd, 2008). Survivors of trauma

who have lost part of their cortex are often still able to perform many of their daily functions but, rather than suggesting the missing parts were not in use, this is evidence for the brain's plastic nature and its ability to compensate with what is left.

4 These arguments also rest on assumptions about the role of synaptic connectivity in human learning, and links between synaptogenesis and human learning, neither of which are entirely understood. However, since these assumptions are commonly seen as reasonable within neuroscience, they are not explored here.

5 More recent references to enriched animal environments supporting increased neurogenesis in the hippocampus should be interpreted in the same way (Olson *et al.*, 2006).

3 Educators on the brain, neuroscientists on education

1 Apart from its visual resemblance to the wrinkled exterior of the human cortex, this idea may be related to the fact the walnut has a higher Omega-3 content than any common nut (Davis and Kris-Etherington, 2003).

4 Neuroscience and education in dialogue

1 Executive Director, South Australian Centre for Lifelong Learning and Development.

2 Available on https://www.bris.ac.uk/education/research/sites/brain/docs

3 However, at the time of writing, no research in this area has been funded by UK research councils.

5 A multi-perspective understanding of learning

1 This anonymously derived expression is often used by popular writers about the brain but, for more accurate representations of the Hebbian learning theory it refers to, see Hebb (1947).

2 In this sense, it could be said that educational thinking has frequently been constrained by explanations that privilege some psycho-social perspectives, to the exclusion of biological insight.

9 Neuroeducational research case study B: Learning games

1 Note that reward is being used here in the psychological sense, i.e. as that which reinforces behaviour.

2 Motivation is being used here in the 'lower level' neuropsychological sense, as reflected in our desire to approach, or as our immediate sense of wanting (e.g. as when we see chocolate cake). In everyday language, we can also say we are motivated by higher level goals, such as paying off a long-term loan or providing benefit to others. The motivation to achieve such higher level goals is less related to this type of reward system activity.

10 Neuroscience, education and the future

1 The author has included dyslexia in this list because present understanding in neuroscience tends to support much existing practice, but this is partly because

existing practice has already been influenced by cognitive psychology and cognitive neuroscience.

2 In the type of N-back task used in this research, participants are asked to observe a sequence of stimuli, and asked to recall the item that was N items back.

3 Memory processes will, however, still remain of key importance in education although semantic memory (for knowing 'how to') may increase its significance relative to declarative memory (explicit recall of facts and events).

4 An extreme view of this redefinition has been provided by Koizumi: '... education should be designed to guide and inspire the construction of the basic architecture for information processing in the brain by preparing and controlling the input stimuli given to the learners' (Koizumi, 2004, p. 435).

5 For example: http://www.ltscotland.org.uk/ictineducation/gamesbasedlearning/sharingpractice/braintraining/introduction.asp

6 WM is usually considered one component of EFL.

7 "Programmes through the curriculum can promote mental health ... important characteristics of such programmes include those that enable children to correctly identify and regulate one's feelings ..." DfEE (2001, p. 10).

8 Invasive BCIs involve the implantation of electrodes, produce cleaner signals and perform a little better, but clearly these are not likely to become acceptable for those who suffer no serious disability and so these devices are not considered here.

References

AAP (1998) Learning disabilities, dyslexia, and vision: A subject review (electronic version), *Pediatrics*. American Academy of Pediatrics.

AACAP (1997) Practice parameters for the assessment and treatment of children, adolescents, and adults with attention-deficit hyperactivity disorder. *Journal of the American Academy of Child and Adolescent Psychiatry*, 36, 85S–121S.

Abdullaev, Y. G. and Posner, M. I. (1997) Time course of activating brain areas in generating verbal associations. *Psychological Science*, 8, 56–59.

Abrahams, E., Ginsburg, G. S. and Silver, M. (2005) The personalized medicine coalition: Goals and strategies. *American Journal of Pharmacogenomics*, 5, 345–355.

Acevedo, A. and Loewenstein, D. A. (2007) Nonpharmacological cognitive interventions in aging and dementia. *Journal of Geriatric Psychiatry and Neurology*, 20, 239–249.

Adcock, R. A. (2006) Reward-motivated learning: mesolimbic activation precedes memory formation. *Neuron*, 50, 507–517.

Adolphs, R., Tranel, D. and Damasio, A. R. (2003) Dissociable neural systems for recognizing emotions. *Brain and Cognition*, 52, 61–69.

AERA (2000) Ethical Standards of the American Educational Research Association.

Ahamed, Y., MacDonald, H., Reed, K., Naylor, P.-J., Liu-Ambrose, T. and McKay, H. (2007) School-based physical activity does not compromise children's academic performance. *Medicine and Science in Sports and Exercise*, 39, 371–376.

Akkoyunlu, B. and Soylu, M. Y. (2008) A study of students' perceptions in a blended learning environment based on different learning style. *Educational Technology and Society*, 11, 183–193.

Alexander, B. A. (2005) Performance ethnography: The reenacting and inciting of culture, in Denzin, N. K. and Lincoln, Y. S. (eds) *The Sage Handbook of Qualitative Research* (third edn). Thousand Oaks, CA: Sage.

Allinson, C. W. and Hayes, J. (1996) The cognitive style index. *Journal of Management Studies*, 33, 119–135.

Amabile, T. (1996) *Creativity in Context*. New York: Springer-Verlag.

Amunts, K., Schlaug, G., Jancke, L., Steinmetz, H., Schleicher, A., Dabringhaus, A. and Zilles, K. (1997) Motor cortex and hand motor skills: Structural compliance in the human brain. *Human Brain Mapping*, 5, 206–215.

Anderson, S. L. (2005) Stimulants and the developing brain. *Trends in Pharmacological Sciences*, 26, 237–243.

Ansari, D. and Coch, D. (2006) Bridges over troubled waters: education and cognitive neuroscience. *Trends in Cognitive Sciences*, 10, 146–149.

Arhib, M. A. (ed.) (2003) *The Handbook of Brain Theory and Neural Networks*, Cambridge, MA: The MIT Press.

Arshavsky, Y. I. (2006) *Progress in Neurobiology*, 80, 99–113.

Arter, J. A. and Jenkins, J. R. (1979) Differential diagnosis – prescriptive teaching: A critical appraisal. *Review of Educational Research*, 49, 517–555.

Atkinson, J. W. (1957) Motivational determinants of risk taking behaviour. *Psychological Review*, 64, 359–372.

Baird, A., Fugelsang, J. and Bennett, C. (2005) 'What were you thinking'? A neural signature associated with reasoning in adolescence, *Journal of Cognitive Neuroscience*, S, 193–193.

Ball, K., Berch, D. B., Helmers, K. F., Jobe, J. B., Leveck, M. D., Marsiske, M., *et al.* (2002) Effects of cognitive training interventions with older adults: A randomized controllled trial. *Journal of American Medical Association*, 288(18), 2271–2281.

Baluch, B. and Kaur, B. (1995) Attitude change toward animal experimentation in an academic setting, *Journal of Psychology*, 129, 477–479.

Bar-David, Y., Urkin, J. and Kozminsky, E. (2005) The effect of voluntary dehydration on cognitive functions of elementary school children. *Acta Paediatrica*, 94, 1667–1673.

Bar-Or, O., Dotan, R., Inbar, O., Rotshstein, A. and Zonder, H. (1980) Voluntary hypohydration in 10 to 12 year old boys. *Journal of Applied Physiology*, 48, 104–108.

BBC (2000) Water improves test results. *BBC News Online*.

Beauchamp, M. S., Lee, K. E., Argall, B. D. and Martin, A. (2004) Integration of auditory and visual information about objects in superior temporal sulcus. *Neuron*, 41, 809–823.

Bechara, A., Damasio, H., Tranel, D. and Damasio, A. R. (1997) Deciding advantageously before knowing the advantageous strategy *Science*, 275, 1293–1295.

Bechara, A., Damasio, H., Tranel, D. and Damasio, A. R. (2005) The Iowa gambling task and the somatic marker hypothesis: Some questions and answers. *Trends in Cognitive Sciences*, 9, 159–162.

Bechtereva, N. P., Danko, S. G. and Medvedev, S. V. (2007) Current methodology and methods in psychophysiological studies of creative thinking, *Methods*, 42, 100–108.

Bekhtereva, N. P., Starchenko, M. G., Klyucharev, V. A., Vorob'ev, V. A., Pakhomov, S. V. and Medvedev, S. V. (2000) Study of the brain organisation of creativity: II. Positron-emission tomography data, *Human Physiology*, 26, 516–522.

Bellisle, F. (2004) Effects of diet on behaviour and cognition in children. *British Journal of Nutrition*, 92, S227–S232.

Bennett, M. R. and Hacker, P. M. S. (2003) *Philosophical Foundations of Neuroscience*. Oxford: Blackwell.

BERA (2004) Revised ethical guidelines for educational research.

Berridge, K. C. and Robinson, T. E. (2003) Parsing Reward. *Trends in Neurosciences*, 26(9), 507–513.

Beyerstein, B. (1999a) Pseudoscience and the brain: Tuners and tonics for aspiring superhumans, in Della Salla, S. (ed.) *Mind Myths*. Chichester: John Wiley and Sons.

Beyerstein, B. (1999b) Whence cometh the myth that we only use ten percent of our brains? in Della Salla, S. (ed.) *Mind-myths: Exploring Everyday Mysteries of the Mind and Brain*. New York: John Wiley and Sons.

Beyerstein, D. F. (1992) Graphology and the philosophy of science, in Beyerstein, B. (ed.) *The Write Stuff*. Amherst, NY: Prometheus Books.

Bjork, J. M., Smith, A. R., Danube, C. L., and Hommer, D. W. (2007) Developmental differences in posterior mesofrontal cortex recruitment by risky rewards. *Journal of Neuroscience*, 27(18), 4839–4849.

Blackwell, L. S., Trzesniewski, K. H. and Dweck, C. S. (2007) Implicit theories of intelligence predict achievement across an adolescent transition: A longtitudinal study and an intervention. *Child Development*, 78, 246–263.

Blakemore, S. J. and Choudhury, S. (2006) Development of the adolescent brain: Implications for executive function and social cognition. *Journal of Child Psychology and Psychiatry*, 47, 296–312.

Blakemore, S. J. and Frith, U. (2000) *The Implications of Recent Developments in Neuroscience for Reseach on Teaching and Learning*. Exeter: TLRP.

Blakemore, S. J. and Frith, U. (2005) *The Learning Brain*. Oxford: Blackwell.

Blakemore, S. J., Winston, J. and Frith, U. (2004) Social cognitive neuroscience: Where are we heading? *Trends in Cognitive Sciences*, 8, 216–222.

Bloom, P. and Weisberg, D. S. (2007) Childhood origins of adult resistance to science. *Science*, 316.

Bochner, S. (1978) Ayres, sensory integration and learning disorders: A question of theory and practice. *Australian Journal of Mental Retardation*, 5, 41–45.

Bookheimer, S. (2002) Functional MRI of language: New approaches to understanding the cortical organization of semantic processing. *Annual Review of Neuroscience*, 25, 151–188.

Bowden, E. M. and Jung-Beeman, M. (2007) Methods for investigating the neural components of insight. *Methods*, 42, 87–99.

Boyd, R. (2008) Fact or fiction?: People only use 10 percent of their brains. *Scientific American*, Feb 7.

Boysen, S. T. and Capaldi, E. J. (eds) (1993) *The Development of Numerical Competence: Animal and Human Models*. Hillsdale, NJ: Erlbaum.

BPS (2006) Code of ethics and conduct.

Brasil-Neto, J. P., Pascual-Leone, A., Valls-Sole, J., Cohen, L. G. and Hallett, M. (1992) Focal transcranial magnetic stimulation and response bias in a forced-choice task. *Journal of Neurology, Neurosurgery and Psychiatry*, 55, 964–966.

Brierley, B., Medford, N., Shaw, P., and David, A. S. (2007) Emotional memory for words: Separating content and context. *Cognition and Emotion*, 21(3), 495–521.

Bruer, J. (1997) Education and the brain: A bridge too far. *Educational Researcher*, 26, 4–16.

Bruner, J. S. (1972) *The Relevance of Education*. London: George Allen & Unwin.

Bruner, J. S. (1974) *Beyond the Information Given: Studies in the Psychology of Knowing*. London: George Allen & Unwin.

Burgess, N. and O'Keefe, J. (1996) Neural computation underlying the firing place cells and their role in navigation. *Hippocampus*, 6, 749–762.

Bull, R., Espy, K. A. and Wiebe, S. A. (2008) Short-term memory, working memory, and executive functioning in preschoolers: Longitudinal predictors of mathematical achievement at age 7 years. *Developmental Neuropsychology*, 33(3), 205–228.

Burns, K. and Bechara, A. (2007) Decision making and free will: A neuroscience perspective. *Behavioral Sciences and the Law*, 25, 263–280.

Busch, C. R., Taylor, H. A., Kanarek, R. B. and Holcomb, P. J. (2002) The effects of a confectionery snack on attention in young boys. *Physiology and Behavior*, 77, PII S0031–9384(02)00882-X.

Byrnes, J. P. (2001) *Minds, Brains, and Learning*. New York: The Guildford Press.

Carey, S. (2004) Bootstrapping and the origins of concepts. *Daedalus*, 59–68.

Casey, B. M., Andrews, N., Schindler, H., Kersh, J. E., Samper, A. and Copley, J. (2008) The development of spatial skills through interventions involving block building activities. *Cognition and Instruction*, 26, 269–309.

Castelli, D. M., Hillman, C. H., Buck, S. M. and Erwin, H. (2007) Physical fitness and academic achievement in 3rd and 5th grade students. *Journal of Sport and Exercise Psychology*, 29, 239–252.

Catherine, S., Burnett, S. and Blakemore, S. (2008). *Neuroscience of Social Cognition in Teenagers: Implications for inclusion in Society*. London: Government Office for Science.

Chapanis, N. P. (1982) The patterning method of therapy: a critique, in Black, P. (ed.) *Brain Dysfunction in Children: Etiology, Diagnosis, and Management*. New York: Raven Press.

Chappell, K. (2006) The dilemmas of teaching for creativity: Insights from expert specialist dance teachers. *Thinking Skills and Creativity*, 2, 29–56.

Charmaz, K. (2000) *Constructed Grounded Theory: A practical Guide Through Qualitative Analysis*. London: Sage.

Charmaz, K. (2005) Grounded theory in the 21st century, in Denzin, N. K. and Lincoln, Y. S. (eds) *The Sage Handbook of Qualitative Research*. London: Sage.

Chen, S. Y., Lin, J. R., Kao, M. D., Hang, C. M., Cheng, L. and Pan, W. H. (2007) Dietary supplement usage among elementary school children in Taiwan: their school performance and emotional status. *Asia Pacific Journal of Clinical Nutrition*, 16, 554–563.

Chenault, B., Thomson, J., Abbott, R. D. and Berninger, V. W. (2004, Nov) Effects of prior attention training on child dyslexics' response to composition instruction. Paper presented at the 24th Annual Meeting of the National-Academy-of-Neuropsychology, Seattle, WA.

Choudhury, S., Blakemore, S. J. and Charman, T. (2006) Social cognitive development during adolescence. *Social Cognitive and Affective Neuroscience*, 1, 165–174.

Christianson, S. A. (1992) Emotional stress and eyewitness memory – a critical review. *Psychological Bulletin*, 112, 284–309.

Christodoulou, J. A. and Gaab, N. (2009). Using and misusing neuroscience in education-related research. Discussion. *Cortex*, 45(4), 555–557.

Churchland, P. M. (2005) Cleansing science. *Inquiry*, 48, 464–477.

Cian, C., Koulman, N., Barraud, P. A., Raphel, C., Jimnez, C. and Melin, B. (2000) Influence of variations in body hydration on cognitive function: effect of hyper-hydration, heat stress, and exercise-induced dehydration. *Journal of Psychophysiology*, 14, 29–36.

Citri, A. and Malenka, R. C. (2008) Synaptic plasticity: multiple forms, functions, and mechanisms. *Neuropsychopharmacology*, 33, 18–41.

Claxton, G. (1998) Knowing without knowing why. *The Psychologist*, 11, 217–220.

Clifford, M. M. (1988) Failure tolerance and academic risk-taking in ten- to twelve-year-old students. *British Journal of Educational Psychology*, 58, 15–27.

Clifford, M. M., and Chou, F. C. (1991) Effects of payoff and task context on academic risk taking. *Journal of Educational Psychology*, 83(4), 499–507.

Coch, D. (2007) Neuroimaging research with children: ethical issues and case scenarios. *Journal of Moral Education*, 36, 1–18.

Coffield, F., Moseley, D., Hall, E. and Ecclestone, K. (2004) Learning styles and pedagogy in post-16 learning: A systematic and critical review (Report no. 041543). London: Learning and Skills Research Centre.

Coghlan, A. (2004) Cambridge's primate research centre axed. *New Scientist*.

Cohen, H. J., Birch, H. G. and Taft, L. T. (1970) Some considerations for evaluating the Doman-Delecato 'patterning' method. *Pediatrics*, 45, 302–314.

Cohen, I. and Goldsmith, M. (2000) *Hands On: How to use Brain Gym ® in the Classroom*. Sea Point, South Africa: Hands On Books.

Cohen, N. J. and Squire, L. R. (1980) Preserved learning and retention of pattern analyzing skill in amnesia: Dissociation of knowing how and knowing that. *Science*, 210, 207–209.

Cohen, S. A. (1969) Studies in visual perception and reading in disadvantaged children. *Journal of Learning Disabilities*, 2, 498–507.

Cohn, S. (2004) Increasing resolution, intensifying ambiguity: an ethnographic account of seeing life in brain. *Economy and Society*, 33, 52–76.

Colcombe, S. J., Framer, A. F., Erickson, K. I., Scalf, P., McAuley, E., Cohen, N. J., Webb, A., Jerome, G. J., Marquez, D. X. and Elavsky, S. (2004) Cardiovascular fitness, cortical plasticity, and aging. *Proceedings of the National Academy of Sciences (USA)*, 101, 3316–3321.

Collet, C., Vernet-Maury, E., Delhomme, G. and Dittmar, A. (1997) Autonomic nervous system response patterns specificity to basic emotions. *Journal of Autonomic Nervous System*, 62, 45–57.

Cooper, R. B. and Jayatilaka, B. (2006) Group creativity: The effects of extrinsic, intrinsic, and obligation motivations. *Creativity Research Journal*, 18, 153–172.

Corkum, P. V., McKinnon, M. M. and Mullane, J. C. (2005) The effect of involving classroom teachers in a parent training program for families of children with ADHD. *Child and Family Behavior Therapy*, 27, 29–49.

Cotman, C. A. and Berchtold, N. C. (2007) Physical activity and the maintenance of cognition: Learning from animal models. *Alzheimer's and Dementia*, 3, S30–S37.

Crick, F. (1984) Memory and molecular turnover. *Nature*, 312, 101.

Crockard, A. (1996) Review: Confessions of a brain surgeon. *New Scientist*.

Csikszentmihalyi, M., and Csikszentmihalyi, I. S. (1988) *Optimal Experience*. Cambridge, UK: Cambridge University Press.

Cummins, R. A. (1988) *The Neurologically Impaired Child: Doman-Delacato Techniques Reappraised*. New York: Croom Helm.

Curtis, C. E. and D'Esposito, M. (2003) Persistent activity in the prefrontal cortex during working memory. *Trends in Cognitive Sciences*, 7.

Davis, A. J. (2004) The credentials of brain-based learning. *Journal of Philosophy of Education*, 38, 21–36.

Davis, B. C. and Kris-Etherington, P. M. (2003) Achieving optimal essential fatty acid status in vegetarians: Current knowledge and practical implications. *The American Journal of Clinical Nutrition*, 78, 640S–6S.

Davis, H. P. and Squire, L. R. (1984) Protein synthesis and memory: a review. *Psychological Bulletin*, 96, 518–559.

Daw, N., O'Doherty, J. P., Dayan, P., Seymour, B. and Dolan, R. J. (2006) Cortical substrates for exploratory decisions in humans. *Nature*, 441, 876–879.

de Quervain, D. J. F., Roozendaal, B., Nitsch, R. M., McGaugh, J. L. and Hock, C. (2000) Acute cortisone administration impairs retrieval of long-term declarative memory in humans. *Nature Neuroscience*, 3, 313–314.

Degrandpre, R. (1999) Just cause? *The Sciences*, March/April, 15–18.

Dehaene, S., Spelke, E., Pinel, P., Stanescu, R. and Tsivkin, S. (1999) Sources of mathematical thinking: behavioral and brain-imaging evidence. *Science*, 284, 970–974.

Delazer, M., Domahs, F., Bartha, L., Brenneis, C., Lochy, A., Trieb, T. and Benke, T. (2003) Learning complex arithmetic – an fMRI study. *Cognitive Brain Research*, 18, 76–88.

Delazer, M., Ischebeck, A., Domahs, F., Zamarian, L., Koppelstaetter, F., Siedentopf, C. M., Kaufmann, L., Benke, T. and Felber, S. (2005) Learning by strategies and learning by drill – evidence from an fMRI study. *Neuroimage*, 25, 838–849.

Dennison, P. E. (1981) *Switching on: A Guide to Edu-Kinesthetics*. Ventura, California: Edu-Kinesthetics.

Dennison, P. E. and Dennison, G. E. (1994) *Brain Gym Teacher's Edition – revised*. Ventura: Edu-Kinesthetics.

Department of Health (UK) (2004) *National Service Framework for Children and Young People and Maternity Services*. London: Department of Health.

DeSantis, A. D., Webb, E. M. and Noar, S. M. (2008) Illicit use of prescription ADHD medications on a college campus: A multimethodological approach. *Journal of American College Health*, 56, 315–323.

Desforges, C. (2001) A report on the consultation exercise on the Blakemore and Frith report, 'The implications of recent developments in neuroscience for research on teaching and learning'. Exeter: Teaching and Learning Programme (TLRP).

Detre, J. A. and Floyd, T. F. (2001) Functional MRI and its applications to the clinical neurosciences. *The Neuroscientist*, 7, 64–79.

DfEE (2001) *Promoting Children's Mental Health within Early Years and School Settings*. Nottingham: Department for Education and Employment.

Diamond, M. C., Greer, E. G., York, A., Lewis, D., Barton, T. and Lin, J. (1987) Rat cortical morphology following crowded-enriched living conditions. *Experimental Neurology*, 96, 241–247.

Doman, C. H. (1968) *The Diagnosis and Treatment of Speech and Reading Problems*. Springfield, IL: Thomas.

Downie, J. and Marshall, J. (2007) Pediatric neuroimaging ethics. *Cambridge Quarterly of Healthcare Ethics*, 16, 147–160.

Downie, J., Schmidt, M., Kenny, N., D'Arcy, R., Hadskis, M. and Marshall, J. (2007) Paediatric MRI research ethics: The priority issues. *Journal of Bioethical Inquiry*, 4, 85–91.

Draganski, B., Gaser, C., Busch, V., Schuierer, G., Bogdahn, U. and May, A. (2004) Changes in grey matter induced by training. *Nature*, 427, 311–312.

Dunbar, K. and Fugelsang, J. (2005) Inside the educated brain: An FMRI study of how physics and non-physics students respond to motion. *Journal of Cognitive Neuroscience*, 22–23.

Dunbar, K., Fugelsang, J. and Stein, C. (2004) Do naïve theories ever go away?, in Lovett, M. and Shah, P. (eds) *Thinking with Data: 33rd Carnegie Symposium on Cognition*. Mahwah, NJ: Erlbaum.

Dunn, R., Sklar, R. I., Beaudry, J. and Bruno, J. (1990) Effects of mismatching students' hemispheric preferences on mathematics scores. *Journal of Educational Research and Extension*, 83(5), 283–288.

Egner, T. and Gruzelier, J. H. (2001) Learned self-regulation of EEG frequency components affects attention and event-related brain potentials in humans. *Neuroreport*, 12, 411–415.

Ehri, L. C. (1995) Phases of development in learning to read by sight. *Journal of Research in Reading*, 18, 116–125.

Elbert, T., Pantev, C., Wienbruch, C., Rockstroh, B. and Taub, E. (1995) Increased cortical representation of the fingers of the left hand in string players. *Science*, 270, 305–307.

Elkins, J. S., Longstreth, W. T., Manolio, T. A., Newman, A. B., Bhadelia, R. A. and Johnston, S. C. (2006) Education and the cognitive decline associated with MRI-defined brain infarct. *Neurology*, 67, 435–440.

Elliot, R., Friston, K. J. and Dolan, R. J. (2000) Dissociable neural responses in human reward systems. *Journal of Neuroscience*, 20(16), 6159–6165.

Elliott, J. (1991) *Action Research for Educational Change*. Buckingham: Open University Press.

Ernst, M. (1948) *Beyond Painting*. New York: Wittenborn and Schultz.

Ernst, M., Pine, D. S. and Hardin, M. (2005) Triadic model of the neurobiology of motivated behavior in adolescence. *Psychological Medicine*, 36, 299–312.

Eshel, N., Nelson, E. E., Blair, R. J., Pine, D. S. and Ernst, M. (2007) Neural substrates of choice selection in adults and adolescents: Development of the ventrolateral prefrontal and anterior cingulate cortices. *Neuropsychologia*, 45, 1270–1279.

Etnier, J. L., Salazar, W., Landers, D. M., Petruzzello, S. J., Han, M. and Nowell, P. (1997) The influence of physical fitness and exercise upon cognitive functioning: A meta-analysis. *Journal of Sport and Exercise Psychology*, 19, 249–277.

Facer, K. (2004) *Designing Educational Technologies with Users*. Bristol: Futurelab.

Farah, M. J. (2002) Emerging ethical issues in neuroscience. *Nature Neuroscience*, 5, 1123–1129.

Fiez, J. A. (1998) Neuroimaging studies of word reading. *Proceedings of the National Academy of Sciences (USA)*, 95, 914–921.

Fink, A., Benedek, M., Grabner, R. H., Staudt, B. and Neubauer, A. C. (2007) Creativity meets neuroscience: Experimental tasks for the neuroscientific study of creative thinking. *Methods*, 42, 68–76.

Fiorillo, C. D., Tobler, P. N. and Schultz, W. (2003) Discrete coding of reward probability and uncertainty by dopamine neurons. *Science*, 299, 1898–1902.

Fitzgerald, K. D., Welsh, R.C., Gehring, W. J., Abelson, J. L., Himle, J. A., Liberzon, I. and Taylor, S. F. (2005) Error-related hyperactivity of the anterior cingulate cortex in obsessive-compulsive disorder. *Biological Psychiatry*, 57, 287–294.

Forgays, D. G. and Forgays, D. K. (1992) Creativity enhancement through floatation isolation. *Journal of Environmental Psychology*, 12, 329–335.

Friedrich, M. (2008) Early neural markers of language learning difficulty in German. *Mental Capital and Wellbeing, State-of-Science Reviews*. London: Government Office for Science.

Friston, K. J., Harrison, L. and Penny, W. (2003) Dynamic causal modelling. *Neuroimage*, 19, 1273–1302.

Frith, U. (1985) Beneath the surface of developmental dyslexia, in Patterson, K., Marshall, J. and Coltheart, M. (eds) *Surface Dyslexia: Neuropsychological and Cognitive Studies of Phonological Reading*. London: Erlbaum.

Gallichan, D. J. and Curle, C. (2008) Fitting square pegs into round holes: The challenge of coping with attention-deficit hyperactivity disorder. *Clinical Child Psychology and Psychiatry*, 13, 343–363.

Ganis, G., Kosslyn, S. M., Stose, S., Thompson, W. L. and Yurgelun-Todd, D. A. (2003) Neural correlates of different types of deception: An fMRI investigation. *Cerebral Cortex*, 13, 830–836.

Gardner, H. (1983) *Frames of the Mind: The Theory of Multiple Intelligences*. New York: Basic Books.

Gardner, H. (1999) *Intelligence Reframed*. New York: Basic Books.

Gardner, H. (2003) Multiple intelligences after twenty years. *American Educational Research Association*.

Gardner, H. and Moran, S. (2006) The science of multiple intelligences theory: A response to Lynn Waterhouse. *Educational Psychologist*, 41, 227–232.

Gaser, C. and Schlaug, G. (2003) Brain structures differ between musicians and non-musicians. *Journal of Neuroscience*, 23, 9240–9245.

Gazzaniga, M. S. (1995) Consciousness and the cerebral hemispheres, in Gazzaniga, M. S. (ed.) *The Cognitive Neurosciences*. Massachusetts: MIT Press.

Gazzaniga, M. S. (2005) Smarter on drugs. *Scientific American: Mind*, 16, 32–37.

Gazzola, V., Rizzolatti, G., Wicker, B. and Keysers, C. (2007) The anthropomorphic brain: The mirror neuron system responds to human and robotic actions. *Neuroimage*, 35.

Geake, J. G. (2008) Neuromythologies in education. *Educational Research*, 50.

Geake, J. G. and Hansen, P. C. (2005) Neural correlates of intelligence as revealed by fMRI of fluid analogies. *Neuroimage*, 26, 555–564.

Gehring, W. J. and Knight, R. T. (2000) Prefrontal-cingulate interactions in action monitoring. *Nature Neuroscience*, 3, 516–520.

Giesinger, J. (2006) Educating brains? Free-will, brain research and pedagogy. *Zeitschrift fur erziehungswissenschaft*, 9, 97–109.

Gordon, W. J. J. and Poze, T. (1980) SES Syntectics and gifted education today. *Gifted Child Quarterly*, 24, 47–151.

Goswami, U. (2004) Neuroscience and education. *British Journal of Educational Psychology*, 74, 1–14.

Goswami, U. (2006) Neuroscience and education: From research to practice? *Nature Reviews Neuroscience*, 7, 406–413.

Goswami, U. (2008) Neuroscience in education. *Mental Capital and Wellbeing, State-of-Science Reviews*. London: Government Office for Science.

Goswami, U., Thomson, J., Richardson, U., Stainthorp, R., Hughes, D., Rosen, S. and Scott, S. K. (2002) Amplitude envelope onsets and developmental dyslexia: A new hypothesis. *Proceedings of the National Academy of Sciences (USA)*, 99, 10911–10916.

Good, C. D., Johnsrude, I. S., Ashburner, J., Henson, R. N. A., Friston, K. J. and Frackowiak, R. S. J. (2001) A voxel-based morphometric study of ageing in 465 normal adult human brains. *Neuroimage*, 14(1), 21–36.

Gottlieb, G. (2004) Normally occurring environmental and behavioral influence on gene activity: From central dogma to probabilistic epigenesist, in Garcia Coll, C.,

Bearer, E. L. and Lerner, R. M. (eds) *Nature and Nurture: The Complex Interplay of Genetic and Environmental Influences on Human Behaviour and Development.* Mahwah, NJ: Lawrence Erlbaum.

Grabner, R. H., Ansari, D., Reishofer, G., Stern, E., Ebner, F. and Neuper, C. (2007) Individual differences in mathematical competence predict parietal brain activation during mental calculation. *Neuroimage*, 38, 346–356.

Gracia-Bafalluy, M. and Noel, M.-P. (2008) Does finger training increase young children's numerical performance? *Cortex*, 44, 368–375.

Graf, P. and Schacter, D. L. (1985) Implicit and explicit memory for new associations in normal and amnesic subjects. *Journal of Experimental Psychology: Learning, Memory and Cognition*, 13, 45–53.

Greely, H., Sahakian, B., Harris, J., Kessler, R. C., Gazzaniga, M. S., Campbell, P. and Farah, M. J. (2008) Towards Responsible Use of Cognitive-Enhancing Drugs by the Healthy, *Nature*, 456, 702–705.

Greenberg, M. T. (2006, Feb 26–28) Promoting resilience in children and youth – Preventive interventions and their interface with neuroscience. Paper presented at the Conference on Resilience in Children, Arlington, VA.

Greenough, W. T., Black, J. E. and Wallace, C. S. (1987) Experience and brain development. *Child Development*, 58.

Grigorenko, E. L. (2007) How can genomics inform education? *Mind, Brain and Education*, 1, 20–27.

Gron, G., Kirstein, M., Thielscher, A., Riepe, M. W. and Spitzer, M. (2005) Cholinergic enhancement of episodic memory in healthy young adults. *Psychopharmacology*, 182, 170–179.

Gruzelier, J. H. and Egner, T. (2004) Physiological self-regulation: Biofeedback and neurofeedback, in Williamon, A. (ed.) *Musical Excellence.* Oxford: Oxford University Press.

Gureasko-Moore, S., DuPaul, G. J. and White, G. (2006) The effects of self-management in general education classrooms on the organizational skills of adolescents with ADHD. *Behavior Modification*, 30, 159–183.

Guttorm, T. K., Leppanen, P. H. T., Poikeus, A.-M., Eklund, K. M., Lyytinen, P. and Lyytinen, H. (2005) Brain event-related potentials (ERPs) measured at birth predict later language development in children with and without familial risk for dyslexia. *Cortex*, 41, 291–303.

Hagelin, J., Carlsson, H.-E. and Hau, J. (2003) An overview of surveys on how people view animal experimentation: some factors that may influence the outcome. *Public Understanding of Science*, 12, 67–81.

Hammill, D., Goodman, L. and Wiederholt, J. L. (1974) *The Reading Teacher*, 27, 469–478.

Hannon, E. E. and Trehub, S. E. (2005a) Metrical categories in infancy and adulthood. *Psychological Science*, 16, 48–55.

Hannon, E. E. and Trehub, S. E. (2005b) Tuning in to musical rhythms: Infants learn more readily than adults. *Proceedings of the National Academy of Sciences (USA)*, 102, 12639–12643.

Harre, R. (2002) *Cognitive Science: A Philosophical Introduction.* London: Sage.

Harter, S. (1978). Pleasure derived from cognitive challenge and mastery. *Child Development*, 45, 661–669.

Haslam, D. W. and James, W. P. T. (2005) Obesity. *Lancet*, 366, 1197–1209.

Hebb, D. O. (1947) *The Organization of Behavior.* New York: Wiley.

Heatherley, S. V., Hancock, K. M. F. and Rogers, P. J. (2006) Psychostimulant and other effects of caffeine in 9- to 11-year-old children. *Journal of Child Psychology and Psychiatry*, 47, 135–142.

Heffler, B. (2001) Individual learning styles and the Learning Style Inventory. *Educational Studies*, 27, 307–316.

Helveston, E. M. (2005) Visual training: Current status in opthalmology. *American Journal of Opthalmology*, 140, 903–910.

Herman, J. P. and Cullinan, W. E. (1997) Neurocircuitry of stress: central control of the hypothalamo-pituitary-adrenocortical axis. *Trends in Neurosciences*, 20, 78–84.

Hermann, N. (1989) *The Creative Brain*. North Carolina: Brain Books, The Ned Hermann Group.

Hillman, C. H., Erickson, K. I. and Framer, A. F. (2008) Be smart, exercise your heart: Exercise effects on brain and cognition. *Nature Reviews Neuroscience*, 9, 58–65.

Hinton, C. D. (2005) A report of the Learning Sciences and Brain Research Third Lifelong Learning Network meeting, Tokyo, Japan, 21–22 January. Paris: OECD.

Hoeft, F., Watson, C. L., Kesler, S. R., Bettinger, K. E. and Reiss, A. L. (2008). Gender differences in the mesocorticolimbic system during computer game-play. *Journal of Psychiatric Research*, 42, 253–258.

Hoffman, E. (2002) *Introducing Children to Their Amazing Brains*. Middlewich: LTL Books Ltd.

Hoover, D. W. and Milich, R. (1992) Effects of sugar ingestion expectancies on mother–child interactions. *100th Annual Convention of the American-Psychological-Association*. Washington, DC: Plenum Publ Corp.

Horn, G. (2008) *Brain Science, Addiction and Drugs*. London: Academy of Medical Sciences.

Horton, J. (2006) Stroppy teenagers can blame the brain. *Edinburgh Evening News*. Edinburgh.

Howard-Jones, P. A. (2002) A dual-state model of creative cognition for supporting strategies that foster creativity in the classroom. *International Journal of Technology and Design Education*, 12, 215–226.

Howard-Jones, P. A. (2007) *Neuroscience and Education: Issues and Opportunities*. London: Teaching and Learning Research Programme.

Howard-Jones, P. A. (2008) *Fostering Creative Thinking: Co-constructed Insights from Neuroscience and Education*. Bristol: Escalate.

Howard-Jones, P. A. (2009) Scepticism is not enough. *Cortex*, 45(4), 550–551.

Howard-Jones, P. A. and Demetriou, S. (in press – now published online) Uncertainty and engagement with learning games. *Instructional Science*.

Howard-Jones, P. A. and Murray, S. (2003) Ideational productivity, focus of attention and context. *Creativity Research Journal*, 15, 153–166.

Howard-Jones, P., Pickering, S. J. and Diack, A. (2007) *Perceptions of the Role of Neuroscience in Education*. London: Innovation Unit.

Howard-Jones, P. A., Taylor, J. and Sutton, L. (2002) The effects of play on the creativity of young children. *Early Child Development and Care*, 172, 323–328.

Howard-Jones, P. A., Winfield, M. and Crimmins, G. (2008) Co-constructing an understanding of creativity in the fostering of drama education that draws on neuropsychological concepts. *Educational Research*, 50, 187–201.

Howard-Jones, P. A., Blakemore, S. J., Samuel, E., Summers, I. R. and Claxton, G. (2005) Semantic divergence and creative story generation: An fMRI investigation. *Cognitive Brain Research*, 25, 240–250.

Howard-Jones, P. A., Bogacz, R., Demetriou, S., Leonards, U. and Yoo, J. (2009) From gaming to learning: A reward-based model of decision-making predicts declarative memory performance in a learning game. *British Psychological Society Annual Conference*. Brighton.

Howard-Jones, P. A., Franey, L., Mashmoushi, R. and Liao, Y.-C. (2009) The neuroscience literacy of trainee teachers, paper presented at the Annual British Educational Research Association Conference, Manchester, UK.

Hughes, C. (1998) Executive function in preschoolers: Links with theory of mind and verbal ability. *British Journal of Developmental Psychology*, 16, 233–253.

Hunter, S. (1958) *Introduction to the Catalogue of the Jackson Pollock Exhibition*. New York: Museum of Modern Art.

Hurculano-Houzel, S. (2002) Do you know your brain? A survey on public neuroscience literacy at the closing of the decade of the brain. *The Neuroscientist*, 8, 98–110.

Hutchinson, S., Lee, L. H., Gaab, N. and Schlaug, G. (2003) Cerebellar volume of musicians. *Cerebral Cortex*, 13, 943–949.

Huttenlocher, P. R. (1979) Synaptic density in human frontal cortex – developmental changes and effects of aging. *Brain Research*, 163, 195–205.

Huttenlocher, P. R. and Dabholkar, A. S. (1997) Regional differences in synaptogenesis in human cerebral cortex. *Journal of Comparative Neurology*, 387, 167–178.

Hyatt, K. J. (2007) Brain Gym: Building stronger brains or wishful thinking? *Remedial and Special Education*, 28, 117–124.

Illes, J., Rosen, A. C., Huang, L., Goldstein, R. A., Raffin, T. A., Swan, G. and Atlas, S. W. (2004) Ethical consideration of incidental findings on adult brain MRI in research. *Neurology*, 62, 888–890.

Immordino-Yang, M. H. (2007) A tale of two cases: Lessons for education from the study of two boys living with half their brains. *Mind, Brain and Education*, 1(2), 66–83.

Immordino-Yang, M. H. and Damasio, A. R. (2007) We feel, therefore we learn: The relevance of affective and social neuroscience to education. *Mind, Brain and Education*, 1, 3–10.

Isaacs, E. B., Edmonds, C. J., Lucas, A. and Gadian, D. G. (2001) Calculation difficulties in children of very low birthweight – A neural correlate. *Brain*, 124, 1701–1707.

Ischebeck, A., Zamarian, L., Siedentopf, C., Koppelstatter, F., Benke, T., Felber, S. and Delazer, M. (2006) How specifically do we learn? Imaging the learning of multiplication and subtraction. *Neuroimage*, 30, 1365–1375.

Jaeggi, S. M., Buschkuehl, M., Jonides, J. and Perrig, W. J. (2008) Improving fluid intelligence with training on working memory. *Proceedings of the National Academy of Sciences (USA)*, 105(19), 6829–6833.

James, J. E. (1997) *Understanding Caffeine: A Biobehavioural Analysis*. Thousand Oaks, CA: Sage.

James, J. E. and Rogers, P. J. (2005) Effects of caffeine on performance and mood: withdrawal reversal is the most plausible explanation. *Psychopharmacology*, 182, 1–8.

Jensen, P. S., Arnold, L. E., Richters, J. E., Severe, J. B., Vereen, D., Vitiello, B., Schiller, E., Hinshaw, S. P., Elliott, G. R., Conners, C. K., Wells, K. C., March, J., Swanson, J., Wigal, T., Cantwell, D. P., Abikoff, H. B., Hechtman, L., Greenhill, L. L., Newcorn, J. H., Pelham, W. E., Hoza, B. and Kraemer, H. C. (1999) A 14-month randomized clinical trial of treatment strategies for attention-deficit/hyperactivity disorder. *Archives of General Psychiatry*, 56, 1073–1086.

Joels, M., Pu, Z. W., Wiegert, O., Oitzl, M. S. and Krugers, H. J. (2006) Learning under stress: How does it work? *Trends in Cognitive Sciences*, 10, 152–158.

Johnson, M. H. (2005). *Developmental Cognitive Neuroscience: An Introduction* (2nd ed.). Oxford Blackwell.

Johnson, S. (2005) *Everything Bad is Good for You*. (London, Penguin/Allen Lane).

Johnson, C. N. and Wellman, H. M. (1982) Children's developing conceptions of the mind and brain. *Child Development*, 53, 222–234.

Johnstone, T. and Shanks, D. R. (2001) Abstractionist and processing accounts of implicit learning. *Cognitive Psychology*, 42, 61–112.

Jones, R., Morris, K. and Nutt, D. (2005) *Drugs Futures 2025? Foresight: Brain Science, Addiction and Drugs State of Science Review*. London: Office of Science and Technology, Department of Trade and Industry (UK).

Jorgenson, O. (2003) Brain scam? Why educators should be careful about embracing 'brain research'. *The Educational Forum*, 67, 364–369.

Judge, M. P., Harel, O. and Lammi-Keefe, C. J. (2007) Maternal consumption of a docosahexaenoic acid-containing functional food during pregnancy: benefit for infant performance on problem-solving but not on recognition memory tasks at age 9 mo. *American Journal of Clinical Nutrition*, 85, 1572–1577.

Kairaluoma, L., Narhi, V., Ahonen, T., Westerholm, J. and Aro, M. (2009) Do fatty acids help in overcoming reading difficulties? A double-blind, placebo-controlled study of the effects of eicosapentaenoic acid and carnosine supplementation on children with dyslexia. *Child Care Health and Development*, 35, 112–119.

Katzman, G. L., Dagher, A. P. and Patronas, N. J. (1999) Incidental findings on brain magnetic resonance imaging from 1000 asymptomatic volunteers. *Jama-Journal of the American Medical Association*, 282, 36–39.

Kaufmann, L. (2008) Dyscalculia: Neuroscience and education. *Educational Research*, 50.

Kaufmann, L., Handl, P. and Thony, B. (2003) Evaluation of a numeracy intervention program focusing on basic numerical knowledge and conceptual knowledge: A pilot study. *Journal of Learning Disabilities*, 36, 564–573.

Kaufmann, L., Vogel, S. E., Wood, G., Kremser, C., Schocke, M., Zimmerhackl, L.-B. and Koten, J. W. (2008) A developmental fMRI study of nonsymbolic numerical and spatial processing. *Cortex*, 44, 376–385.

Kavale, K. A. and Forness, S. R. (1987) Substance over style: Assessing the efficacy of modality testing and teaching. *Exceptional Children*, 54, 228–239.

Kelly, G. (1955) *The Psychology of Personal Constructs*. New York: W. W. Norton.

Kendall, T., Taylor, E., Perez, A., Taylor, C. and on behalf of the Guideline Development, G. (2008) Diagnosis and management of attention-deficit/hyperactivity disorder in children, young people, and adults: summary of NICE guidance. *BMJ*, 337, a1239.

Keogh, B. K. and Pelland, M. (1985) Vision training revisited. *Journal of Learning Disabilities*, 18, 228–236.

Kim, B. S., Illes, J., Kaplan, R. T., Reiss, A. and Scott, W. (2002) Incidental findings on pediatric MR images of the brain. *American Journal of Neuroradiology*, 23, 1674–1677.

Kim, H.-Y., Frongillo, E. A., Han, S.-S., Oh, S.-Y., Kim, W.-K., Jang, Y.-A., Won, H.-S., Lee, H.-S. and Kim, S.-H. (2003) Academic performance of Korean children is associated with dietary behaviours and physical status. *Asia Pacific Journal of Clinical Nutrition*, 12, 186–192.

Kirchhoff, B. A. and Buckner, R. L. (2006) Functional-anatomic correlates of individual differences in memory. *Neuron*, 51, 263–274.

Kirschbaum, C. (1996) Stress- and treatment-induced elevations of cortisol levels associated with impaired declarative memory in healthy adults. *Life Sciences*, 58, 1475–1483.

Klingberg, T., Fernll, E., Olesen, P. J., Johnson, M., Gustafsson, P., Dahlstrom, K., *et al.* (2005) Computerized training of working memory in children with ADHD – A randomized, controlled trial. *Journal of the American Academy of Child and Adolescent Psychiatry*, 44(2), 177–186.

Knutson, B., Adams, C. M., Fong, G. W. and Hommer, D. (2001) Anticipation of monetary reward selectively recruits nucleus accumbens. *Journal of Neuroscience*, 21(RC159), 1–5.

Koelsch, S., Kasper, E., Sammler, D., Schulze, K., Gunter, T. and Friederici, A. T. (2004) Music, language and meaning: Brain signatures of semantic processing. *Nature Neuroscience*, 7, 302–307.

Koepp, M. J., Gunn, R. N., Lawrence, A. D., Cunningham, V. J., Dagher, A., Jones, T., *et al.* (1988). Evidence for striatal dopamine release during a video game. *Nature*, 393, 266–268.

Koizumi, H. (2004). The concept of 'developing the brain': A new science for learning and education. *Brain and Development*, 26, 434–441.

Kolb, D. A. (1999) *The Kolb Learning Style Inventory, Version 3*. Boston: Hay Group.

Kosslyn, S. M. (2005) Mental images and the brain. *Cognitive Neuropsychology*, 22, 333–347.

Kounios, J., Fleck, J. I., Green, D. L., Payne, L., Stevenson, J. L., Bowden, E. M. and Jung-Beeman, M. (2008) The origins of insight in resting-state brain activity. *Neuropsychologia*, 46, 281–291.

Kratzig, G. P. and Arbuthnott, K. D. (2006) Perceptual learning style and learning proficiency: A test of the hypothesis. *Journal of Educational Psychology*, 98, 238–246.

Kris, E. (1952) *Psychoanalytic Explorations in Art*. New York: International Universities Press.

Kuhl, P. K., Williams, K. A., Lacerda, F., Stevens, K. N. and Lindblom, B. (1992) Linguistic experience alters phonetic perception in infants by 6 months of age. *Science*, 255, 606–608.

Kuhlmann, S. (2005) Impaired memory retrieval after psychosocial stress in healthy young men. *Journal of Neuroscience*, 25, 2977–2982.

Lam, S. S. K. (1997) Reliability and classification stability of Learning Style Inventory in Hong Kong. *Perceptual and Motor Skills*, 85.

Larson, E. B., Wang, L., Bowen, J. D., McCormick, W. C., Teri, L. and Crane, P. (2006) Exercise is associated with reduced risk for incident dementia among persons 65 years of age and older. *Annals of Internal Medicine*, 144, 73–82.

Lashley, K. S. (1929) *Brain Mechanisms and Intelligence: A Quantitative Study of Injuries*. Chicago: University of Chicago Press.

Leclerc, C. M. and Hess, T. M. (2007) Age differences in the bases for social judgments: Tests of a social expertise perspective. *Experimental Aging Research*, 33, 95–120.

Lerner, R. M. (2005) *Promoting Positive Youth Development: Theretical and Emprical Bases*. Washington D.C.: National Research Council/Institute of Medicine.

Leshner, A. I. (2005) It's time to go public with neuroethics. *American Journal of Bioethics*, 5, 1–2.

Loo, R. (1997) Evaluating change and stability in learning style scores: A methodological concern. *Educational Psychology*, 17.

Luna, B. (2004) Algebra and the adolescent brain. *Trends in Cognitive Sciences*, 8.

Lundy, L. (2007) 'Voice' is not enough: conceptualising Article 12 of the United Nations Convention on the Rights of the Child. *British Educational Research Journal*, 33, 927–942.

Lythgoe, M. F. X., Pollak, T. A., Kalmus, M., de Haan, M. and Khean Chong, W. (2005) Obsessive, prolific artistic output following subarachnoid hemorrhage. *Neurology*, 64, 397–398.

Machino, T. and Yoshizawa, T. (2006) Brain shrinkage due to acute hypernatremia. *Neurology*, 67, 880–880.

Maguire, E. A., Gadian, D. S., Johnsrude, I. S., Good, C. D., Ashburner, J., Frackowiak, R. S. and Frith, C. D. (2000) Navigation related structural change in the hippocampi of taxi drivers. *Proceedings of the National Academy of Sciences (USA)*, 97, 4398–4403.

Mahncke, H. W., Connor, B. B., Appelman, J., Ahsanuddin, O. N., Hardy, J. L., Wood, R. A., *et al.* (2006). Memory enhancement in healthy older adults using a brain plasticity-based training program: A randomized, controlled study. *Proceedings of the National Academy of Sciences of the United States of America*, 103(33), 12523–12528.

Makrides, M., Neumann, M. A., Byard, R. W., Simmer, K. and Gibson, R. A. (1994) Fatty acid composition of brain, retina, and erythrocytes in breast- and formula-fed infants *American Journal of Clinical Nutrition*, 60, 189–194.

Malone, T. W. (1981). Toward a theory of intrinsically motivating instruction. *Cognitive Science*, 4, 333–339.

Marshall, J. C. and Merritt, S. L. (1986) Reliability and construct validity of the Learning Style Questionnaire. *Educational and Psychological Measurement*, 47, 257–262.

Martin, S. J., Grimwood, P. D. and Morris, R. G. (2000) Synaptic plasticity and memory: an evaluation of the hypothesis. *Annual Review of Neuroscience*, 23, 649–711.

Maquet, P., Laureys, S., Peigneux, P., Fuchs, S., Petiau, C., Phillips, C., *et al.* (2000). Experience dependent changes in cerebral activation during human REM sleep. *Nature Neuroscience*, 3(8), 831–836.

Mazza, M., Pomponi, M., Janiri, L., Bria, P. and Mazza, S. (2007) Omega-3 fatty acids and antioxidants in neurological and psychiatric diseases: An overview. *Progress in Neuro-Psychopharmacology and Biological Psychiatry*, 31, 12–26.

McCabe, S. E., Knight, J. R., Teter, C. J. and Wechser, H. (2005) Non-medical use of prescription stimulants among US college students: prevalence and correlates from a national survey. *Addiction*, 100, 96–106.

McCann, D., Barrett, A., Cooper, A., Crumpler, D., Dalen, L., Grimshaw, K., Kitchin, E., Lok, K., Porteous, L., Prince, E., Sonuga-Barke, E., Warner, J. O. and Stevenson, J. (2007) Food additives and hyperactive behaviour in 3-year-old and 8/9-year-old children in the community: a randomised, double-blinded, placebo-controlled trial. *Lancet*, 370, 1560–1567.

McCarthy, B. (1987) *The 4MAT System: Teaching to Learning Styles with Right/Left Mode Techniques*. Barrington, IL: Excel.

McCarthy, B. (1997) A tale of four learners: 4MAT's learning styles. *Educational Leadership*, 54, 46–51.

McClelland, J. L. and Rogers, T. T. (2003) The parallel distributed processing approach to semantic cognition. *Nature Reviews Neuroscience*, 4, 310–322.

McDaniel, M. A. (2005) Big-brained people are smarter: A meta-analysis of the relationship between in vivo brain volume and intelligence. *Intelligence*, 33, 337–346.

McGaugh, J. L. (2004) The amygdala modulates the consolidation of memories of emotionally arousing experiences *Annual Review of Neuroscience*, 27, 1–28.

McGivern, R. F., Andersen, J., Byrd, D., Mutter, K. L. and Reilly, J. (2002) Cognitive efficiency on a match to sample task decreases at the onset of puberty in children. *Brain and Cognition*, 50, 73–89.

Mel, B. W. (2002) Have we been hebbing down the wrong path?, *Neuron*, 34, 175–177.

Mercer, N. and Wegerif, R. (1999) Is 'exploratory talk' productive talk?, in Littleton, K. and Light, P. (eds) *Learning with Computers*. London: Routledge.

Mercer, N., Dawes, L., Wegerif, R. and Sams, C. (2004) Reasoning as a scientist: ways of helping children to use language to learn science. *British Educational Research Journal*, 30(3), 359–377.

Merrienboer, J. J. G. and Sweller, J. (2005) Cognitive load theory and complex learning: Recent developments and future directions. *Educational Psychology Review*, 17, 147–177.

Mills, D. (2005) The dyslexia myth. *Dispatches*. UK: Channel 4.

Miranda, A., Presentacion, M. J. and Soriano, M. (2002) Effectiveness of a school-based multicomponent program for the treatment of children with ADHD. *Journal of Learning Disabilities*, 35, 546–562.

Mishkin, M., Malamut, B. and Bachevalier, J. (1984) Memories and habits: Two neural systems, in Lynch, G., McGaugh, J. L. and Weinberger, N. M. (eds) *Neurobiology of Learning and Memory*. New York: Guilford.

Molfese, D. L. (2000) Predicting dyslexia at 8 years of age using neonatal brain responses. *Brain and Language*, 72, 238–245.

Moore, H. and Hibbert, F. (2005) Mind Boggling! Considering the possibilities of brain gym in learning to play an instrument. *British Journal of Music Education*, 22, 249–267.

Morgane, P. J., Galler, J. R. and Mokler, D. J. (2005) A review of systems and networks of the limbic forebrain/limbic midbrain. *Progress in Neurobiology*, 75, 143–160.

Morrison, J. H. and Hof, P. R. (1997) Life and death of neurons in the aging brain. *Science*, 278, 412–419.

Morse, S. J. (2006) Brain overclaim syndrome and criminal responsibility: A diagnostic note. *Ohio State Journal of Criminal Law*, 3, 397–412.

Mortensen, E. L., Michaelsen, K. F., Sanders, S. A. and Reinisch, J. M. (2002) The association between duration of breastfeeding and adult intelligence. *Jama-Journal of the American Medical Association*, 287(18), 2365–2371.

Morton, J. (2004) *Understanding Developmental Disorders: A Causal Modelling Approach*. Oxford: Blackwell.

Morton, J. and Frith, U. (1995) Causal modelling: A structural approach to developmental psychopathology, in Cicchetti, D. and Cohen, D. J. (eds) *Manual of Developmental Psychopathology*. New York: Wiley.

Motherwell, R. (1981) *The Dada Painters and Poets: An Anthology*, Boston, MA: G.K. Hall.

NACCE (1999) *All our Futures: Creativity, Culture and Education*. London National Advisory Committee on Creative and Cultural Education.

Neuper, C., Muller-Putz, G. R., Scherer, R. and Pfurtscheller, G. (2006) Motor imagery and EEG-based control of spelling devices and neuroprostheses, in *Event-Related Dynamics of Brain Oscillations* (Vol. 159, pp. 393–409). Amsterdam: Elsevier Science Bv.

Nicolson, R. (2005) Dyslexia: Beyond the myth. *The Psychologist*, 18, 658–659.

Nieuwenhuis, S., Heslenfeld, D. J., von Geusau, N. J. A., Mars, R. B., Holroyd, C. B. and Yeung, N. (2005) Activity in human reward-sensitive brain areas is strongly context dependent. *Neuroimage*, 25(4), 1302–1309.

Noel, M.-P. (2005) Finger gnosia: A predictor of numerical abilities in children? *Child Neuropsychology*, 11, 413–420.

Norton, A., Winner, E., Cronin, K., Overy, L., Lee, D. J. and Schlaug, G. (2005) Are there pre-existing neural, cognitive, or motoric markers for musical ability? *Brain and Cognition*, 59, 124–134.

Novella, S. (1996) Psychomotor Patterning. *The Connecticut Skeptic*, 1.

Nunez, J. M., Casey, B. J., Egner, T., Hare, T. and Hirsch, J. (2005) Intentional false responding shares neural substrates with response conflict and cognitive control. *Neuroimage*, 25, 267–277.

OECD (2002a) Report on the first meeting of the Lifelong Learning Network, Tokyo, Japan, 10–11 December. Paris: OECD.

OECD (2002b) *Understanding the Brain:Towards a New Learning Science*. Paris: OECD Publications.

OECD (2003) Brain Research and Learning Sciences: 'Emotions and Learning'. Planning Symposium.

OECD (2004) Summary of the second meeting of the Lifelong Learning Network held in Tokyo, Japan, 13–14 January 2004. Paris: OECD.

OECD (2007) *Understanding the Brain: Birth of a New Learning Science*. Paris: OECD.

Ofsted (2001) *Improving Attendance and Behaviour in Secondary Schools*. London: Ofsted.

Olff, M., Langeland, W. and Gersons, B. P. R. (2005) The psychobiology of PTSD: coping with trauma. *Psychoneuroendocrinology*, 30, 974–982.

Olson, A. K., Eadie, B. D., Ernst, C. and Christie, B. R. (2006) Environmental enrichment and voluntary exercise massively increase neurogenesis in the adult hippocampus via dissociable pathways. *Hippocampus*, 16, 250–260.

Orton, S. T. (1937) *Reading, Writing and Speech Problems in Children*, New York: Norton.

Paivio, A. and Csapo, K. (1973) Picture superiority in free recall: imagery or dual coding? *Cognitive Psychology*, 5, 176–206.

Paracchini, S., Scerri, T. and Monaco, A. P. (2007) The genetic lexicon of dyslexia. *Annual Review of Genomics and Human Genetics*, 8, 57–79.

Parkinson, L. (2006) Boy's behaviour 'out of control'. *Bristol Evening Post*. Bristol.

Paus, T. (2008) Mapping brain maturation and development of social cognition during adolescence. *Mental Capital and Wellbeing, State-of-Science Reviews*. London: Government Office for Science.

Phelps, E. A. (2006) Emotion and cognition: Insights from studies of the human amygdala. *Annual Review of Psychology*, 57, 27–53.

Pickering, S. J. (ed.) (2006) *Working Memory and Education*. London: Elsevier Academic Press.

Pickering, S. J. and Howard-Jones, P. (2007) Educators' views on the role of neuroscience in education: Findings from a study of UK and international perspectives. *Mind, Brain and Education*, 1, 109–113.

Pineau, E. L. (1994) Teaching is performace – reconceptualizing a problematic metaphor. *American Educational Research Journal*, 31, 3–25.

Pinnegar, S. and Carter, K. (1990) Comparing theories from textbooks and practicing teachers. *Journal of Teacher Education*, 41, 20–27.

Plomin, R. (2008) Genetics and the future diagnosis of learning disabilities. *Mental Capital and Wellbeing, State-of-Science Reviews*. London: Government Office for Science.

Plomin, R., Kovas, Y. and Haworth, C. M. A. (2007) Generalist genes: Genetic links between brain, mind, and education. *Mind, Brain and Education*, 1, 11–19.

QCA (2000) *Science: The national Curriculum for England Key Stages* 1–4. London: HMSO/Qualifications and Curriculum Authority.

Qin, Y., Silk, E. M., Fissell, K., Carter, C. S. and Anderson, J. R. (2003) Modality independent brain areas in mental manipulation. *Society for Neuroscience Abstract Viewer and Itinerary Planner*, 2003, Abstract No. 195.22.

Qin, Y., Carter, C. S., Silk, E. M., Stenger, V. A., Fissell, K., Goode, A. and Andersen, J. R. (2004) The change of the brain activation patterns as children learn algebra equation solving. *Proceedings of the National Academy of Sciences (USA)*, 101.

Rack, J. (2003) The who, what, why and how of intervention programmes. Comments on the DDAT Evaluation. *Dyslexia*, 9, 137–139.

Rakic, P. (1995) Corticogenesis in human and non-human primates. in Gazzaniga, M. S. (ed.) *The Cognitive Neurosciences*. Cambridge, MA: MIT Press.

Rampp, S. and Stefan, H. (2007) On the opposition of EEG and MEG. *Clinical Neurophysiology*, 118, 1658–1659.

Rasch, B. H., Born, J. and Gais, S. (2006) Combined blockade of cholinergic receptors shifts the brain from stimulus encoding to memory consolidation,. *Journal of Cognitive Neuroscience*, 18(5), 793–802.

Raymond, J., Sajid, I., Parkinson, L. and Gruzelier, J. H. (2005) The beneficial effects of alpha/theta and heart rate variability training on dance performance. *Applied Psychophysiology and Biofeedback*, 30, 65–73.

Reynolds, D., Nicolson, R. I. and Hambly, H. (2003) Evaluation of an exercise-based treatment for children with reading difficulties. *Dyslexia*, 9, 48–71.

Richards, I. L., Moores, E., Witton, C., Reddy, P. A., Rippon, G., Rochelle, K. S. H. and Talcott, J. B. (2003) Science, sophistry and 'commercial sensitivity': Comments on the 'Evaluation of an exercise-based treatment for children with reading difficulties', by Reynolds, Nicolson and Hambly. *Dyslexia*, 9, 146–150.

Richardson, A. J. (2006) Omega-3 fatty acids in ADHD and related neurodevelopmental disorders. *International Review of Psychiatry*, 18, 155–172.

Richardson, A. J. and Puri, B. K. (2002) A randomized double-blind, placebo-controlled study of the effects of supplementation with highly unsaturated fatty acids on ADHD-related symptoms in children with specific learning difficulties. *Progress in Neuro-Psychopharmacology and Biological Psychiatry*, 26, 233–239.

Riding, R. (1998) *Cognitive Styles Analysis*. Birmingham: Learning and Training Technology.

Rizzolatti, G. and Craighero, L. (2004) The mirror neuron system. *Annual Review of Neuroscience*, 27, 169–192.

Rizzolatti, G., Fadiga, L., Fogassi, L. and Gallese, V. (2002) From mirror neurons to imitation: Facts and speculations, in Meltzoff, A. N. and Prinz, W. (eds) *The Imitative Mind: Development, Evolution, and Brain Bases*. New York: Cambridge University Press.

Robbins, M. P. and Glass, G. V. (1968) The Doman-Delacato rationale: a critical analysis, in Hellmuth, J. (ed.) *Educational Therapy*. Seattle: Special Child Publications.

Rodriguez, P. (2006) Talking brains: A cognitive semantic analysis of an emerging folk neuropsychology. *Public Understanding of Science*, 15, 301–330.

Roehrs, T. and Roth, T. (2008) Caffeine: Sleep and daytime sleepiness. *Sleep Medicine Reviews*, 12, 153–162.

Rogers, P. J., Kainth, A. and Smit, H. J. (2001) A drink of water can improve or impair mental performance depending on small differences in thirst. *Appetite*, 36, 57–58.

Roman, G. C. and Rogers, S. J. (2004) Donepezil: a clinical review of current and emerging indications. *Expert Opinion on Pharmacotherapy*, 5, 161–180.

Roshon, M. S. and Hagen, R. L. (1989) Sugar consumption, locomotion, task orientation, and learning in pre-school children. *Journal of Abnormal Child Psychology*, 17, 349–357.

Rossi, S., Miniussi, C., Pasqualetti, P., Babiloni, C., Rossini, P. M. and Cappa, S. F. (2004) Age-related functional changes of prefrontal cortex in long-term memory: A repetitive transcranial magnetic stimulation study. *Journal of Neuroscience*, 24, 7939–7944L.

Rusconi, E., Walsh, V. and Butterworth, B. (2005) Dexterity with numbers: rTMS over left angular gyrus disrupts finger gnosis and number processing. *Neuropsychologia*, 43, 1609–1624.

Sailer, L., Robinson, S., Fischmeister, F. P. S., Moser, E., Kryspin-Exner, I. and Bauer, H. (2007) Imaging the changing role of feedback during learning in decision-making. *Neuroimage*, 37, 1474–1486.

Salem, N., Litman, B., Kim, H.-Y. and Gawrisch, K. (2001) Mechanisms of action of docosahexaenoic acid in the nervous system. *Lipids*, 36, 945–959.

Salvia, J. and Ysseldyke, J. E. (2004) *Assessment in Special and Inclusive Education*. New York: Houghton Mifflin.

Scheff, S. W., Price, D. A. and Sparks, D. L. (2001) Quantitative assessment of possible age-related change in synaptic numbers in the human frontal cortex. *Neurobiology of Aging*, 22, 355–365.

Schlaug, G., Jancke, L., Huang, Y., Staiger, J. F. and Steinmetz, H. (1995) Increased corpus callosum size in musicians. *Neuropsychologia*, 33, 1047–1055.

Schneider, P., Scherg, M., Dosch, H. G., Specht, H. J., Gutschalk, A. and Rupp, A. (2002) Morphology of Heschl's gyrus reflects enhanced activation in the auditory cortex of musicians. *Nature Neuroscience*, 5, 688–694.

Schumacher, R. (2007) The brain is not enough: Potential and limits in integrating neuroscience and pedagogy. *Analyse and Kritik*, 29.

SCMH (2005) *The Future of Mental Health: a Vision for 2015*. London: The Sainsbury Centre for Mental Health.

Seger, C. A., Desmond, J. E., Glover, G. H. and Gabrieli, J. D. E. (2000) Functional magnetic resonance imaging evidence for right-hemisphere involvement in processing of unusual semantic relationships. *Neuropsychology*, 14, 361–369.

Sharp, J. G., Bowker, R. and Byrne, J. (2008) VAK or VAK-uous? Towards the trivialisation of learning and the death of scholarship. *Research Papers in Education*, 23, 293–314.

Shastri, L. (2002) Episodic memory and cortico-hippocampal interactions *Trends in Cognitive Sciences*, 6, 162–168.

Shaywitz, B. A., Shaywitz, S. E., Pugh, K. R., Mencl, W. E., Fullbright, R. K., Skudlarski, P., Constable, R. T., Marchione, K. E., Fletcher, J. M., Lyon, G. R. and Gore, J. C. (2002) Disruption of posterior brain systems for reading in children with developmental dyslexia. *Biological Psychiatry*, 52, 101–110.

Shaywitz, B. A., Shaywitz, S. E., Blachman, B. A., Pugh, K. R., Fullbright, R. K., Skudlarski, P., Mencl, W. E., Constable, R. T., Holahan, J. M., Marchione, K. E., Fletcher, J. M., Lyon, G. R. and Gore, J. C. (2004) Development of left occipitotemporal systems for skilled reading in children after a phonologically-based intervention. *Biological Psychiatry*, 55, 926–933.

Shaywitz, S. E., Shaywitz, B. A., Fulbright, R. K., Skudlarski, P., Mencl, W. E., Constable, R. T., Pugh, K. R., Holahan, J. M., Marchione, K. E., Fletcher, J. M., Lyon, G. R. and Gore, J. C. (2003) Neural systems for compensation and persistence: young adult outcome of childhood reading disability. *Biological Psychiatry*, 54, 25–33.

Shellock, F. G. and Crues, J. V. (2004) MR procedures: Biologic effects, safety, and patient care. *Radiology*, 232, 635–652.

Sheridan, K., Zinchenko, E. and Gardner, H. (2006) Neuroethics in education, in Illes, J. (ed.) *Neuroethics: Defining the Issues in Theory, Practice and Policy*. Oxford: Oxford University Press.

Shizgal, P. and Arvanitogiannis, A. (2003) Gambling on dopamine. *Science*, 299, 1856–1858.

Shors, T. J., Miesegaes, G., Beylin, A., Zhao, M. R., Rydel, T. and Gould, E. (2001) Neurogenesis in the adult is involved in the formation of trace memories *Nature*, 414, 938–938.

Sibley, B. A. and Etnier, J. L. (2003) The relationship between physical activity and cognition in children: A meta-analysis. *Pediatric Exercise Science*, 15, 243–256.

Sieban, R. L. (1977) Controversial medical treatments of learning disabilities. *Academic Therapy*, 13, 133–147.

Sifft, J. M. and Khalsa, G. C. K. (1991) Effect of educational kinesiology upon simple response-times and choice response-times. *Perceptual and Motor Skills*, 73, 1011–1015.

Silver, L. B. (1995) Controversial therapies. *Journal of Child Neurology*, 10, 96–100.

Simon, O., Mangin, J.-F., Cohen, L., Bihan, D. L. and Dehaene, S. (2002) Topographical layout of hand, eye, calculation, and language-related areas in the human parietal lobe. *Neuron*, 33, 475–487.

Simopoulos, A. P. (2002) The importance of the ratio of omega-6/omega-3 essential fatty acids. *Biomedical Pharmacotherapy*, 56, 365–379.

Simos, P. G., Fletcher, J. M., Bergman, E., Breier, J. I., Foorman, B. R., Castillo, E. M., Davis, R. N., Fitzgerald, M. and Papanicolaou, A. C. (2002) Dyslexia-specific brain activation profile becomes normal following successful remedial training,. *Neurology*, 58, 1203–1213.

Singleton, C. and Stuart, M. (2003) Measurement mischief: A critique of Reynolds, Nicolson and Hambly. *Dyslexia*, 9, 151–160.

Sinn, N. and Bryan, J. (2007) Effect of supplementation with polyunsaturated fatty acids and micronutrients on learning and behavior problems associated with child ADHD. *Journal of Developmental and Behavioral Pediatrics*, 28, 82–91.

Sloan, T., Daane, C. J. and Giesen, J. (2002) Mathematics anxiety and learning styles: What is the relationship in elementary preservice teachers? *School Science and Mathematics*, 102, 84–87.

Snider, V. E. and Roehl, R. (2007) Teachers' beliefs about pedagogy and related issues. *Psychology in the Schools*, 44.

Snowling, M. J. and Hulme, C. (2003) A critique of claims from Reynolds and Hambly (2003) that DDAT is an effective treatment for children with reading difficulties – 'lies, damned lies and (inappropriate) statistics?' *Dyslexia*, 9, 127–133.

Sowell, E. R., Peterson, B. S., Thompson, P. M., Welcome, S. E., Henkenius, A. L. and Toga, A. W. (2003) Mapping cortical change across the human life span. *Nature Neuroscience*, 6(3), 309–315.

Springer, S. P. and Deutsch, G. (1989) *Left Brain, Right Brain*. New York: Freeman.

Squire, L. R. (2004) Memory systems of the brain: A brief history and current perspective. *Neurobiology of Learning and Memory*, 82, 171–177.

Stare, F. J. and McWilliams, M. (1974) *Nutrition for Good Health*. Fullerton, CA: Plycon.

Starkey, P. and Cooper, R. G. (1980) Perception of numbers by human infants. *Science*, 4473, 1033–1035.

Stein, J. (2003) Evaluation of an exercise based treatment for children with reading difficulties. *Dyslexia*, 9, 122–126.

Stern, E. (2005) Pedagogy meets neuroscience. *Science*, 310, 745–745.

Steven, M. C., Kiehl, K. A., Pearlson, G. D. and Calhoun, V. D. (2007) Functional neural networks underlying response inhibition in adolescents and adults. *Behavioural Brain Research*, 181(1), 12–22.

Stevens, R. (1998) Trimodal theory as a model for inter-relating perspectives in psychology, in Sapsford, R. J., Still, A., Miell, D. E., Stevens, R. and Wetherell, M. (eds) *Theory and Social Psychology*. London: Sage and the Open University.

Stevens, C., Fanning, J., Coch, D., Sanders, L. and Neuille, H. (2008) Neural mechanisms of selective auditory attention are enhanced by computerized training: Electrophysiological evidence from language-impaired and typically developing children. *Brain Research*, 1205, 55–69.

Stewart, L. and Williamon, A. (2008) What are the implications of neuroscience for musical education? *Educational Research*, 50.

Stewart, W. J. (2008) *Technology Futures*. London: Government Office for Science.

Stitch, S. (1990) *The Fragmentation of Reason*, Cambridge, MA: MIT Press.

Sullivan, J. (1972) The effects of Kephart's perceptual motor-training on a reading clinic sample. *Journal of Learning Disabilities*, 5, 32–38.

Swift, B. (2006) Preparing numerical data, in Sapsford, R. J. and Jupp, V. (eds) *Data Collection and Analysis*. London: Sage.

Szucs, D. and Goswami, U. (2007) Educational neuroscience: defining a new discipline for the study of mental representations. *Mind, Brain and Education*, 1, 114–127.

Szucs, D., Soltesz, F., Jarmi, E. and Csepe, V. (2007) The speed of magnitude processing and executive functions in controlled and automatic number comparison in children: an electro-encephalography study. *Behavioral and Brain Functions*, 3, 20.

Tancredi, L. R. (2007) The neuroscience of 'free will'. *Behavioral Sciences and the Law*, 25, 295–2007.

Taylor, C. and Gorrard, S. (2004) *Combining Methods in Educational and Social Research.* McGraw-Hill International.

Temple, E., Poldrack, R. A., Salidis, J., Deutsch, G. K., Tallal, P., Merzenich, M. M. and Gabrieli, J. D. E. (2001) Disrupted neural responses to phonological and orthographic processing in dyslexic children: an fMRI study. *Neuroreport,* 12, 299–308.

Temple, E., Deutsch, G., Poldrack, R. A., Miller, S. L., Tallal, P. and Merzenich, M. M. (2003) Neural deficits in children with dyslexia ameliorated by behavioral remediation: Evidence from functional fMRI. *Proceedings of the National Academy of Sciences (USA),* 100, 2860–2865.

Tettamanti, M., Buccino, G., Saccuman, M. C., Gallese, V., Danna, M., Scifo, P., Fazio, F., Rizzolatti, G., Cappa, S. F. and Perani, D. (2005) Listening to action-related sentences activates fronto-parietal motor circuits. *Journal of Cognitive Neuroscience,* 17, 273–281.

Thorndike, E. L. (1926) *Educational Psychology. Volume 1: The original nature of man.* Phd Thesis, New York: Teachers College.

Tindell, A. J., Berridge, K. C., Zhang, J., Pecina, S. and Aldridge, J. W. (2005) Ventral pallidal neurons code incentive motivation: amplification by mesolimbic sensitization and amphetamine. *European Journal of Neuroscience,* 22(10), 2617–2634.

TLRP (2006) *Improving Teaching and Learning in Schools: A Commentary by the Teaching and Learning Research Programme.* London: TLRP.

TLRP (2007) *Principles into Practice: A Teacher's Guide to Research Evidence on Teaching and Learning.* London: TLRP.

Toga, A. W. and Thompson, P. M. (2005) Genetics of brain structure and intelligence. *Annual Review of Neuroscience,* 28, 1–23.

Tokuhama-Espinosa, T. N. (2008) The scientifically substantiated art of teaching: A study in the development of standards in the new academic field of neuroeducation (mind, brain, and education science). Capella University.

Turkeltaub, P. E., Gareau, L., Flowers, D. L., Zeffiro, T. A. and Eden, G. F. (2003) Development of neural mechanisms of reading. *Nature Neuroscience,* 6, 767–773.

Tvesrky, B. and Morrison, J. B. (2002) Animation: can it facilitate? *International Journal of Human-Computer Studies,* 57, 247–262.

Vaidya, C. J., Audtin, G., Kirkorian, G., Ridlehuber, H. W., Desmond, J. E., Glover, G. H. and Gabrieli, J. D. E. (1998) Selective effects of methylphenidate in attention deficit hyperactivity disorder: A functional magnetic resonance study. *Proceedings of the National Academy of Sciences (USA),* 95, 14494–14499.

Valtin, H. (2002) 'Drink at least eight glasses of water a day.' Really? Is there scientific evidence for '8x8'? *American Journal of Regulatory Comparitive Physiology,* 283, 993–1004.

van Gog, T., Paas, F., Marcus, N., Ayres, P. and Sweller, J. (2008) The mirror neuron system and observational learning: Implications for the effectiveness of dynamic learning. *Educational Psychology Review,* online first.

van Praag, H., Christie, B. R., Sejnowski, T. J. and Gage, F. H. (1999) Running enhances neurogenesis, learning, and long-term potentiation in mice. *Proceedings of the National Academy of Sciences (USA),* 96, 13427–13431.

Varma, S. and Schwartz, D. L. (2008) How should educational neuroscience conceptualize the relation between cognition and brain function? Mathematical reasoning as a network process. *Educational Research,* 50.

Vaynman, S., Ying, Z. and Gomez-Pinilla, F. (2004) Hippocampal BDNF mediates the efficacy of exercise on synpatic plasticity and cognition *European Journal of Neuroscience*, 20, 2580–2590.

Voigt, R. G., Llorente, A. M., Jensen, C. L., Fraley, J. K., Berretta, M. C. and Heird, W. C. (2001) A randomized, double-blind, placebo-controlled trial of docosahexaenoic acid supplementation in children with attention-deficit/hyperactivity disorder. *The Journal of Pediatrics*, 139, 189–96.

Vreeman, R. C. and Carroll, A. E. (2007) Mixed messages: medical myths. *British Medical Journal*, 335, 1288–1289.

Vygotsky, L. S. (1978) *Mind in Society: The Development of Higher Psychological Processes.* Cambridge, MA: Harvard University Press.

Wagner, U., Gais, S., Haider, H., Verleger, R. and Born, J. (2004) Sleep inspires insight. *Nature*, 427(6792), 352–355.

Walker, S. O. and Plomin, R. (2005) The Nature-Nurture Question: Teachers' Perceptions of How Genes and the Environment Influence Educationally Relevant Behaviour. *Educational Psychology*, 25, 509–516.

Waterhouse, L. (2006) Multiple intelligences, the Mozart effect, and emotional intelligence: A critical review. *Educational Psychologist*, 41, 207–225.

Weber, A., Hahne, A., Friedrich, M. and Friederici, A. D. (2004) Discrimination of word stress in early infant perception: Electrophysiological evidence. *Cognitive Brain Research*, 18, 149–161.

Wegner, D. M. (2003) The mind's best trick: How we experience conscious will. *Trends in Cognitive Sciences*, 7, 65–69.

Weiner, B. (1985). An Attributional Theory of Achievement-Motivation and Emotion. *Psychological Review*, 92(4), 548–573.

Weisberg, D. S., Keil, F. C., Goodstein, J., Rawson, E. and Gray, J. (2008) The seductive lure of neuroscience explanations. *Journal of Cognitive Neuroscience*, 20, 470–477.

Werner, H. (1948) *Comparative Psychology of Mental Development.* New York: International Universities Press.

Willingham, D. T. (2009) Three problems in the marriage of neuroscience and education discussion. *Cortex*, 45(4), 544–545.

Willis, S. L., Tennstedt, S. L., Marsiske, M., Ball, K., Elias, J., Mann Koepke, K., *et al.* (2006). Long-term effects of cognitive training on everyday functional outcomes in older adults. *Journal of American Medical Association*, 296(23), 2805–2814.

Wilson, A. J., Dehaene, S., Pinel, P., Revkin, S. K., Cohen, L. and Cohen, D. (2006) Principles underlying the design of 'The Number Race', an adaptive computer game for remediation of dyscalculia. *Behavioral and Brain Functions*, 2.

Wilson, R. S. (2005) Mental challenge in the workplace and risk of dementia in old age: is there a connection? *Occupational and Environmental Medicine*, 62, 72–73.

Wilson, R. S., Mendes de Leon, C. F., Barnes, L. L., Schneider, J. A., Bienias, J. L., Evans, D. A., *et al.* (2002) Participation in cognitively stimulating activities and risk of Alzheimer disease. *Journal of the American Medical Association*, 287(6), 742–748.

Winter, B., Breitenstein, C., Mooren, F. C., Voelker, K., Fobker, M., Lechtermann, A., Krueger, K., Fromme, A., Korsukewitz, C., Floel, A. and Knecht, S. (2007) High impact running improves learning. *Neurobiology of Learning and Memory*, 87, 597–609.

Wolf, S. M., Lawrenz, F. P., Nelson, C. A., Kahn, J. P., Cho, M. K., Clayton, E. W., Fletcher, J. G., Georgieff, M. K., Hammerschmidt, D., Hudson, K., Illes, J., Kapur, V., Keane, M. A., Koenig, B. A., LeRoy, B. S., McFarland, E. G., Paradise, J., Parker, L. S., Terry, S. F., Van Ness, B. and Wilfond, B. S. (2007) Managing incidental findings in human subjects research: Analysis and recommendations. *Symposium on Findings in Human Subjects Research – From Imaging to Genomics.* Minneapolis, MN: Blackwell Publishing.

Wolfe, P. (1998) Revisiting effective teaching. *Educational Leadership*, 56, 61–64.

Wolraich, M. L., Wilson, D. B. and White, J. W. (1995) The effect of sugar on behavior or cognition in children – a metaanalysis. *Jama-Journal of the American Medical Association*, 274, 1617–1621.

Wood, D., Bruner, J. S. and Ross, G. (1976) The role of tutoring in problem solving. *Journal of Child Psychology and Psychiatry and Allied Disciplines*, 17, 89–100.

Wundt, W. (1896) *Lectures on Human and Animal Psychology.* New York: Macmillan.

Zimmerman, E. and Fortugno, N. (2005) Soapbox: Learning to Play to Learn – Lessons in Educational Game Design. *Gamasutra*.

Index

Action research 105, 114–16, 120,
    149–62, 179
Adenosine 17, 200
ADHD 32, 88–9, 112–14, 127, 134,
    189–90, 200
Adolescence 5–6, 11, 13, 26, 126, 131,
    134, 187–8, 195
Agency – see free will
Animal research 129
Attention
    and the brain 107, 154
    educators' views on 46–8
    focus of in creativity 17, 151, 154
    in learning contexts 10, 16, 148,
        178, 190
    orienting of 5, 154, 164, 177–8, 187
    and working memory 9, 189
Autonomy – see free will

Biology – as determining outcome
    51–3, 39–44, 91
Brain development 3–7
Brain Gym see educational kinesiology
Brain, educator's knowledge of 38–53,
    69, 196
Brain-based science of education 194–5
Brain-computer interfaces 193–4

Caffeine 17–18, 49–50
Children, as research participants 128–9
Co-construction of concepts 149–61
Cognitive contrast 106–7
Cognitive enhancers 53–4, 71–2,
    134–5, 192–3, 196
Cognitive training 189–91
Cogs – see cognitive enhancers
Communication of research 68–72,
    75, 130–3

Creativity 16–17, 138–63, 180, 186
Critical periods – see sensitive periods
Curriculum 6, 63, 109, 134, 138,
    189–92, 195–6

Design of research 115–19, 120
Dopamine 10, 164–5, 177–9, 200
Dualism 87–9
Dyscalculia 13, 66, 118, 187, 200
Dyslexia
    and the brain 93, 103, 186
    controversy surrounding 131–2
    interventions for 28, 43, 94, 102,
        186, 190
    screening for 14–15, 135–6, 189

Ecological validity 98, 116, 117, 141–4,
    162, 200
Educational kinesiology 27–30, 44, 50,
    63, 111, 191
Electrodermal activity (EDA) – see skin
    conductivity
Electroencephalography (EEG)
    102–3, 200
Emotion
    and the brain/body 9–10, 16, 72,
        80, 87, 90, 103
    and creativity 147–8, 160, 162
    development 57, 71, 190–1
    educators' views on 43, 46–7
    evidence involving 115
    and games 165–8, 170–80
    stress 8
Emotional intelligence 21, 60
Enriched environments 5, 26–7, 41
Ethics 122–37, 144, 174, 192–4
Evidence
    distortion/absence of 34–5

in neuroeducational research 61–2,
66–70, 74, 85–7, 98–121, 151,
162, 194–5
Executive function 154, 190, 196
Exercise 7, 18–19, 28–31, 35, 49–50,
191, 196
Experiential methods 95–6, 99–101,
104–6, 111–15, 118–20, 146–8,
160, 166
Experimental methods to study
cognition 108, 120, 166–9, 174–7

Fish oils – see Omega-3
Food additives 33
Free will 84, 94–6, 99, 115, 126,
131–2, 162, 195
Functional magnetic resonance imaging
(fMRI) 72, 101–2, 106–8, 120,
123–9, 140–6, 151–3
Future, the 185–96

Games involving learning 164–82
Genetics
and brain development 4
educators' views on 38–42, 51–3
profiling in education 136, 192–3
Goals of neuroeducational research 98,
120, 138, 165
Grounded theory 112

Imitation 10–11, 158
Implicit learning 48
Interpretative methods 79, 109–11,
115, 120, 169–74

Language
and the brain 14, 25, 27, 48, 93–5,
103, 140–1, 186, 189–90
issues for neuroscience and education
34–5, 70–1, 79–87, 130–1, 159,
161, 179–80
the study of 110–11, 136, 94
Learning
and the brain 79–83, 11, 191
meaning of 79–85
Learning games – see games
Learning styles 23–6, 44, 50, 60,
111, 194
Left-brain/right-brain theory 24–6, 34,
49–50, 160
Levels of action model 91–7
Long-term depression (LTD) 81, 201

Long-term potentiation (LTP) 29, 81,
86, 201

Magnetoencephalography (MEG) 102
Mathematics 9, 11–13, 21, 28–9, 66,
107–10, 118, 166, 187, 189
Meaning – approaches to 87–9, 92–7,
104–5, 110–12, 115–18, 147–63,
195–6
Memory 7–9, 19, 24–6, 29, 39, 46–7,
79–82, 134, 165, 174, 177–80
Mental health 190–1, 196
Metacognition 156, 160, 161
Mind, relation to brain 45, 66–7,
85–91, 108–9, 140,
Mirror neurons 10–11, 157–8, 201
Monism 85–87
Motivation 10–11, 110, 115, 135, 151,
164–6, 173–4, 177, 180, 188
Multiple intelligences theory 21–3, 44
Music 15–16, 21, 41, 54

Neurogenesis 4, 29, 46–7, 201
Neuromyth 20–36, 41, 48–51, 63, 118,
130–2, 154, 160–1, 190–2, 194
Neuroscience
power and authority 23, 34, 48, 56,
65–6, 73
understanding of the term 66
Neuroscientists on education 53–7

Omega-3 31–3, 35, 49–50

Performance methodology 146–8
PET 102, 201
Philosophy of neuroeducational research
67–8, 79–97
Plasticity 4–7, 46, 48, 60, 81–2, 86,
186, 201
Policy 133–6
Professional aims of researchers
65–7, 133

Reading, see also dyslexia 4, 13–14
Research design 115–20
Reward 6, 10, 164–5, 177–9, 188
Risk, ethical consideration of 123–7

Science, teaching and learning of 15
Screening, for educational purposes 15,
135–6, 188–9, 192–3, 195
Sensitive periods 5, 26, 48, 109, 201

Skin conductivity 103, 174–7
Sleep 17–18, 47, 60
Smart pills/drugs – see cognitive
    enhancers
Sociocultural methods 110–11, 120
Studies, types of – see research design
Sugar 33, 42, 44, 49, 51, 123
Synaptic pruning 4–5, 26, 90, 187, 201

Synaptogenesis 4–5, 26, 46, 48,
    90, 201

Visualization 10–11, 148, 155–6, 186

Water 30–1, 44, 49–50
Working memory 6, 9, 12, 15, 43, 60,
    82–3, 90, 189, 195, 202